Be Still

Lessons from an Angel

E.D. Perry

Be Still

This book was printed in the United States of America by Be Still Publications.

Identifiers:
979-8-9911297-0-1 (paperback)
979-8-9911297-1-8 (ebook)
979-8-9911297-2-5 (hardcover)

GOD'S Recommended WAY OF LIFE

A Study of
Philippians, Colossians, Philemon and Ephesians

E. D. Perry

March 1997

CONTENTS

THE LETTER TO THE PHILIPPIANS—HOW INNER HAPPINESS IS ACQUIRED

THE LETTER TO THE COLOSSIANS—"WHY JESUS IS WORTHY OF OUR TRUST"

THE LETTER TO PHILEMON— AN APPLICATION OF CHRISTIAN DOCTRINE

THE LETTER TO THE EPHESIANS— "THE BODY OF CHRIST"

Foreword by Ron L. Frey

I WAS WAITING in an unassuming office on the very important day I met Ed. It wasn't the place you would expect God to show his hand . . . but isn't that exactly how He works?

That office was the office of Ray Jordan, a CPA in downtown Portland, Oregon.

At the time, my new business was getting complicated. It consisted of helping credit unions and their members select and purchase any make and model of new or used car with no negotiation or dealing directly with a dealer. And, while the business was very successful, there were many locations placed inside of credit unions, and it was getting to be way too much for me to keep track of.

I always knew I wanted to be in business, and from my earliest memories, I had been on that path. I got started out of the back of a Chicago-style hot dog and U-Bake pizza restaurant I purchased when I was eighteen. I worked in the restaurant with my high school sweetheart, now wife of thirty-eight years. Once I started the new business, I sold the restaurant and turned my attention full-time to this venture in 1985.

Seems like an odd pivot, I know. In the most unlikely of ways, it was, and the rest of this story is no different.

That day, I explained my business to Ray Jordan and what I felt I needed; Ray appeared to understand completely. He hit the intercom button on his desktop phone and asked his assistant to please send Ed in. I can remember it like it was yesterday.

I was sitting in front of Ray's desk in this big office overlooking the city. I felt like I was out of place and in way over my head. I had no idea what I was doing, but somehow God had led me here.

In walks Ed. He was the quintessential accountant, lifted straight from a Rockwell painting. Ed was well into his seventies which put a huge divide between him and me. Yet, his gentle smile hinted at his welcoming personality, which seemed to bridge any age gap. He stood in the big office facing Ray, holding a notepad in his left hand and a pen, poised and ready for action, in his right. Ray explained the situation as Ed took copious notes all while standing there. Ray finished the explanation and instructed Ed to show up at my office Monday morning. The plan was for him to stay for the next two weeks to see what's what and get the accounting squared away.

I remember this day so vividly because it literally changed my life.

So, Ed showed up that Monday. I cannot tell you exactly how events unfolded, but I will share that Ed continued to show up every day until I sold the business some years later. Ed continued to support me with my personal finances until shortly before he went to Glory in 2010. Ed and I had a very special relationship. I swore for years that he wasn't even real, that he was an angel sent to me from God. And while Ed was indeed real, with a long and remarkable life, to this day, I know with certainty that he was sent to me from God.

What I later came to learn was that Ed had a very successful career in business along with a lot of life experience that he was willing to share, but never in a pushy way. Ed was a very quiet, gentle man with a huge smile on his face all the time. As I look back now, as with so many life experiences, Ed knew what was in front of me with my business aspirations and could anticipate what life may bring to this journey along the way.

We would meet every Monday morning for breakfast to talk about the week, which always turned into a conversation about life lessons. Today, I can see how deliberate he was, knowing where I was, and I believe the Holy Spirit was working through Ed to lead me with just what I needed at the time, planting seeds that I have learned to value ever since. I will share just a few.

Ed and I were at a restaurant, and true to my personality, I was excited to share my thoughts and point of view, interrupting the conversation to get it out. Ed put his hand on my leg and said, "Ron, if you don't let people finish what they are saying, you might miss something really important." So true. I still have to stop myself as I hear Ed reminding me. Also, when my determination came on strong, and I would tell Ed, "I can do this," Ed would softly correct me and say, "Ron, you can't do anything, but God can."

He would tell me to keep flying, and He would navigate.

And he'd sign off every written communication with me with "Keep Looking Up." I was young with a young family, not overly religious. I had faith but not a real understanding and was in search of what I believed and why. I was not one to accept religion just because I happened to be born into a family belief or because of a good-sounding argument, but I was seeking truth for myself. Ed helped me understand how God played an important role in my business and formed so much of my thinking and behavior.

Ed devoted the last ten years of his life to writing and teaching Bible lessons. Ed sent me, and I believe maybe another twenty people, these lessons every week. I was at full throttle in business and family and would read one of the lessons every now and then. They were wonderful, but I just did not have time to keep up with them. That was foolish, looking back. But God always has a plan. What I did not realize was Ed was a scholar with a deep, deep understanding of theology in his studies of the Bible. Oh, if I could go back, I have so many conversations I wish I could have had with him. Anyway, I kept every lesson Ed sent me. In his later years, Ed took his studies and bound them for us. I saved each one and promised myself that "one day," when I slowed down, I would read them. I kept them in a file drawer, in order of dates, books, and lessons for that "One Day."

My business life has treated me well. I accomplished all the things I had dreamed of. I say this not as a boast but as a warning. Everything comes at a price. What I know for certain is earthly success, while it is nice, is not satisfying or lasting.

Relationships are the only thing that matters, and they point us to the ultimate and most worthy relationship with our savior, Jesus Christ. The hardest thing for me was and still is to simply BE STILL and make room for God.

So today, I am still enjoying business but advising others who are now on their journeys, sharing any wisdom that I might be able to provide to help make their paths easier. In one of my one-on-one virtual meetings, a very accomplished executive asked me about my faith. I was thrilled to share some of my thoughts, but I was compelled, maybe led, to start the conversation by explaining the role Ed had in my life. I told her to wait, and I went off-screen to go get the stack of lessons from Ed. They stand about two feet high. I then sat the stack down by my desk and finished our conversation. For two weeks, this stack—that "One Day"—was screaming at me. So, I grabbed a lesson off the top called "MARRIAGE: A Great Institution." Ed wrote this in 1998. I picked it up, read the lesson, and sat at my desk in silence, thinking how powerful it was and if only I had read this twenty-five years ago. So, in my quietness, I went through some more of the writings and grabbed the binder I decided to start. "One Day" had arrived.

God works, not in our ways or our timing, but in His. We want to be in charge, in control, and set the path, the future, and the timing, but God has His plan, and it's far better. I believe all the events of Ed's long and amazing experiences led him to me, and my most unlikely path to where life has brought me today, was in His perfect time. Yes, that "One Day" is now because He chose it in His perfect timing.

I opened the writings, and as I read, I simply knew that this couldn't just be for me. My clients had to read it, and my friends. And now I know that you need this too, so here we are. Ed's family graciously consented to me sharing these lessons with all of you—with everyone looking for answers to the what's what about God, in plain talk but also in truth. I hope you get as much out of this life's work as I have. Our Lord instructs us as He says, "Be still, and know that I am God." (Psalm 46:10).

As for Ed and his theology background, in the back you will find a more extensive bio.

He's still my angel, looking over me. So much of how I operate in life and business is based on the influence and impact Ed had on my life in business, personally and spiritually.

*Note: Please know that while E.D. Perry (the author of these lessons) and I enjoyed a close friendship, any views regarding events (political, societal, etc.) expressed in the book are his and were current to his day.

Translation Information

Except as specifically noted, the translations given are the King James Version, with the "thees" and "thines" changed to our modern pronouns of "you," "yours," etc. Also, many of the verbs have been expanded to better translate the Greek verb forms that were not understood around the year 1611, when the King James Version was made.

Actual words have been changed only where these changes conform to the more ancient Greek texts that have been found since the King James Version was translated, and these changes agree with translations found in the New American Standard Bible.

My words, which are intended to expand or more fully express the meaning of some of the Greek words, are contained in parentheses.

E.D. Perry

*Note: This book was published posthumously. E.D. Perry used a family Bible and may have made Bible references in his lessons from memory and/or his personal study notes. While all lessons are scripture-based, the citations may not match cross references to other Bible sources.

Introduction

We Humans seem to be so constructed that we will receive words from one person but reject virtually the same words when spoken by another person. This has to do with something called "credibility," and it is one of God's mysteries.

It is for those who happen to be tuned to me that I have carefully and thoughtfully compiled this collection of words.

I appreciate being in this relationship, and I am also very appreciative of those who have made this compilation possible, some through their moral support and some through the addition of financial assistance. You know who you are—and I am thankful for you and grateful to you!

I know that the teachings of Christianity, as God gave them to us, are not too widely understood, and this results in too many people not giving the contents of the Bible the weight it deserves. This, in turn, results in some Christians missing blessings that they could be enjoying during this phase of "Life," and also, in some who have not accepted Christianity, missing blessings now, plus a whole lot more.

This collection of words, the results of many hours of careful study (both by this "collector" and by others whose works I have carefully studied) has been assembled, based on a "hope." A "hope" that, as a result of someone reading them, he or she will see the magnitude of "The Bible" as I have come to see it and, as a result, his or her life will be equally enriched.

E. D. Perry
March 1997

God's Code of Christian Conduct

From Paul's Letter to the Ephesians, Chapters 4 through 6

As He did for Israel, God has also written out the simple list of His Instructions to us; how He knows we should operate in this "life" for our best life and to bring this "best life" to those around us. As you see here, I have placed my "paraphrase" of His List in the very front of this little book, since it's what this "little book" is all about.

It's a relatively short list and its instructions are "do-able." Further, there is not an "unpleasant" thing among the items on the list. However, these things, again, are a little different from the way the majority of the people around us choose to operate. Yet the rewards for adhering to His List are great, and the consequences of disregarding His List are not very pleasant, to say the least.

Verse

4:24 "… that you put on the new man, which, after God, is created in righteousness and true holiness."

25 Putting away "The Lie" (Satan's Lie), speak truth with your neighbor.

26 Be mentally upset at that which God is upset yet handle it as God handles it—with longsuffering, remembering that "Vengeance belongs to the Lord."

Do not let the sun go down on an anger against someone, that is boiling within you.

27 Never give place to Satan—to his Lie, to his enticings.

28 If you have been in the habit of stealing, stop it! Instead, work with your hands at things that are intrinsically "good," so that you can give to him who has a need.

29 Watch what comes out of your mouth; let it be that which builds up the hearer!

30 Do not grieve God's Holy Spirit by allowing sin to remain unconfessed in your life.

31 Allow the Holy Spirit to put out of your pattern of living—all bitterness, violent anger, the habit of yelling at people ("clamor,"—*KRAUGE*—"the outcry of controversy").

32 Instead, cultivate kindness to one another, tenderhearted, forgiving—because God forgave you!

5:1 Like little children, be imitators of God, walking in concern for one another as Christ does with us.

3 Put fornication and uncleanness and covetousness out of your life.

4 Likewise, put away filthiness, foolish talking, out-of-place conversations and jokings; instead, be expressing appreciation and be keeping this in mind, that no whoremonger, nor unclean person, nor covetous person (an idolater) has any inheritance in the Kingdom of Christ and of God.

6 Be on guard that no one deceives you with empty words, and don't associate with those who are Deceivers. You are now associated with The Light—things of The Truth. Act like it! Instead of participating with them, reprove them!

15 Walk carefully—not as a foolish person, but as a wise person.

16 Redeem the time you have been given, don't waste it with the time-wasting things of this age that we live in, realizing the Lord's Plan is moving ahead right on schedule.

18 Do not allow wine to distort your thinking or your actions. Instead, *be always under the control of the Holy Spirit!*

19 Speak constantly to yourself the psalms and hymns and songs that praise God.

20 Be giving thanks constantly for all things unto God and do it in the name of our Lord Jesus Christ.

21 Be submitting yourself to the Order of God's Establishment, in respect and awe of God.

Wives, to your own husbands, as the husband is the head of the wife, just as Christ is the head of the "Body of Christ," and is its Savior. Husbands, be as concerned for your wife as Christ is for the members of His Body, even to the point of giving His life for us members! Remember, husbands, he that is concerned for his wife is concerned for himself, since you two are one.

6:1 Children, obey your parents. Give respect and honor to your father and mother, keeping in mind that this command has a promise to you: "That it may be well with you, and that you may live long on this earth."

4 Fathers, do not provoke your children to wrath; instead, bring them up in the nurture and admonition of the Lord.

5 Employees, be obedient to those who society has put in authority over you; and don't do it superficially, but sincerely from your heart, knowing that you are serving your true Master, who is Christ. And keep this in mind: whatever good thing a person does, no matter who you are, the same you will receive back from the Lord! That's a Promise from Him!

6 Masters—you who have been placed in charge of people—regard your responsibility to those in your charge; do not use threats, but keep always in mind that you, too, have a Master; He is in Heaven, and He is not impressed with "who you are".

10 Finally, to all, be strengthened in the Lord, putting on the armor He has provided, so that you are able to withstand the Devil and his wiles.

The "Armor of God"

"**WHEREFORE TAKE UNTO** yourself the whole armor of God, so that you may be able to withstand in the evil day, and, having done all, to stand.

Stand, therefore, having your loins girt about with Truth, and having on the Breastplate of Righteousness;

And your feet shod with the preparation of the Gospel of Peace;

Above all, taking the Shield of Faith, wherewith you shall be able to quench all the fiery darts of the wicked.

And take the Helmet of Salvation, and the Sword of the Spirit, which is the Word of God;

Praying always with all prayer and supplication, in the Spirit, and watching thereunto with all perseverance and supplication for all the Saints." (Eph. 6:13-18)

God's Armor Against Satan's Attacks:

- His "belt," which is "The Truth," that which is contained in His Word; and we "stand" on that!

- His "breastplate," which is "right doing"; living in accordance with these standards that He has just given us.
- His "foot covering," that which keeps us mobile and for which we prepare ourselves ahead of time, which is a full understanding of all that is "The Gospel of Peace" (It's stated for us in First Corinthians 15).
- His "shield" to ward off the "fiery darts" that are shot at us is our Faith. And we remember that the Holy Spirit produces Faith, as we allow Him to work.
- His "helmet," our head (brain) protector, which is our knowledge of all that our "Salvation" (our "Deliverance") provides—future *and* present.
- The Spirit's "sword" (the Word of God), with which we can parry any lunges from Satan or his friends.

All the time praying IN The Spirit. All the time watching, alert to our Enemy, alert to Him and to His leading. And watching for His Return.

The "Gospel of Peace"

Excerpted from Paul's First Letter to the Corinthians Chapter 15:

"Moreover, brethren, I declare unto you the Gospel which I preached unto you, which also you have received, and wherein you stand;

By which you also are saved, seeing you keep in memory what I preached unto you, unless you have believed in vain.

For I declared unto you first of all, that which I also received,
How that Christ died for our sins according to the Scriptures;

That he was buried, and that he rose again the third day, according to the Scriptures;

That He was seen by Peter, then by the Twelve;

After that he was seen by about five hundred Brethren all at one time, of whom the greater part are alive now—but some have passed on.

After that, he was seen by James, then by all of the Apostles;

And last of all, He was seen by me also, as one born out of due time." (1 Cor. 15:1-8)

"But now is Christ risen from the dead, and become the first fruits of them that slept.

For since through man came Death, by Man came also the resurrection from the dead.

For as in Adam all die, even so, in Christ shall all be made alive.

But every man in his own order; Christ, the first fruits; afterward they that are Christ's at His Coming.

Then comes the end, when he shall have delivered up the Kingdom to God the Father, when he shall have put down all rule and all authority and power.

For He must reign, until He has put all enemies under His feet.

The last enemy that shall be destroyed is Death.

And when all things shall be subdued unto Him, then shall the Son also Himself be subject unto Him that put all things under Him, SO THAT God may be All in All." (1 Cor. 15:20-28)

THE LETTER TO THE PHILIPPIANS

How Inner Happiness Is Acquired

Lesson 1 Philippians Chapter 1

Introduction to "The Four Prison Epistles"

GREETINGS! THIS STUDY that we are about to begin takes off immediately following the action in the Book of Acts. It is a study of the material that the Holy Spirit gave to the world through Paul in the city of Rome during his imprisonment there.

The Book of Acts ends with Paul in prison, waiting for his appearance before the Roman Caesar Nero for a "hearing" to which he was entitled as a Roman citizen as an appeal from the court of Festus, the governor of Judaea. We know that he waited there under a sort of "house arrest" for a period of two years, and during this time, he was chained constantly to a Roman soldier.

When he was finally given his hearing, Nero released him, and he was allowed to go his way. No details are left for us concerning that hearing, but we do know that he left Rome and apparently went next to Spain, as he had hoped to do, and in this, he would have completed Christ's command to the Apostles, to carry this New Message "to the end of the world." Spain was, then, literally the "end of the world" as far as they knew.

Now during Paul's enforced stay in Rome, he was able to move into a residence of some sort that he paid for out of the funds that his faithful followers provided to him, and he was allowed as much freedom as his chains to his Roman guard would have allowed. Undoubtedly the soldiers who guarded him were changed on four-hour shifts, as was the Roman custom in things like this, and we can't help wondering how many of these Roman soldiers accepted Jesus Christ and this New Way during this time!

During these two years, Paul had many visitors. Among them were Epaphroditus, who was the leader of the assembly in Philippi; Epaphras, who was the leader of the assembly in Colossae; and Tychicus, who was the leader of the assembly in Ephesus. And then there was Onesimus, who was a slave who had run away from a man who, it turned out, was a convert of Paul's. The name of the man Onesimus raw away from was Philemon, and he lived in the city of Colossae. Onesimus talked with Paul, himself became a Christian, and then was encouraged by Paul to return to Philemon. Only this time, Paul was confident that the relationship between the master and the slave would be very different from before since major changes had occurred in both their lives.

As we know, Paul wrote letters to each of these groups I've mentioned here, and near the end of his imprisonment there in Rome, Paul sent these four letters back with the men involved: Epaphroditus took one back to Philippi; Epaphras took one back to Colossae; Tychicus took one back to Ephesus, and Onesimus took the little letter about himself back to his master Philemon.

Four Letters—all that we have preserved from us from Paul's two-year stay there in Rome, but these are letters that are priceless to Christianity since together they set forth all the basic teachings of Christianity. As Christians, we should really know all four of them by heart, word for word, because, really, our lives depend on the information they contain!

They are as "timely" now as the day they were written! And they are totally relevant to the time in which you and I live, since the conditions that existed in the cities to which they were addressed closely parallel the conditions in our country and world today.

So, I would like to cover these four familiar letters with you. I realize that you may well have been over these letters many times, and I know that the teachings in them are undoubtedly thoroughly familiar to you. So, my challenge is to avoid boring you with things you already know, and still point you to some things, as we go along, that may cause the Light of the Gospel of Christ Jesus to be a little brighter in your minds, and, most of all, that may help these remaining days of our lives to be a little more productive and satisfactory.

It seems also important that we have the sequence of the books of the New Testament clear in our minds, as I think we need that in order to better understand what Paul is doing for us here in these letters.

It seems pretty clear that Paul had no preconceived plan or order that would cover all the letters that he wrote, and he probably wrote others that we don't have. These four letters were written (or dictated, undoubtedly) toward the end of his stay there in Rome, and probably all within a year's time around 63 AD. And as he wrote them, he knew that any day, he would be brought before Nero, and who knew what the outcome would be—very likely his death.

Then from the indications within the letters themselves, scholars who have studied these things carefully agree that the letter to the Philippians was first, then Colossians, then Ephesians, and last, Philemon. So, we're going to take them up in that order and pay special note to the development of Paul's thinking as he wrote these successive treatises, each directed to a specific Assembly of Believers whose differences were well known to Paul.

Philippi was up at the north end of the Aegean Sea in what is now northern Greece on the continent of Europe; it was truly a Greek city, very metropolitan and thoroughly "Greek" in its way of life.

The other two cities, Colossae and Ephesus, were down in Asia Minor in the country we know now as Turkey. The people there were also "Greek" in their thinking, but they were of a different temperament than the Europeans. And Philemon, the slave owner whom the fourth of these letters was about, was a Colossian.

Then I want to point out another difference between these four letters of Paul's and the other letters that we have of his. The other letters were what we would call "problem-solving" letters, written in response to some special problem that Paul learned existed.

On the other hand, these letters have a different tone. They express his care and concern for these people. They express his gratitude for their care and concern for him, and then, further, he used these letters to help build them up in their faith.

Paul has given us a great example here to follow in our own contact with the people we're involved with; we should be quick to express our appreciation for what others do for us. That's number one. And then, the words that we speak to them should always be aimed at building them up emotionally, mentally, and spiritually!

God even offers a reward to us if we DO this. Paul tells us about it right here in this letter, in Chapter 4, Verse 9, he states:

> "Those things, which you have both learned, and received, and heard, and seen in me, practice (PRASSO) and the God of Peace shall be with you!" (THEN here's the reward)

Notice this closely: this verse says clearly that IF you follow what Paul has been telling us, and showing us by example, THEN, it tells us, "The God of Peace shall be with us!"

So, are we to read this as if we don't, then He won't be with us? Well, we know He will always be with us, because He's promised to be, but he will be with us in a different way. We're going to look at this thought more closely in a few minutes, but here we have a clear expression from the Holy Spirit, which will be a great help to us if we keep it in mind!

> "Those things, which you have both learned, and received, and heard, and seen in me, practice; and the God of Peace shall be with you." (Phil 4:9)

So, what we have here are four letters concerned with "Christian Living"! The first two letters of Paul's that have been preserved for us—the two

Letters to the Thessalonians—he wrote early in his ministry, probably in AD 50 or 51, and they were written specifically to answer questions those people had raised about the Resurrection and the return of Christ to the Earth.

Then, about four years later, he wrote two letters to the people in the city of Corinth: First and Second Corinthians. These were written to try to get the Corinthians straight on some non-Scriptural practices and way of life that, apparently, many of their members had drifted into.

Another year or so later, Paul then learned that the "Judaizers" that had given him so much trouble in Jerusalem had moved into the area of Galatia, and into Rome itself, and were pressing the issue with those people that Believers in Christ still must adhere to the practices taught by the Mosaic Law. So, Paul wrote a rather scathing letter to the Assembly in Galatia, and, shortly after that, he composed a longer and more detailed letter to the Believers in the city of Rome—the Book of Romans, that we regard as really the "Primer" of Christianity!

God's Re-Arrangement of the Order of the Books

Now, since this is the *chronological* order of these letters, then why is the order of these Books different in the Bible? I see this as another notable example of Divine Intervention in the creation of this Book.

The way the "New Testament" section of our Bible is organized is very logical; the way we expect a book to be. First come the four "Gospel" Books and they start with Matthew's account, which helps a newcomer connect this "Good News from God" with the nation of Israel, whose history IS the Old Testament and is the logical progression of God's Revelation of Himself to Mankind. Those four "Gospels" acquaint us with God's human revealing of Himself to the human race; they present "Our Lord Jesus Christ."

Next comes the Book of Acts, describing to us the launching of Christianity to the world and the means of spreading it (we need to know that), which is by the Holy Spirit, working through Believers, using the Holy Scriptures. The Book of Acts is a necessary bridge between the accounts of the Life of Jesus, the Messiah, and the Teachings that He gives to us in the remainder of the New Testament.

Next comes the Book of Romans; it's the "Primer"; it gives a person who knows little or nothing about God and His dealings with Mankind the reason why we need divine help for our life; it tells us just how that help can be received; it tells us all about the Holy Spirit and, it tells us how to live this life, and still stay in God's good graces in the process.

And even for a Jew, knowledgeable in God's dealings with Israel, the Book of Romans explains carefully where Jesus Christ fits into this whole picture.

Then the two Letters to the Corinthians, and the Letter to the Galatians, each have more information for a person presently involved in what we call "the world," and they explain the adjustments that people need to make in their old life so that the Blessings of God will come to them.

And now, having given the world this information, Paul is now in Rome, awaiting his trial before Nero—a trial that, he knows could well result in his death. But during this time, he has reached the most effective and productive time of his life!

Our Position as "Slaves of Christ Jesus"

And so, he begins his first letter, the Letter to the Philippians:

> "Paul and Timothy, slaves of Christ Jesus, to all those set apart in Christ Jesus at Philippi, along with the *EPISKOPOS* and the *DIAKANOS*..."

That's his salutation, and it's loaded with information! To begin, Paul describes himself and the members of his company as "slaves of

Christ Jesus." Paul never uses the words "Jesus" and "Christ" in any combination other than "Christ Jesus" unless it's with the word "Lord" out ahead, as in "Lord Jesus Christ." To Paul, Jesus, the unique Man, is subservient to "The Christos," the "Messiah." So, with Him, it's always with the emphasis on the Divine Position of this unique Person, Jesus.

Then, he refers to himself and Timothy as "slaves." Not "servants," but "slaves." The Greek word is *DOULOS* that Dr. Trench defines as "the permanent surrender of personal rights in an attitude of total submission."

In that time, there were also what we'd call "household servants" or "servants" and these often were hired and working for money. This is covered by another Greek word, *OIKETES*.

But in those days, a great many people were owned by another person. Half the population of Rome at that time was made up of people who were owned by a Roman citizen—people who had been captured in some military action by the Roman armies. These "slaves" had no personal rights.

Then there were "bond slaves"; these were often freed slaves, but who chose to devote themselves to their former masters.

Or, in some cases, a person would voluntarily indenture himself to another as a "slave." This is the situation that Paul placed himself and Timothy in—totally the property of Christ Jesus, and at His entire disposal! Which, of course, should be the mental attitude that you and I have toward Him! After all, why not!

We note that this letter is addressed to Believers—to "saints," and "set apart ones." This letter will make very little sense to a non-believer, because this is a letter that is only, as the Bible expresses it, "spiritually discerned." We should not expect a non-Christian to make sense out of what's here.

On the other hand, a non-Christian can plunge into the Gospels, or even into the Book of Hebrews, and probably come away with a sense of some comprehension—but don't expect a non-believer to read through Paul's letters and then tell you that what he or she read or what makes sense to them.

Two Groups Set Apart from the Rest: "Teachers" and "Helpers"

The last thing I want you to note in this first verse is that there are, among these Believers, two classes of people set apart from "all" the Believers: *EPISKOPOS,* which is the word for "overseers," who were the Pastor-Teachers; and then there were *DIAKANOS*, which is the word for "helpers." That Greek word comes from a combination of words in their language that spoke of "hurrying and creating a cloud of dust."

This office of "Helpers" was created back in Acts 6, and their duty was to take the physical pressure off the Pastor-Teachers, leaving them free to minister to the spiritual needs of the people in their Assembly.

Nothing I was able to find in later passages in the New Testament has added to or altered the job description of the *DIAKANOS.*

Likewise, the super-imposing of "Bishops" or "District Pastoral Committees," or other hierarchical personages OVER the local Pastor-Teacher, is also conspicuous by its absence in the rest of the New Testament Scriptures. All of this "church organization" business is totally manmade.

So, that's the first verse of this Letter to the Believers at Philippi. That's a lot of important information, isn't it!

Our Introduction to the Meaning of "Grace"

Next, we find a verse that has intrigued me greatly; it appears in all four of these letters of Paul's, and in most of his other letters:

> "Grace to you, and peace from God our Father, and the Lord Jesus Christ!"

Now, obviously it is a "greeting," and I guess you could ask why I should try to read something deeper into it than just a normal "greeting" but I am convinced that there is nothing in the original text of God's Word that is NOT important, and so I ask myself a few questions about this one.

First, we know that the greeting "Grace to you" was a common word of greeting in the entire Greek world, and I understand that it still is. It's *CHAIREIN!* And we find that greeting in other passages where it is used as such (Acts 15:23; Acts 23:26).

And since the root word *CHARIS* meant "a cause for rejoicing" or "something that causes pleasure," and since the Greeks had many "gods" in their pantheon, the meaning of their greeting was, "May the gods smile on you; may they be kind to you; may they allow your days to be good." We Americans have shortened it down to just two words: "Good luck!" Or, as the Chinese say it: "May your joss be good!"

These Greeks knew that they had little or no influence on their "gods" no matter what they did. The best they could do for a friend was to "hope" that they could brighten their day by a cheery greeting and, at the same time, "put in a good word for him," as we say.

Now, it was common in the Old Testament to ASK God to "be gracious" to others. We remember the words that the Lord spoke to Moses at the time He was giving Moses their Rules of Conduct that we call the Mosaic Law. These words have been used over and over again as a "benediction" ENTIRELY out of order for our Dispensation—but here they are—and this is the Book of Numbers, beginning at 6:22:

> "And the Lord spoke to Moses saying: 'Speak to Aaron and to his sons, saying: On this wise you shall bless the children of Israel, saying to them:
> The Lord (Jehovah) bless you and keep you;
> The Lord make His face shine upon you, and be gracious to you;
> The Lord lift up his countenance upon you, and give you peace."
> (Num. 6:22-26)

Then God added these words:

> "And they shall put My Name upon the children of Israel, and I will bless them." (Num 6:27)

You and I know that God *would have* been "gracious" to the Jewish people and *would have* given them "peace" had they followed His instructions, but they consistently did not. For these Jews, this would have been a fair request, to plead for God's grace. And for the Greeks, who had only lifeless gods to worship, you might as well wish them "Good Luck!"

But is that true with us? Certainly not!

Paul has told us that his ministry, and his position with Christ, was a matter of pure grace, and he made this very interesting statement to these Philippian Believers, right here in Verse 7, that they are all "partakers of his grace"!

We know that it is through God's grace that we're redeemed (Ephesians 1:7), that we're "made alive with Christ" (Ephesians 2:5) and that "unto every one of us is given grace, according to the measure of the gift of Christ" (Ephesians 4:7).

So, each of us HAS God's Grace. We're IN it; it's all over us!

So, do we profit from someone shooting up a prayer on our behalf that "God be gracious to us" or that "His Grace fall on us"? It hardly seems so.

Well, do we really appreciate His Grace? Do we "wallow" in it? Do we think about it and give thanks for it? Do we stop to think that it provides us with daily care and help and guidance? And then do we relax and enjoy our position, which is "under His wing" and "in His hand"?

Does it cause us, as the Apostle Peter urged on us in, First Peter 2:

> "Since you have tasted that the Lord is gracious, then lay aside all malice, and all guile, and hypocrisies and envies, and all evil speakings, and, as newborn babes, seek after the pure milk of God's Word, so that, by it, you may grow up in your salvation!"

Does our knowledge of His Grace that we are showered with cause us to do these things? It should! Paul closed this letter to the Philippians with these words of assurance, where he tells us, "The grace of our Lord Jesus Christ IS with you all!"

That verse is a "present tense" verse—not a hope, nor a wish! And an appreciation of this gives a Believer peace! That's the other part of this greeting of Paul's.

The greeting of "Grace to you" (*CHAIREIN*) was the Greek greeting; the usual Jewish greeting was—and still is—*SHALOAM*.

The Jews have always prayed for peace—personal, individual and national peace, and they never have found it. And they won't, as we know, until they turn to the Person that they rejected, and still reject.

But Paul, now, brings a new message of hope to us all. In "Grace," God made wonderful provisions, and in "Grace" He included us in them. As we operate "in Grace," then a new and wonderful peace is ours, as you and I have come to know.

However, there are a couple of strings attached to this, as many of God's promises have attached to them. Here at the end of Philippians 4:9, we note that Paul instructed us:

> "Those things which you have both learned, and received, and heard, and seen in me, practice; and the God of Peace shall be with you." (Phil. 4:9)

God is always with us, and IN us, but we are all prone to deviate. And in our deviations from what we have learned from God's Word, and have observed in Paul's life, we deprive ourselves of the closeness with our Heavenly Father that brings us both guidance, and fellowship, and peace. But in HIS Grace, God has given us the technique of First John 1:9; we use it, and again, the peace that God has graciously arranged for us is ours!

So, we can close this little lesson as Paul closed his message to these people here at the end of Philippians:

"The Grace of our Lord Jesus Christ IS with you all! Amen!"

Lesson 2 Philippians Chapter 1

Our Assurance of Progress in the Christian Life

THIS LETTER TO the people at the city of Philippi is the first of four letters that the Apostle Paul wrote during his time of imprisonment in the city of Rome. He was being held under "house arrest," awaiting his hearing before the Roman Emperor Nero.

Paul really expected his hearing to result in a death sentence for him; yet during this time he was held there, which had been dragged out for nearly two years, Paul was constantly teaching and (probably) writing. Although, these four letters (Philippians, Colossians, Ephesians, and Philemon) are all that have been preserved for us.

But together, these letters constitute a great revelation of the Mind of God toward us members of the human race. On the scale of things, these four letters constitute an Upper-Division course in Christianity and Christian Living; we might say that the Gospels and the Book of Acts are "Christianity 101; the Books of Romans, Corinthians and Galatians are 201."

When we look at Verses 1 and 2 of Philippians 1, we marvel a bit at the depth of his combined greeting in Verse 2, combining the *CHAIREIN* (that was the common greeting of the Greek people of that day, and even today) that says, "Grace to you!" with the common greeting of the Jewish people, *SHALOM* that says, "Peace to you!"

To those people, both Greek and Jew, these greetings were only "wishes" at best, since the Greeks worshipped only dead "gods," who could not help a person anyway, and the Jews knew what it took to secure a state of personal and national "Peace" from God—and that was obedience to His Commands to them, which they consistently chose to disregard.

But Paul took these two national greetings and combined them into one that should mean a great deal to a Believer in Jesus Christ and that says to us:

> "You are the beneficiary of God's Grace; it is constantly with you; you are a part of it! So enjoy it, and then enjoy the Peace that will go with your enjoyment of His Grace!"

Now Paul continues his Letter to these European Believers, many of whom were the results of his first efforts on the continent of Europe. These people were dear to him, as he explains to them in Verse 3:

> "I thank my God upon every remembrance of you; always, in every prayer of mine for you all, I pray with joy because of your partnership in the Gospel from the first day until now." (Phil. 1:3-5)

They have shared with him in his love and devotion to the "Good Word from God," and he appreciates that! I can understand that. It's actually exciting when we come across someone who is enthused about what we're enthused about. For me, that doesn't happen too often in daily life, and when it does, it's actually exhilarating, right?

Then, Verse 6 gives us another great truth; one that can give us great comfort with our own lives, but also can be a source of comfort as we view a life of a person we love that has maybe not lived very close to the things of God and of Christ as he or she could have:

> "For I am absolutely confident (perfect tense, active voice) of this very thing, that He who began a good work in you will perform it to completion *(EPI-TELEO)* until the Day of Christ Jesus."

At a person's "moment of salvation" (and only God knows when that is or was) God begins a work in that person, and no matter what happens in that person's life from that point on, God continues His process of work on that person until he leaves this Earth.

But when that person stands before our Lord Jesus Christ, that person will be in a state of perfection because of the Grace of God, which includes the Work that Jesus did on the Cross for each member of the human race.

THAT is a source of comfort! And He will do that!

I remember something that Dr. Jack Mitchell used to say, "I know you see lots of faults in me now, but just be patient; God is not through with me yet. Just wait until you see me in Heaven! I will be just like Him!" Then Paul added these further words to them in Verse 7:

> "For it is only right for me to feel this way about you all, because I have you in my heart, since both in my imprisonment and in the defense and confirmation of the Gospel, you all are partakers of grace with me. For God is my witness, how I long for you all with the affection of Christ Jesus."

Here is the expression of his sense of "fellowship" with those who also have a strong pull to Christ and to Christianity. And here is the key verse of the Letter to the Philippians, which is in Chapter 4, Verse 9:

> "Those things which you have both learned, and received, and heard, and seen in me, practice; and the God of Peace shall be with you!"

Here, in Paul, is an example for us to follow!

Paul's Prayer for Our Knowledge and Discernment

And now, starting here in Verse 9 is Paul's prayer for them (and it would be for us as well as it was his request that these letters of his be read by all the Assemblies) and it contains his analysis of what should be the pattern of the life and the thinking of every Believer—so that, as he says in Chapter 4, Verse 9, "the God of Peace shall be with us!"

Philippians 1:9 begins. Here is a literal translation:

> "And this I pray, that your love (your 'Divine Concern') may abound more and more in full knowledge and all discernment, so that you may test and establish the things that are right in God's sight, with the result that you are clean, yourself, and that you will cause no one else to stumble until the Day of Christ Jesus, having been filled with the fruit of righteousness, that comes through Jesus Christ, to the glory and praise of God."

Now there is another passage that is packed full of doctrinal information! First, there are two things that he urgently wants for us: the first is "full knowledge," and the second is "discernment."

We are going to be running into the expression "full knowledge" frequently in the studies of these four letters; the Greek word is *EPI-GNOSIS.* "GNOSIS" was their word for just plain "knowledge"; *EPI-GNOSIS* was "full knowledge," and there is a great difference, as we well know. It's one thing to have "some" knowledge of a subject but "full knowledge" puts us in a vastly different position, and that's where Paul wants us Believers to be.

"Full knowledge" is obtained only by digging a matter out, then by studying it and then by applying it to our experience.

Then this "Divine Concern"—this *AGAPE* that we've attached the word "love" to—is an end result of "full knowledge" of God's Word, because out of it all comes a "fellowship" with our Heavenly Father that allows the Holy Spirit to produce this "Divine Concern" in our life.

The second thing he urgently wants for all Believers is "discernment"; the ability to "judge" things that come our way and determine accurately what's right, from God's Viewpoint, and what's not right.

"Full knowledge" helps us to make good judgments, but we need even more than just that, because there are so many things thrown at us these days, most of which are insidious, or covered over with otherwise seemingly-desirable qualities, so that, as Matthew warned us in Matthew 24:24, in these end times there will be things presented to us as "good" that aren't! And "even the very elect shall be deceived"!

The sad thing is that when you and I are not accurately discerning good from bad, others in our "sphere of influence" are led astray because of us!

Verse 11 then tells us the results that will characterize our lives as a result of our efforts to gain "full knowledge" and to measure all things against God's Word, so as to rightly "discern" them. The results are that the "fruit of Righteousness" will be produced in us.

These "fruit" are defined for us by Paul in Galatians 5:22 and 23, where he lists the "fruit of the Holy Spirit." (You're familiar with them: "Love, Joy, Peace, Longsuffering, Gentleness, Goodness, Faith, Meekness, Self-control.") Jesus Christ, our Creator and our Benefactor, arranged for us to have the Holy Spirit at our Moment of Salvation, and the Character traits that the Holy Spirit wants to produce will bring, as he says here at the end of Verse 11:

> "...will bring glory and praise to God!"

God wants mankind to recognize Him and to honor Him—not ourselves, or the things we think we are creating. He wants us to do what I call a "reality check" and to realize that, literally, "without Him, we can do nothing!" (John 15:5). Which, of course, gets our eyes off ourselves and our "good fortune" and onto Him.

Here we have God's great desire for the human race expressed through the Apostle Paul, given to us for our benefit, so that (Chapter 4:9) if we *practice* these things, then will the God of Peace be with us. Certainly, the most wonderful possession we could have, this side of Heaven.

A Model for Our Reactions to Adversity

Now, in these following verses, Paul reviews with us the correct reaction that we all should have to adversity.

I have this little saying posted in front of me at my study desk: *"A Christian should never flinch!"* Well, here's the example that the Apostle Paul left for us in Verse 12:

> "Now I want you to know, brethren, that my circumstances have turned out for the greater progress of the Gospel, so that my imprisonment in the cause of Christ has become well known throughout the whole Praetorian Guard, and to everyone else;
>
> ...and that most of the brethren, trusting in the Lord because of my imprisonment, have far more courage to speak the Word of God without fear." (Phil. 1:12-14)

We know that ever since his arrival there in Rome, Paul has been chained to a member of the Praetorian Guard. And, as was their practice, the guards were changed every four hours, so you can imagine the string of men that would have been listening to Paul's words as he continued to meet and talk with all sorts of people that came to see him.

Now the members of this "Praetorian Guard" were "elite troops" (actually they were members of Caesar's household) and we know this exposure to the Roman soldiers was successful because the Roman Historian Tertullian wrote that the Roman government became disturbed when it found that there were Christians in positions of authority. Many of these men later died for their Faith in Jesus Christ, by the way.

So not only was Caesar's household touched with the Message of the New Way, but Paul's inability to get out and around seemed to put some boldness into the minds of other Believers, encouraging them to go out in Paul's place.

Then we have another effect of his imprisonment, and that is in the fact that as a result, he wrote these four letters that are a vital part of the knowledge that you and I have, of God's Mind toward us. Plus, of course, they have given us another example of perseverance in the face of adversity. Then in these verses, starting with Verse 15, Paul says something that is a bit puzzling:

> "Some, to be sure, are preaching Christ even from envy and strife, but some also from good will; the latter do it out of love, knowing that I am appointed for the defense of the gospel;
>
> ...the former proclaim Christ out of selfish ambition, rather than from pure motives, thinking to cause me distress in my imprisonment—but, whether in pretense or in truth, Christ is proclaimed; and in this I rejoice, yes, and I will rejoice."

Dr. Vernon McGee commented that at the beginning of his ministry he had trouble understanding how anybody could preach the Word "out of selfish ambition." Then, he said, it wasn't long until he saw it happening.

Today, of course, you and I have seen a number of well-known men being caught up in the money-making aspect of the Ministry—and for other purely selfish reasons—so we can understand what was undoubtedly going on also in Paul's day, since, as we know, there is really *"nothing new under the sun."*

Now Verse 19 has an important thought for us:

> "For I know that this shall turn out for my deliverance through your prayers and the provision of the Spirit of Jesus Christ."

Notice that Paul expects his "deliverance" to come as a result of two happenings:

- First, through their prayers; AND
- through the provision of the Holy Spirit.

Then note what this "deliverance" is that he has in mind; it's not that he be released from his confinement, nor is it for his good health. He states what he's looking for, here in Verse 20:

> "...that I shall not be put to shame in anything, but that with all boldness, Christ shall even now, as always, be exalted in my body, whether by life or by death."

There, by the way, is NOT the kind of prayer that most of us continually pray, is it! Our usual prayer is for our good health, for our success in whatever we're trying to accomplish, etc., etc. This is the model prayer:

> "...that I shall not be put to shame in anything, but that with all boldness, Christ shall even now, as always, be exalted in my body, whether by life or by death." (Phil. 1:20)

But now let's look back at Verse 19, and the two "happenings" that Paul says will bring about this state in his life. It will come about:

1. "Through your prayers" AND
2. "Through the provision of the Holy Spirit!"

It's interesting, isn't it, that God encourages us to pray for one another, and, as we have here, He indicates strongly that the outcome of things really *is* influenced by our prayers for one another.

We see so many instances where the things we pray for to happen don't happen, and yet we are urged by Him to pray for one another! So, we ARE to pray for one another, and, as we're also told, "The fervent prayer of a person in right-standing with God, avails much!" (James 5:16).

But then we note also that our praying is coupled with the Work of the Holy Spirit. I remember Dr. Mitchell telling his congregation that, "I know you are concerned for me, but, knowing some of you, I'm glad that I'm not dependent on your prayers for my wellbeing; the Holy Spirit is praying for me also!"

The Problem of a "Divided Assembly"

God wants us to have fellowship not only with Him, but also with each other. We refer to the passage in First John, where John reminded us that,

> "That which we have seen and heard, declare we unto you, SO THAT you also may have fellowship with us, and truly our fellowship is with the Father, and with His Son, Jesus Christ." (1 John 1:3)

Then he goes on to say, in Verse 7:

> "But if we walk in the light, as He is in the light, we HAVE fellowship one with another, and the blood of Jesus Christ His Son cleanses us from all sin."

He wants us to have a spirit of "fellowship" with Him, and with His people. "Fellowship" (*KOINONIA*) is one of the keywords of Christianity, as is *AGAPE*, which we translate as "Divine Concern," and as is *SO-TER-IA*, which we translate as "Salvation," which is deliverance from all the evils of this world.

Now, having expressed to us what the central thinking of his life is, Paul explains the dilemma that this thinking places a person in. He has just stated it, here in Philippians 1:20:

> ...that he would not ever be put to shame, but "that with all boldness, Christ shall even now, as always, be exalted in my body, whether by the process of my life, or by the effects of my death."

And here's his dilemma in Verse 21:

> "For to me, to live is Christ, and to die is gain."

Here's what happens if he continues to live, in Verse 22:

> "But if I live on in the flesh, this will mean fruitful labor for me."

And he continues that thought in Verse 24:

> "...to remain on in the flesh is more necessary for your sake."

But the pull to be with the Lord is very strong with him, also. In Verse 21 he calls dying "gain"; and, in Verse 23, he says simply that "being with Christ, is very much better!" So, he is hard-pressed from both directions! We can understand his dilemma!

But, either way, he will do what God expects of him, even though it involves more suffering, so that he can be a further example for them, to encourage them, as they move ahead.

First, here is his hope for them in Verse 27, there at the end:

> "...that you are standing firm in one spirit, with one mind, striving together for the faith of the gospel; in no way alarmed by your opponents..."

Paul is reminding us of two things here; first, that there is no rational reason for a divided Assembly, if all parties are conscientiously seeking the One Mind, which is the Mind of God.

And the second thing is that we not be "set into panic" by our opponents. We need to be alert as to what they're up to, so that we can defend ourselves against them … but *what they're up to* must not destroy our inner peace.

The increase in the opposition to the "Things of God" is well documented as being a part of the End Times. God knows this. However, we still have our work to do; it will still have its rewards, because it is His Work!

In Verse 29, he also wants us to be alert to what may be ahead for us:

> "For to you it has been granted for Christ's sake, not only to believe in Him, but also to suffer for His sake, experiencing the same conflict which you saw in me, and now hear to be in me."

There have been times when being identified with Christianity has caused great suffering; it still is in many places of the world, and may be for us, someplace along the line. If we DO "suffer for the cause of Christ," we are to recognize the fact that we are thereby taking our place of honor, and a place where we WILL BE honored.

Some Thoughts on "Undeserved Suffering"

There is, of course, no *virtue* in suffering, so there is no virtue in deliberately putting ourselves in a place where we will be "beat upon," either physically or verbally, just simply to make the point that we are a Christian. But if we DO find ourselves in that position, we realize that it has always been that way, and many have suffered through the years—and we also realize that God is well aware of what is going on with us. In James 1:12, we are assured that:

> "Blessed is the man that endures testing; for when he is tried, he shall receive the crown of life, which the Lord has promised to them that are concerned for Him."

Now, speaking of "suffering," let's talk about that for a couple of minutes and let me pass along a couple of thoughts to you.

The subject of "suffering" is very much in our minds. As we observe all that is going on in the world, and, as you and I get older, we see and feel more and more of it. It is with us, and around us. And the question is always: "Why, Lord?" And, sometimes, "Why ME, Lord?"

Well, first of all, you and I know that much of the suffering that is going on around us is self-induced. We also know that much more is also for discipline.

But what you and I are mostly concerned with is what is called "undeserved suffering"; the suffering of Believers who have done no wrong, and whose faith is already seemingly very strong.

I would remind us again of what we already know. Jesus told us plainly that, "In this world we will have tribulation, but (He added) be of good cheer, I have overcome the world" (John 16:33).

Tribulation ("testing") will be a part of our life. There's no escaping it. But we also know, from James Chapter 1, that "tribulation" or "testing" has a purpose; it builds our faith as we respond positively to it. It is a part of the process we recognize as "boot camp," where we are being trained for greater responsibilities in the next phase of our life.

So, we don't fight it, we thank Him for it, knowing that He will see us through it and will use what we are going through for our benefit, and for the benefit of those around us.

But the struggle for us all is to view it positively, as a personal benefit, for which we are thankful; there lies the struggle for most of us.

One pastor that I listen to, who was an Air Force pilot and who has flown many combat missions, likens Suffering to flying a plane in bad weather; he points out that the moment you get into stormy conditions, immediately you have to get onto your Instruments, and get off "flying by the seat of your pants."

When you run into a storm, if you are flying by visual contact only, as though you had no instruments, the first sensation is usually panic, the next sensation is despair and the next action is probably a dumb move, or at least an alteration of your course, whether you realize it or not. You must get onto your instruments at once!

Now relating that to "life" and a person is told that he has, say, cancer; again, the first reaction is usually panic, which is usually followed by despair.

From there it can move to various forms of "escape." Drugs, alcohol, TV absorption, tantrums, self-destruction, and on and on, as we know. All of these avenues, of course, have to be called negative responses to "testing."

The positive response, on the other hand, is a quick switch to our instruments, which, of course, is God's Word; His Promises, His Assurances, His Record of Promise Keeping, His Grace toward us, as His Children, and His Concern for us. Then we rely on what we read, and we rest on what we read.

And, as a result, we make it through, those around us are blessed, and God is honored.

And since our anchor IS the Word of God, I would encourage you to take every opportunity to read things that are readily available, that record and present the many confirmations that establish the validity and the authenticity of our Bible.

Satan would like to weaken our faith and will throw everything at us that he can; therefore, every opportunity we can use to strengthen our Faith will be time well spent. When "tribulation" suddenly appears, and when we reach for the switch from "visual flying" to "instruments," this is our prime opportunity.

Lesson 3 Philippians Chapter 2

God's Provision for "Christian Living"

We know that this letter of Paul's we are studying was a "thank you" letter to these Believers in the city of Philippi, thanking them for their thoughtfulness and kindness they had shown to Paul, but to those of us who have followed along, we realize that it is a tremendous spelling out of what God's idea of Christian living should be.

And if I can capsulize what it tells us IS "Christian living," I'd say it's a life in which, first of all, we recognize how gracious God was to us:

- to make a provision for the forgiveness of our shortcomings and failures;
- to "mark paid" the penalties that missing God's standards require; and
- to provide for us a wonderful future life with Him and in His Presence after this one is completed.

That is "Grace," and it's only the beginning! *Then* as we understand and appreciate this Grace, we are able to enjoy a total sense of peace, no matter what is going on around us or what we happen to be going through.

Then, on top of that, God has arranged for His Own Spirit to live within us as a separate entity, here to guide us, protect us, and instruct us AS we give Him the opportunity.

Then, we find that as the Holy Spirit is allowed to operate within us, our personality begins to change; new characteristics begin to form and begin to be seen by others around us. The Bible calls these the "fruit of the Spirit." They're listed in Galatians 3 and they consist of:

- a "concern for others" that we didn't have before;
- an "inner sense of fullness" that the Bible calls "joy." A friend of mine used to say that she "felt like a chocolate sundae—all covered over with good stuff!";
- then there develops the quietness within our minds that we call "peace," that is so wonderful;
- then there is the quality called "longsuffering" that gives you quietness even though you're being "provoked" either by people, or by circumstances;
- then the qualities of gentleness and goodness appear, or are intensified; AND, what most of us have a great need for;
- self-control begins to be added to us!

All of these develop in this original shell that was stinky-old-us, and they re-form us, if and as we give the Holy Spirit the opportunity to work! And you and I know how to keep Him working, I'm sure. It's by the application of First John 1:9, as needed!

Now with all of these things included in the Benefits of Christianity, who would NOT want to be a part of it? But obviously many just don't care!

But in this letter, we can see these things at work in these people at Philippi, and we can see them at work in the Apostle Paul, so we will watch him operate, and we will listen to the advice he gives us—advice directly from the Holy Spirit to us!

The first bit of advice that we have found here was in Verse 10 of Chapter 1, and it calls for some mental effort that we call "mind control." We CAN control our mind and, further, the Holy Spirit will help us, if He is operational in our lives!

The point is that we now have (and are gaining, as Verse 9 of Chapter 1 tells us) a "full knowledge!" And with it, we are gaining the ability to discern what's good in God's eyes and what's NOT good in God's eyes; and now we are expected, Verse 10 tells us, to test things that come along, accepting what is "good" and pulling away from what's not good. Not just "going along, rather than creating waves," but divorcing ourselves from what's not good.

People don't like to "take a stand" anymore. But God expects us, with this new knowledge and discernment, to apply it to our life—to "take a stand" when necessary and not just "float along."

If you are a timid person, you don't have to go on a campaign against something evil if you don't feel comfortable in doing so, but you also don't have to accept it as a part of your own life, as so many Christians are doing more and more these days!

Paul tells us this, in so many words, in Philippians 1:27. Here it is expressed as a command—as something that God says we are expected to do:

> "Conduct yourselves in a manner worthy of the Gospel of Christ..."

Then he actually tells us what he means by this, as he continues:

> "...whether I am there or here..."

(In other words, no matter who is looking at you)

> "...see that you are standing firm in one spirit, with one mind, striving together for the faith of the gospel."

Standing together, not struggling with petty doctrinal differences. If some other Assembly has their trust in Jesus as the Christ, as God's Provision for Eternal Life, then why should we brush them off because they like to raise their hands at certain times in their meeting? Then Paul adds to that thought in Philippians 2:2. He again commands us:

> "Make my joy complete by being of the same mind, maintaining the same concern, united in spirit, intent on one purpose."

Then the sentence continues with a string of commands that are valid to us, because even though the Holy Spirit resides in us, and may be fully operative in our life, we still have our original nature in us, too, and our impulse is to put ourselves first, to try to build ourselves up in the eyes of others.

When the occasion arises, the Holy Spirit will nudge us so that we are conscious that a time of decision is upon us, but He won't shut our mouth for us! After all, we are not robots, nor are we vegetables! We are free agents. So, Paul cautions us in Verse 3 to:

> "Do nothing from selfishness or empty conceit, but with lowliness of mind, let each of you regard one another as more important than himself, not looking out ONLY for your own personal interests, but also for the interests of others."

Then here is the example Verse 5:

> "Have this attitude in yourselves which was also in Christ Jesus!"

In other words, here is an "attitude of mind" that we are to assume. If it were simply a fruit that the Holy Spirit were to present us with, then we would not be commanded to do this. It is an "attitude" that we are expected to adopt as our own, and the Holy Spirit will help us in the adoption process!

Paul further explains here, starting in Verse 6, what Jesus went through as He adopted this mental attitude:

> "Even though He was a form of God, He did not cling to that, but emptied Himself, taking the form of a servant, and being made in the likeness of men, He humbled Himself by becoming obedient to the point of death—even death on a cross."

If you're like I am, you may have trouble comprehending exactly what The Christ, the Son of God, did actually go through mentally as He changed Himself into a human being and left the glory of Heaven to come to live on this Earth. His memory would certainly have come with Him and would have brought with Him His full knowledge of Heaven.

But also, He would have had with Him God's compassion and feelings for each member of the human race, knowing the prevalent attitude of rejection that exists so widely, and the bitter end result of that rejection. This would have been a heavy burden!

We weep over the waywardness we see around us in our very limited circle of contact but think of what He would be conscious of!

Now, the physical pain of His total experience here on Earth, we know He could stand, just as you and I can and will be able to stand it, but the mental anguish must have been monumental.

However, He wanted to do it. It had to be done to accomplish God's Plan, and so He did what had to be done. We see in Verse 9, "Therefore God highly exalted Him, and bestowed on Him the name that is above every name…" In a like manner, as Paul is instructing us here, again in Verse 5, we are to, "…have this attitude in ourselves which was also in Christ Jesus!"

When what we are to do calls for us to assume the role of a servant, then we are expected to do it willingly, graciously, as unto our Lord, looking out for, as our first interest, the interests of others.

The Only Message Worth Getting Out

Then he continues the thought down in Verse 14, where he adds this command:

> "Do all things without grumbling (whining, complaining) or disputing (arguing about it) so that you may establish yourselves to be blameless and innocent, children of God above reproach, in the midst of a crooked and perverse generation, among whom you shine as lights in the world, holding fast the Word of Life..."

And Paul also reminds us of what this "Word of Life" has to tell the world; it starts here in Philippians 2:9. Because of His coming to Earth, and His Death:

> "Therefore God highly exalted Him, and bestowed on Him the name which is above every name, so that at the name of Jesus every knee should bow, of those who are in heaven, and on earth, and under the earth, and that every tongue should confess that Jesus Christ is Lord, to the glory of God the Father."

I know this is a trite statement, and much overworked in what we call "Christian circles," but it is true nevertheless. This message to the world is the only message worth trying to get out to the world. The message is:

- that Jesus Christ is The Exalted of God;
- that one day His Name will be exalted above every other name;
- that at His Name every knee will literally bow;
- that our Deliverance is based on our recognition of the fact that He IS the Lord of our life; and
- that we therefore put ourselves in the position of his bond-slave.

You and I are "lights to the world" and we are, I know, "ready to give an answer to everyone who asks us, of the hope that is within us," But our sphere of influence is limited, as you and I well know. The Evangelical broadcasters have been given a wide, personalized opportunity, to reach an audience on an intimate basis and under conditions so that the listeners can respond favorably. Supporting them is how you and I can let this Light shine way out there!

So, the Message from the Holy Spirit that Paul is passing on to us here is:

- that we stand firm in one spirit;
- with one mind striving together for the faith of the gospel (Chapter 1, Verse 27);
- that we maintain the same concern for others that He has, regarding one another as more important than ourselves, looking out for the interest of others as we do our own (Chapter 2, Verse 3);
- that we take on, as our own, the same attitude toward our assignments in life that Jesus took—of humility and acceptance even unto death (Verse 5); and
- that (Verse 14) we do all this without grumbling or disputing.

All this causes us to "shine as lights" in the midst of this crooked and perverse generation, as we "hold fast the Word of Life."

Paul, as are we, was very conscious of the smallness of the number of people, even among Believers, who are truly interested in others, who are concerned for them to the point of doing something about their concern. Notice here in Verse 19 of Chapter 2:

> "I hope in the Lord Jesus to send Timothy to you shortly, so that I also may be encouraged when I learn of your condition; for I have no one else of kindred spirit who will genuinely be concerned for your welfare. For they all seek after their own interests, not those of Christ Jesus."

Undoubtedly Paul had Believers all around him, in and out of his place but, as with so many of us, their main interest was their own affairs.

Timothy's "light was shining" however, as was their pastor Epaphroditus that Paul talks about in the verses that follow. All of this is what Paul is referring to here in Verse 12 of Chapter 2, where he has also commanded us to:

> "...work out our deliverance (or our 'salvation') with fear and trembling, for it is God who is at work in you, both to will and to work His good pleasure."

And I know that I have through the years (as I know that you have) watched the efforts of so many people in business, many of whom have built success for themselves, only to wind up with split-up families, children who disappoint them, and the business they worked so hard to build up, deteriorate into nothing.

They were looking for "joy" and "peace" in their lives and they found, in the end, that they had nothing, because their focus was NOT on "appearing as lights in the world" and it was NOT on establishing themselves as "blameless and innocent, children of God above reproach in the midst of a crooked and perverse generation."

They were not focused, as Verse 16 states, on:

> "...holding fast the word of life, so that in the day of Christ, they may have cause to glory, and that they did not run in vain, or toil in vain."

They were looking for joy and peace in the wrong place and from the wrong source. Yet the Bible, God's Word, has the instruction as to where any member of the human race can find it. In Verse 18 here in Chapter 2, Paul reminds us that:

> "...he has been poured out as a drink offering"; he says, "he rejoices and shares his joy with all of them."

Then, he continues in Verse 18:

> "And you too, I urge you, rejoice in the same way and share your joy with me!"

The real Joy comes from "shining out as lights in the world," and in "... holding fast the word of life, so that in the Day of Christ we may have cause to glory because we did not run in vain, nor toil in vain" (Phil. 1:16).

I know we all HATE to do unneeded, unnecessary tasks! But think of all the things that are done by well-meaning people that are going to be proven to have been "in vain"; unneeded, unnecessary!

WE have the information to help them see which tasks ARE needed and necessary, and which are not! And they will see it, not only from what we SAY, but mostly from the "light" that shines out of our lives.

Beginning in Chapter 3, Paul starts to list out for us more operating instructions from our Heavenly Father for our benefit, and then, toward the end of the final chapter, Chapter 4, he has this word for us in Verse 9:

> "Those things, which you have both learned, and received, and heard, and seen in me, do; and the God of Peace shall be with you."

And then there is the promise that he has just told us in Chapter 4, Verse 7, that:

> "The peace of God, which passes all understanding, shall keep your hearts and minds, through Jesus Christ."

"Joy" comes from doing these things that please God; "peace" comes from our knowledge of our relationship with His Son, Jesus Christ. This is the message that the world needs, and it's the only one that will change lives.

May we be conscious of every opportunity, as the Holy Spirit gives us opportunity, to get that message out!

Lesson 4 Philippians Chapters 1 and 2 Review

God's Plan for Christian Living

LET'S REVIEW A little bit: we have pointed out that these four "prison epistles" together provide the Body of Christ (that's us "Believers") with our God-given instructions for living a life that will bring the follower of these instructions Peace and Joy on a daily, continuing basis.

The first lesson that I noted here was the example of Paul's mental attitude in all of this; he was a prisoner, robbed of all his privacy and completely restricted, as far as being able to move around and do what he might have otherwise wanted to do. Plus, there was a very good likelihood that he was headed for his death. He was very much like a person who is confined to a wheelchair or a sick bed, or otherwise "laid low," yet he did not fuss or complain. His mental attitude was that he was "a prisoner of Christ Jesus." He kept his mind busy, writing what he did here in Philippians 1:12:

> "But I want you to understand, brethren, that the things that have happened to me have fallen out rather unto the furtherance of the Gospel!"

Paul KNEW the result of "letting your light shine." God will always be honored by our trust in Him and in what He is continually doing in our life!

The next thing we see here is a spelling out of the way God would like to see every Believer—we can call it God's "Profile of a Believer." Paul states it in Philippians 1:9-11:

> "This I pray: that your love (your 'Divine Concern') may abound more and more in full knowledge and all discernment, so that you may test and establish the things that are right in God's sight;
>
> ...with the result that you are clean, yourself, and that you will cause no one else to stumble until the Day of Christ Jesus;
>
> ...having been filled with the fruit of righteousness that comes through Jesus Christ, to the glory and praise of God."

There's our "model." It would be a valuable thing for us to read that over to ourselves on a daily basis, and to think about all the components contained in this message! The result of living this way will be "to the glory and praise of God" ... which is what we really want of our life, right?

Then, while we are living this way, we will be seen to be "filled with the fruit of righteousness" (that's the "fruit" that the Holy Spirit will have been able to produce in our life, including Love, Joy, Peace, Longsuffering, Gentleness, Goodness, Faith, Meekness, and Self-Control), all of which comes to the Believer THROUGH Jesus Christ!

We will be seen by God as "clean," and there will have been no waywardness in our life that will have caused any other person to stumble, because he or she was using us as a role model.

Also, we will have diligently studied His Word to us—His Book of Instruction—and as a result we will have gained a "full knowledge" of It and of Him, which will have produced discernment in us; Discernment of what's right and what's not right in God's eyes.

And, as all this divine insight develops in us, God's attitude of "concern" for those around us will, as he expresses it here, "abound more and more" in us.

This is the pattern He wants in us. I hope you will study this passage, and then look at it again from time to time!

Notice again: it begins with Jesus Christ. As we read and study and apply His Word, we learn what He wants and what He hates, so we steer a straight course. The Holy Spirit, then, is able to produce the "fruit of righteousness" in us, at the top of the list of which is Divine-type concern for those around us. The result is that we are seen as "clean"; we cause no one watching us to stumble; the Fruits of the Holy Spirit are produced in us, including joy and peace, and praise and glory goes to God.

There is "The Christian Life."

Next, Paul moves to another example for us and our mental attitude as we move along through life; it's summarized in his statement here:

> "For to me, to live is Christ, and to die is gain. But if I live in the flesh, this is the fruit of my labor, yet what I should choose, I do not know, I can't perceive.
>
> For I am in a strait between the two, having a desire to depart, and to be with Christ, which is far better, nevertheless, to abide in the flesh is more needful for you." (Phil. 1:21-24)

Now that last is an interesting statement, isn't it! "...to abide in the flesh is more needful for you." You'll note that he sees his present position, even though he knows he is a burden to his friends, yet his presence is nevertheless something that God considers to be important to all involved, otherwise God would have removed him!

That's an interesting thought, isn't it? It's a good thought to tuck away in your memory, for in the future we may need it when we think we're being a burden to someone!

Then Paul continues to give us words of strength and wisdom, starting in Verse 27:

> "Only let your daily walk be worthy of the Gospel of Christ, so that no matter who is looking at you, you will be seen as standing fast in one spirit, with one mind striving together for the faith of the Gospel; and in nothing terrified by what you are facing!"

Isn't it amazing how Paul can pack so much truth into so few words! Then, in Chapter 2, Verse 3 he has given us more Divine Instruction for our daily living:

> "Do nothing from selfishness or empty conceit, but with humility of mind, let each of you regard one another as more important than himself; do not merely look out for your own personal interests, but also for the interests of others."

Another restatement of "The Golden Rule!" And then he gave the best example of all—the way that Jesus set aside His own exalted position, became like us, faced these most difficult trials that we humans would ever have to face, and did it all for us!

Then, in Verse 14, he asks that we:

> "Do all things without grumbling or arguing about it (for a purpose) that we may become blameless and harmless, in the midst of a crooked and perverse generation, among whom you shine as lights..."

And what does God see us as doing? "...holding forth the word of life." What better of a life for us to live! Useful to God, helpful to others out there—many of whom we're not even aware of, of course.

And now, at the start of Chapter 3, Paul uses a word that the Greek-speaking people commonly used when they were winding up a letter or a speech. A speaker would say: "Now in conclusion…" Or, if you were writing to a friend, you'd maybe say: "Well, I have to go now, but..."

The Greek word that is translated here as "finally" translates literally as "for the rest…" or "beyond what I have already said," so we can say that here is really the "wrap up" of what Paul had primarily in mind for these people that meant so much to him.

He begins this "final word" to them by saying: "Keep on rejoicing in the Lord!"

And this process of "rejoicing," of course, means to take time to think on what He really did for us, unworthy as we are, and think on what He is continually doing for us!

And then he says what a good teacher has undoubtedly said to himself many times, "I know that what I say may seem repetitious to you, but I'm going to do it, nevertheless, because it is a safeguard for you!"

And what Paul has to say to them—and to us—here in the remainder of this short but packed letter of instruction, is very probably the best advice and counsel that he has for Believers in all of his writings.

What Paul is clearly trying to impart to us is how we are to live our life so that we each have the maximum amount of this joy and peace in our life. And that life will be the byproduct of a life that is useful, and a life that is pleasing to our Creator.

Sound good? Then "listen up!"

Paul's Appraisal of Human Knowledge

Paul brings it all into focus by pointing to things in his own life. He had worked very hard at his studies; he had been very zealous in his accomplishments; he had worked diligently to become "looked up to" and revered. We recognize these accomplishments of his are typical of what a great many of us have spent our working lives on. Paul's efforts were in the field of Academics; ours may have been in the field of Business, Medicine, Investments, Sports, or any other activity that would accumulate accolades and would cause people to look at us and say, "That is a very good person."

However, of these things Paul says this, here at the end of Verse 8 of Chapter 3 (and this is the way the King James translated it):

> "...I count them but dung..."

The new versions try to clean up that word a little, and translate it as "rubbish", but that isn't the way the Greek-speaking people used the word. The Old King James says it as it was.

And I think that's the way Paul meant it on the scale of true values. These material achievements that we sweat and slave over, and are so proud of and happy about are, on the scale of true values, worth absolutely nothing.

Paul puts them in their proper perspective at the end of Verse 8:

> "...that I may gain Christ, and may be found in Him, not having a righteousness of my own derived from my keeping the Law, but that (right standing) which is through faith in Christ, the righteousness which comes from God on the basis of faith."

Then he states the true goal, the real purpose, there in Verse 10:

> "...so that I may (first and foremost) know Him, and (secondly) know the power of His resurrection and (thirdly) know the fellowship of His sufferings, being conformed to His death, in order that I may attain to the resurrection from the dead."

Now Paul is not counseling that we quit trying to excel at what we are called to be doing or, as some urge Christians to do, to give all that up and "go into full time Christian service." As a matter of fact, he wrote a little later a command to the Colossians:

> "Whatever you do in word or deed, do all in the name of the Lord Jesus, giving thanks to God and the Father by Him!" (Colossians 3:17)

If we do that, would it be anything but our very best effort? Of course not!

How We Are to "Run the Race That We're Given to Run"

Paul recognized that each of us Believers has a "race to run" and a "course to follow" that God has set us on and we are expected to pursue that course to the best of our ability, looking to God daily as we run it; however, our focus is to be on what God wants in our life and wants our life to be! Jesus said:

> "Seek first the Kingdom of God and His righteousness, and all these (other) things shall be added to you." (Matthew 6:33)

So, that is the beginning of our gaining peace and joy in our life: focusing on the right goal! And now, note again what Paul gave as the identification of that goal at the end of Verse 8:

> "...that I may gain Christ..."

Followed by Verse 10:

> "...that I may (first and foremost) know Him. and (secondly) know the power of His resurrection and (third) know the

fellowship of His sufferings, being conformed to His death, in order that I may attain to the out-resurrection from the dead."

We realize that Paul KNEW he would be a part of the resurrection; he also knew that the Believers from Old Testament times were not to be raised until the end of the Great Tribulation period, as Daniel 12:1-3 makes clear. He also knew that the rest of the dead will not be raised until the end of the 1,000 years, "The Millennium." Paul added a prefix to the word he used here for "resurrection" that makes it translate to "out-resurrection." In other words, the "*Rapturo*," the "lifting out" of the Body of Christ, its "homegoing."

Paul looks forward to playing a part in the excitement of that great event! Also, as he says there in Verse 10 that he longs to know more fully Him, Jesus!

I'm sure Paul wished many times that he had been able to know Jesus personally when He was here on Earth, as had those other Apostles. I would like to have known Him personally; I'm sure you would like to have known Him as well.

I will never forget my meeting with Billy Graham back in 1950; it only lasted a few minutes. A couple of us fellows who were ushering were standing in the back of the great tent where the meetings were about to begin, and Billy walked up, shook our hands and talked for a minute as he looked out over that great expanse of benches. But I will never forget his eyes and the sense of a great presence; that experience has affected my attitude toward him ever since that day.

But what if we could know Jesus even that well! This is the longing that Paul expresses here in his heart. And with it, to know the tremendous power that He possesses; the power that raised Him from death, that moved Him up off the earth and into the Heavens. This is the power that operates in the life of each Believer, and we can only slightly sense the magnitude of that power.

Then Paul mentions, here in Verse 10, his desire to participate in the fellowship of the suffering that Jesus went through. Paul's own sufferings on behalf of Christ's Work, as we know, were extreme, yet he seems to want a deeper understanding of what Jesus went through so that he could more fully appreciate all that was done by Jesus for him.

Then Paul recognizes this matter of "gaining Christ" as an on-going thing in our lives, and he expresses that starting here in Verse 12, and the translation of the Greek words into English is hard. The NIV gives us the thought pretty well:

> "Not that I have already obtained all of this, or have already been made 'perfect,' but I press on to take hold of that for which Christ Jesus took hold of me. Brothers, I do not consider myself yet to have taken hold of it. But one thing I do: forgetting what is behind, and straining toward what is ahead, I press on toward the goal to win the prize for which God has called me heavenward, in Christ Jesus." (Phil. 3:12-14)

Again, Paul reminds us that each of us has a calling; a course to follow that God has arranged and has set us into. God wants us to pursue that course "as unto Him," and He has this great power source out there to help us complete it in an honorable fashion. Paul said this in his letter to the people of Galatia, in Galatians 2:20:

> "I am crucified with Christ, nevertheless I live. Yet not I, but Christ lives in me. And this life that I live now in the flesh, I live by the faith of the Son of God, who loved me, and gave Himself for me."

He expresses it a little differently to these Believers at Philippi in Verse 15 of Chapter 3:

> "All of us who are mature should take such a view of things. And if on some point you think differently, that, too, God will make clear to you. Only let us live up to what we have already attained. Join with others in following my example, brothers..."

We remember the little poem by C.T. Studd that says:

> *Only one life, 'twiII soon be past...*
> *Only what's done for Christ, will last!*

Here we have a Scriptural presentation of that great truth!

How we wish we could pass this mental attitude along to the people we see every day who are without peace and without joy, and who are struggling to attain goals that are going to turn out to be empty. But, again, God has us positioned where He wants us to be. And He wants us to be "...ready to give an answer to everyone who asks us, the reason for the Hope that is in us" (I Peter 3:15).

And He has the strength available for us to do that. He tells us, on here in Chapter 4, Verse 13:

> "I can do all things through Christ, who keeps on strengthening me!"

So, there is God's statement of what our goal should be, which, if followed, will result in peace and joy in our lives.

However, we can't leave this without examining the warning that Paul gave us back in the opening verses of Chapter 3. In Verse 2, he warned against three categories:

> "Beware of dogs, beware of evil workers, beware of the concision..."

That's how the King James has it; the New American Standard translates this *last* word as "the false circumcision," which is the sense in which Paul is using it here.

First is the word "Dogs." Who is he referring to? The word is used in this adverse sense only a few times in the New Testament. Jesus used this word that is translated "dogs" (*KU-ON*) only once; that is in Matthew

7:6 when He was giving what we call "The Sermon on the Mount," where He spoke to "the world." To anyone who would listen, he said:

> "Give not that which is holy unto the dogs, neither cast your pearls before swine, lest they trample them under their feet, and turn again and tear you apart!"

Also, the same word is used in Revelation 22:15, where Jesus is making His Final Offer to mankind. Starting in Verse 14 of the last Chapter in the Bible, Jesus had this to say:

> "Blessed are they that do His commandments, that they may have right to the tree of life, and may enter in through the gates into the city.
>
> For outside are dogs, and drug dealers, and whoremongers, and murderers, and idolaters, and whosoever loves and makes a lie..."

So, we can safely say that the reference here in Philippians 3 is against people who would ridicule the things that God stands for and would tear apart those who hold to them, as the packs of dogs did that roamed the streets and countryside in those days.

A Warning Against What's in the World Around Us

Who in all the world today are dedicated to our destruction, to the Destruction of all who follow Christianity? What does God say here?

> "Beware of those whose goal is your destruction."

What does "beware" mean? It means to watch out for them; to be prepared to defend and protect yourself from them. And how do we protect ourselves from them? Obviously NOT by making alliances with them that make their chieftains rich and powerful!

The second group to watch out for are those who work "evil." This Greek word for "evil" is the word they used to identify the opposite of that which is morally and ethically "right." Its Scriptural use is the opposite of what God considers to be "good."

God has identified these people, as we saw earlier, in Revelation 22:15:

> "Drug dealers, those who traffic in prostitution, murderers, idolaters, and those who practice deception." (the "con" artists, in other words)

How are we to handle these people? As Romans 13 tells us, with Capital Punishment—punishment to the body of the offender.

Then the third category is the Greek word *KATATOME,* which was the word Paul used here as the opposite of the rite of Spiritual Circumcision. The rite of Physical Circumcision that God had decreed for the descendants of Israel was to be, for them, an identifying mark of their belonging to God. A permanent identifying mark and a constant reminder to each individual male Jew that he belongs to God.

When Jesus fulfilled the requirements of the Mosaic Law, the rite of Circumcision was no longer a requirement for Christians; then, the set-apartness to God was the Baptism of the Holy Spirit—God "Identifying" the new Believer with the Holy Spirit.

Now, God has given to Christianity the rite of Water Baptism to give the new Believer a permanent reminder of his or her dedication to God and to give the testimony to the world (and to angels) also of that dedication.

However, there are those people who would confuse Believers by distorting God's Word. Paul was continually being plagued with these people. We are to watch out for them, too, since they are as dangerous to our peace and joy as are the "dogs" and those who work evil.

Paul warns us against these people again, in Philippians 3:19, where he points out that:

> "Their end is destruction; their 'god' is their stomach (their fleshly desires), their glory winds up being their shame, as they are focusing on things of the earth."

Which gets us back to Paul's main theme here and, in Verse 20, he reminds us again of it:

> "For our way of life is in heaven; from whence also we look for the Savior, the Lord Jesus Christ, who shall change our vile body, that it may be fashioned like unto His glorious body, according to the working whereby he is able even to subdue all things unto Himself."

There is Our God. We want to keep focused on Him!

Lesson 5 Philippians Chapters 3 and 4

"When We See, Our Focus Will Be—Jesus!"

We're now at the end of our look at the first of four letters that Paul wrote while he was a prisoner in the city of Rome. They convey to all Believers the pattern of how God wants His People to be operating. Dr. McGee describes the contents of this Letter, particularly, as "...dealing with Christian experience at the level on which all believers should be living. It is not a level on which all of us are, but it is where God wants us to be."

We got a look at that as we moved through the high example that Paul gave to us here in Chapter 3, where he has urged us to realize the emptiness and futility of setting and pursuing the goals that are typical of most of us, and that instead, our main goal in life should be, as he expresses it here in Philippians 3:10:

1. to know Him—Jesus; and
2. to know His power—the power of His Resurrection; and
3. to know the fellowship of his sufferings.

All of this so that we might attain and "appreciate to the fullest" the "out-resurrection" of the dead. Now, this probably seems like a rather unusual goal to press onto someone, to fully appreciate our being a part in that great "homegoing of all members of the Body of Christians." Our "graduation" in other words, but we keep in mind that Paul had been places and seen things during the three years that Jesus had him in a training school; things that you and I have never experienced and won't during this lifetime. And it was such a vivid experience that it revolutionized his life and made him into the greatest evangelist the world has ever known!

Paul is telling us here that if we, too, can truly *know Jesus*, and as we come to *fully appreciate the Power* that He possesses, and get a *glimpse* of the wonders that are "out beyond" where we live today, we will be focusing our life on that time of transition that we call the "Homegoing of the Church" (the "Rapture" as many call it) excitedly looking forward to the wonder of it! As the songwriter expressed it:

> "The things of earth will grow strangely dim, in the light of His glory and grace!"— Turn Your Eyes Upon Jesus

Then, in Verse 12, Paul makes it clear that he didn't get this viewpoint overnight, but he is diligently making every effort in trying, as he says, to "...lay hold of that, for which also I was laid hold of by Christ Jesus." And in Verse 14:

> "I press on toward the mark for the prize of the high calling of God, in Christ Jesus."

Jesus is the center of Life and should be the center of our life since He is our Creator. He is the One who made our future life in the Heavens possible; He is the one who wants to guide us and direct us while we are here in this life! And He will, if we make Him the focal point of it! The One to whom we look first!

Paul says this another way, down in Philippians 3:20-21 where he says:

> "Our whole way of life is in Heaven, and it's from there, also, that we look for the return of Christ Jesus; and, when He comes, He will change our corrupt and frail body, so that it will be fashioned like His glorious body, by the power that He possesses, the Power that makes all things to be under His control."

What a wonderful day! Right? I know it is the hope of the Holy Spirit, since Paul is articulating it here so urgently. It's His hope that we, too, can get the feel for what's ahead, because here is the key to peace and real happiness in our life; the happiness that comes from knowing "all is well."

The "Wrap Up"—"Stand Fast in the Lord!"

It will give us the privilege of saying, as Paul did later to his friend Timothy:

> "I have fought the good fight, I have finished the course, I have kept the faith; henceforth there is laid up for me a crown of righteousness, which the Lord, the righteous judge, shall give me at that day; and not to me only, but unto all them also that love his appearing!" (2 Timothy 4:8)

And so, we now come to the word that's always interesting: "therefore" (Chapter 4). "Therefore"—"in view of all of this, my dearly beloved," … what? "Stand fast in the Lord!"

Here we are, down to the wrap up—the final instructions! And here's the prime one: "Stand fast in the Lord!"

The Greek word *STEKO* that is translated "stand fast," is used over and over in the Epistles as a part of the absolutely vital personality element—the mental attitude—that God expects of His People. No matter what is going on around you, "stand firm in your Faith!"

We all know how relatively easy it is to give lip service to our faith when things are going smoothly, but when your ship goes aground and when things begin to fall apart, THEN what do you think of the concept of faith and the promises that tell us that "He will never leave us nor forsake us"? Things take on a little different look, don't they!

But it is then that we need to remember this final admonition from the Holy Word: "Stand fast in the Lord!"

And that means, "Stand firm like a rock; don't look at the waves that are crashing all around you! The Lord allowed you to get into this situation, for your good, and He will certainly see you through it!"

That phrase contains the source of our power for the Christian Life and for "Life" itself! The people around us who are faltering and flailing and groping around for any kind of pacifier are not making use of this Power Source that you and I have.

Notice how Paul stays with this great message as he winds up his letter to these people that he dearly loves:

> Verse 4: "Rejoice in the Lord always, rejoice!"
>
> Verse 6: "Be full of care for absolutely nothing; instead, pray, with thanksgiving!"
>
> Verse 11: "No matter what, be inwardly quiet!"
>
> Verse 12: "I know how to be abased, and I know how to abound,"
>
> Verse 13: "I can do all things through Christ, who keeps on pouring His Power into me!"
>
> Verse 19: "My God shall supply all your need, according to His riches in glory by Christ Jesus!"

So, we have been shown the "source of joy," which is wrapped up in our relationship to Jesus Christ, and now we have been shown the source of the Power to make that a part of our life.

I gave you a line from one of my favorite hymns a moment ago, and I'll say it again. It's the one that says:

"Turn your eyes upon Jesus
Look full in His wonderful face
And the things of earth will grow strangely dim
In the light of His glory and grace."

Well, it's interesting that right in the middle of his wind-up thoughts here, he interrupts himself to speak about a couple of the members of this group that apparently were feuding, "I beseech Euodia, and I beseech Syntyche that they think the same thoughts in the Lord" (Philippians 4:2).

The Problem of "Feuding Members of the Assembly"

We have no clues as to what their problem was. The language technicians tell us that the name "*Euodia*" was a Jewish name, and "*Syntyche*" was of Greek origin; maybe here was the old conflict of Jew vs. Gentile in their approach to Christianity. Whatever it was, Paul's hope was that they would bring their thinking together, as far as the Lord was concerned.

Paul knew, even at that early point in the history of Christianity, that differing thoughts on matters of doctrine are disruptive. This statement of his also brings out the point that there should be NO doctrinal differences among Believers. There is the way that the Scriptures teach, and then there are the ways that man (and women) have devised. Proverbs 14:12 tells us, however:

> "There is a way that seems right unto a man, but the end thereof are the ways of death."

And the inclination of a great many Believers to put their own special "twist" into the Scriptures has created a great many problems through the years, hasn't it! There's another verse of Scripture that bears on this—it's Second Peter 1:20 and it says:

> "Knowing this first, that no teaching of the Scripture is of any private interpretation; for the teaching came not by the will of man, but holy men of God spoke as they were moved by the Holy Spirit."

So, Paul was trying already at this early time in history to encourage "like-mindedness" among God's People! However, "like-mindedness" can come only as people are encouraged to study God's Word for themselves. That's the only way that sound doctrine can be spread!

Now let's remind ourselves of Paul's experience with these people there at Philippi. It started from a vision that Paul had, which is recorded for us in Acts Chapter 16, a vision of a man calling to him from the country of Macedonia to come and help them.

At that time, Paul and his companions had no strong leadership from the Lord as to where to go next and they took this vision as a directive. They left Troy immediately and sailed for the mainland of the Continent of Europe and landed at Philippi.

But, instead of finding a "man" waiting for them, their first contact was with a gathering of women who had assembled there on that Sabbath morning and were praying together. So, women played an important role in the launching of Christianity on the Continent and Paul acknowledges them here in Verse 3; their names, he said "are in the Book of Life!"

Instead of bickering over "private interpretations" of doctrine, he says in Philippians 4:4:

> "Be rejoicing in the Lord always; again I say, Be Rejoicing!"

Be *continually* doing this! "Rejoicing in the Lord" is an awareness of what He did and what He is continually doing, and that should be the focus of our attention—not allowing ourselves to be distracted by the oddballs around us! Let us keep our eyes on the main issue and that is Jesus and what He means to us and to the world!

And what is called for? The next verse (5) ties into this thought:

> "Let your quiet spirit be known unto all men. The Lord is near!"

The key word is *EPIEIKES*; it's translated as "moderation" in the Old King James. The New American Standard has translated it as a "forbearing spirit." The NIV calls it "gentleness." I called it "quiet spirit."

James, the half-brother of Jesus who wrote the "Book of James," goes further into this very important personality attribute in James 3 that I want to look at for a minute.

In this part of his letter, he is urging us to control our tongues; which, as you know, a great many people, including Christians, do not. In Verses 9 and 10 he reminds us that Believers use the same tongue to "bless God and then turn around and curse people"; this, he says, "ought not to be."

We CAN train ourselves to control our tongues, and the Holy Spirit will help us in that process if we allow Him to do so, because "self-control" is one of the fruits of the Holy Spirit, as Galatians 5:22 tells us. But James pokes us a little harder here, in James 3:13-17. Notice this:

> "Who among you is wise and skilled in knowledge? Let him show out of a good walk, his deeds, and do it with the humility that wisdom gives.
>
> But if you have bitter jealousy and selfish ambition in your heart, do not be arrogant, and so lie against the truth. This wisdom is NOT that which comes down from above, but is earthly, from our old nature, and even from the devil.

> But (Verse 17) the wisdom that is from above is first pure, then peaceable, gentle (here's our word *EPIEIKES* again), full of mercy and good fruits, unwavering, without hypocrisy."

That seems to pretty well identify the source of the bickering that so often goes on among Believers, and it's brought on by the human tendency toward jealousy and by our inborn attitude of "I want my own way." James had the uncomfortable knack of saying things as they are, without varnish.

James presented to us the high goal of living, here in Verse 17. Let me say it again:

> "But the wisdom that is from above is first pure, then peaceable, gentle, full of mercy and good fruits, unwavering, without hypocrisy."

"From above" is God's wisdom; the wisdom provided to willing Believers by the Holy Spirit!

Comments on the Expression "Born Again"

I have to digress a little further here (for another minute), to call your attention to the words "from above" (or "from Heaven", as the NIV translates it). It's a single word in the Greek, *ANOTHEN*.

Do you remember when Jesus was talking to Nicodemus? It's recorded for us in John 3 that Jesus made this statement to him:

> "Except a man be born again..."

That's the way it's translated in all the versions, but here we have the same word, and in the Book of James, everyone translates it as "from above" or "from Heaven." This, by the way, was the common use of the word by the Greeks; it means literally "from up" or "from above."

Jesus made it clear to Nicodemus that this was a "second birth," and He also made it clear that it was a Spiritual process. I've often thought that it would make more sense to someone not familiar with Christianity, to ask that person if he or she has had a Spiritual rebirth; a "rebirth from above," rather than asking them, "Have you been born again?" Anyway, our translation problems are interesting, aren't they. Well, there is one more thing to note, while we're still here in the Book of James, and that is what he says in 3:16:

> "For where jealousy and selfish ambition exist, there is disorder and every evil thing."

And you and I know how true that is. It's the source of trouble in the Assembly! All right, back now to Paul and his letter to his beloved friends in Philippi, in facing this issue of in-fighting among Believers, he is literally commanding us to:

> "Rejoice in the Lord!" (And, to let our "wisdom from on high" be clearly obvious to everyone around us)

That wisdom will be characterized, as James has told us, by being:

> "…first pure, then peaceable, gentle, full of mercy and good fruits, unwavering, without hypocrisy."

That seems to end that thought of Paul's, so he switches to another aspect of what we call "mind control"; an exercise that is vital to every one of us.

He has just warned us to not be diverted by the oddball people that are around, that are misreading the Scriptures and/or mis-applying the Scriptures. Now he talks to us about letting the "things of this earth" cause us to get our eyes off Jesus.

He gives us this wonderful verse that I hope you have in your memory bank and that you pull it up constantly. Philippians 4:6 and 7, which states:

> "Be full of care, anxiety, about absolutely nothing; but in everything, by prayer and supplication, with thanksgiving, let your requests be made known unto God. And the peace of God, which passes all understanding, will guard (keep and protect) your hearts and minds through Christ Jesus."

"Do These Things, and the God of Peace Will Be with You!"

And, further, don't allow your mind to dwell on these people and these problems that seem to be staring you in the face. Instead, consider Verse 8:

> "Whatever is true, whatever is noble and honorable, whatever is 'right', whatever is pure, whatever is lovable, whatever is admirable, SEEING there is true goodness, and SEEING there is praise, think on these things!"

Then in Verse 9:

> "The things that you have learned and received and heard and seen in me, HABITUALLY DO these things AND the God of Peace shall be with you."

Now I'm sure that we have read and said these verses many, many times, but have we really noted this last statement here in Verse 9? IF we do what we have studied here in these passages in this Letter to the Philippians, then what is going to happen?

"The God of Peace will be with you!"

"Will be" is a simple statement of what will happen to you. "God—that brings peace—will be very close to you!" Now we know that God is always with Believers but stated in this way it indicates a closeness, a "fellowship."

Do you want peace in your life? Joy? "Inner happiness?" Then carefully read, study, and follow what you have been given here in this very foundational working guide for a Christian's daily life: the Letter to the Philippians!

Then, in Verse 11, Paul gives us another lesson in the acquiring of peace and inner happiness. First, he tells us WHAT he has learned and then he tells us how it was possible for him to acquire that wonderful, blessed quality. It's there at the end of Verse 11:

> "I have learned, in whatever state I find myself, to be content. I have learned both how to be abased, and I know how to abound, everywhere and in all things I am taught both to be full and to be hungry, both to abound, and to suffer need."

If you happen to be a part of what we call "the Depression generation," you will have learned this lesson by now.

I know that this is a part of the stoic philosophy that has been practiced by many people through the years, but you and I have acquired the ability to have inner happiness along with it—and the reason we have it is the same reason that Paul had it, and he states it here in Verse 13:

> "I can do all things through Christ, who continuously puts strength into me!"

If and as we look to Him and not to what our own resources are capable of providing for us, then life takes on an entirely different perspective.

And how we wish we could be more effective in communicating that way of life to the many people that are around us.

Paul concludes this Letter by commending these people at Philippi who had been so unselfish in their support of him and the contributing to his need, even though they, themselves, had very little material substance out of which to share with him. Nevertheless, Paul points out to them at the end of Verse 18 that:

> "...what they have done is a sweet aroma to God, an offering to Him that is thoroughly accepted by Him."

Further, he tells them and us:

> "My God shall supply all your need, according to His riches in glory, BY MEANS OF or through the entity of Christ Jesus!"

Here is our source of peace and our source of inner happiness. It can come from no one else, because no one else has the power and the wisdom to provide it.

Now, just what have we learned from our little study here with these five sessions, from this letter to these people in the ancient city of Philippi?

In the Gospels and in the Book of Romans we were shown the wonders of the Birth from Above, the great blessing of the Indwelling of the Holy Spirit, the wonders of Forgiveness and Fellowship.

But Jesus also warned us that, "In this world you shall have tribulation..."

Now He is causing Paul to teach us how to operate safely and peacefully in the midst of the tribulation that we will face in this time of trial and learning.

Let me quickly review his own experiences, which he points to as examples, and his mental attitude in the midst of these experiences.

The first was in Chapter 1, Verse 12, where he was literally taken out of service by an imprisonment, to which he said:

> "But I want you to understand, brethren, that the things that have happened to me have fallen out rather unto the furtherance of the Gospel!"

God, in other words, was living out the principle of Romans 8:28 through Paul; what happened was "for good." Everything that comes into a Believer's life is for his good. Period.

He also used the example of the concern that the people of Philippi showed for Paul and his associates, to draw us a "profile picture" of the model Believer. He states this just before that, in Philippians 1:9-11:

> "This I pray, that your Concern may abound more and more in full knowledge and all discernment, so that you may test and establish the things that are right in God's sight, with the result that you are clean, yourself, and that you will cause no one else to stumble until the Day of Christ Jesus, having been filled with the fruit of righteousness that comes through Jesus Christ, to the glory and praise of God."

Mark that one down and refer to it often; it's our model! Philippians 1:9.

Next, we have him pointing us to what should be the most basic truth in all of a Believer's life, yet it is one that so few Christians seem to accept as an operating principle; it is stated in Philippians 1:21:

> "For to me, to live is Christ, and to die is gain. But if I live in the flesh, this is the fruit of my labor; yet what I should choose, I do not know.
>
> For I am in a strait between the two, having a desire to depart, and to be with Christ, which is far better; nevertheless, to remain in the flesh, is more needful for you."

The message is: "I would rather die, and be with Christ, but while I am here on Earth, the fruit I produce will be that which is done for Christ; and assuming that to be the case, my presence here will be a benefit to those around me." How's that for a goal to live by?!

Then, in Chapter 2:14, using Christ's life as an example, he has this command for us:

> "Do all things without grumbling or argument so that we may become blameless and harmless, in the midst of a crooked and perverse generation, among whom you shine as lights, holding forth the word of life."

That's God's purpose for us! And then here's how that purpose will be achieved in you and I. We find this in Chapter 3, Verse 10:

> "...to know Him" (that's Number One)

> "...to know His Power, the power that brought about His resurrection";

> "...to know the fellowship of His sufferings, being conformed to His death, in order that I may fully comprehend and look forward to the resurrection from the dead."

And now, lastly, we learn to keep our eyes on Him; we consciously practice mind control, focusing on Him and not on the storm around us; Chapter 4, Verses 6 and 7 command us to:

> "Be full of anxiety about absolutely nothing, but looking to Him, with Thanksgiving..."

Verse 8 challenges us to control our minds, so that we think only good and pure thoughts. And, if we follow these commands, then we arrive at Verse 9:

"The God of Peace will be very close to us!"

An intimate fellowship will exist between you and your Heavenly Father, through and because of His Son, Jesus Christ.

There is the Letter to the Philippians and to us. The way to joy, peace, and inner happiness "in the midst of a crooked and perverse generation."

THE LETTER TO THE COLOSSIANS

"Why Jesus is Worthy of Our Trust"

Thought Line of Colossians Chapter 1

Verse

1,2 Paul, an apostle of Christ Jesus through the will of God, and the
brother Timothy, to the faithful brothers in Christ: Grace to you
and peace, from God our Father.
3 We give thanks to God, praying always for you, since we heard:
4 of your Faith, and
of your concern for all Believers, giving thanks for the Hope laid
up for you in Heaven which is coming to you—as it is also to
the whole world, and which is bearing fruit.
9 And we continue to pray for you: that you may be filled with the
knowledge of His will in all spiritual wisdom and spiritual
10 understanding, so that you might walk worthy of the Lord
being fruitful, and
increasing in the knowledge of God;
11 strengthened with all His glorious power to all patience and
longsuffering with joyfulness,
while giving thanks to the Father. Who has made us fit to be
partakers of this inheritance,
13 since He has delivered us
from the power of darkness, and has
translated us into the Kingdom of His Son.
14 Through His Son, we have
redemption through His Blood;

the forgiveness of sins!
15 He is the Image of God
16 the firstborn of every creature. since He created all things,
18 and He created them for Himself! He is First!
20 In order to reconcile all things to Himself, He made this Peace through the Blood of His Cross, even for you who were once enemies because of your mind and your evil deeds; He did it in order to present you holy and unblameable; seeing you do continue in the faith, grounded and settled.
25 Paul considers himself a *DIAKANOS* (a "Helper"), teaching all this to the Gentiles, in fulfilment of God's Word.
26 What you have heard is the Mystery hid from all in the Past, but is now revealed to the Believers; this is the "Mystery":
"Christ in you, the hope of glory."
28 We teach this, powered by God's mighty power, in order to present every person complete and mature in Christ Jesus.

Lesson 1 Colossians Chapter 1

"Christ is the embodiment of Deity"

We now begin a look at the second of Paul's four letters that were written during his imprisonment in Rome.

The people Paul is writing to this time are of a different ethnic background from the people of Philippi, who were what we think of as "Europeans"; a "gentle" people. On the other hand, these people in Colossae and also the people of Ephesus (originally descended from the Hittites) were a blend of Turks and Arabs and a "rough and tough," hard—living people. The area those cities were in we call "Asia Minor," and the area itself we now know of as Turkey.

So, they were different. Yet the Believers, having come under the influence of the Doctrines of Christ and God's Holy Spirit, had been transformed into people who were caring, "gracious" people who had become definitely "different" from the majority of the people around them.

We are living, as were those Believers in Colossae, in the midst of a what we can rightly call a "crooked and perverse generation." And we certainly need Divine Wisdom to steer a straight course in our day-by-day living!

Now, if we think back a bit over the words that Paul wrote to the Believers in Philippi, first was his thankfulness expressed for their concern, not only for him and his welfare, but also for the welfare of other Assemblies.

Then followed his expression of appreciation for their prayers for him, a reminder to them of the value that God places on our prayers on behalf of others; then his reminder to them of the way the Holy Spirit works on our behalf, as we give Him opportunity to work; then he reminded them of his own mental attitude in the face of trouble and suffering—the continual awareness that we can do all things through Christ, who keeps on pouring Power into us, and that while dying and being with Christ is better than living here on Earth, God still has us here for His Purpose, and those around us will benefit from our presence here, if and as we reflect God's Grace out to them.

Paul then urged us to follow his example as well as his teaching, and we noted that most important verse that he gave us, in Philippians 4:9 that says:

> "Those things which you have both learned and received and heard and seen in me, practice! And the God of Peace shall be with you!"

A special place of blessing is reserved right here on Earth for those who will do as Paul has outlined here for us. And that place of blessing is a combination of inner joy, inner happiness, and peace inside. Not many people have that today, as we well know. It is our gift from God, and if you are not enjoying it, then read and re-read the Letter to the Philippians until you find it!

So, it has been rightly said that the Letter to the Philippians, as Dr. G. Campbell Morgan expresses it, points us to "Christ as the Source of Joy."

When Paul wrote to the Believers at Colossae, who were of a, shall we say, "less civilized" background, and whose moral practices were more barbarian than those of the Europeans of Philippi, Paul clearly felt a need to strengthen their recognition of who this Jesus really is—which is something that all Believers could certainly more fully comprehend.

Dr. Morgan describes the Letter to the Colossians as pointing us to "Christ, the embodiment of Deity."

We're going to see in this Letter first Paul's acknowledgement, which is of their "fruit-bearing," as he did to the Philippians; then, he's going to remind them of their basic needs which are, again, for "full knowledge" and "discernment" as he did to the Philippians. But then he goes in two additional directions, both of which are very important for you and me, also. The first is an effort to bring to us a full understanding of the position of Jesus the Christ in the world, and, therefore, in our lives, and the second, which takes up the last two chapters of this Letter, is an effort to give us some special rules for our personal relationships. These rules were different from those commonly practiced by the population in general, and rules that are certainly different from those commonly practiced by the people whom we live in the midst of. So, he begins this letter very much as he did the letter to the Philippians:

> "Paul, an apostle of Christ Jesus through the will of God, and Timothy our brother, to the set-apart and faithful brethren in Christ who are at Colossae: Grace to you, and peace, from God our Father."

He provides the same reminder to them of the two great benefits that God has provided for His People: His Grace, and His Peace!

Our Hope, and Where it Comes From

Now we note that Paul immediately gives thanks to God for several things in their connection:

- First for the fact that here is a group of people that he had never met, but who, nevertheless, had acquired a knowledge of The Christ, and had placed their faith in Him;

- second, that their faith had produced "fruit," the foremost of which is AGAPE, "concern" for ALL Believers, that we in English translate as "love";
- and then he expresses his thankfulness

This thankfulness, expressed in Verse 5, is for:

> "...the Hope that is laid up for you in Heaven."

And we all deeply appreciate this Hope! You and I have this Hope—a wonderful future "laid up for us in Heaven," "face to face with our Lord," where God has promised that He:

> "...shall wipe away all tears from their eyes; and there shall be no more death, neither sorrow, nor crying, neither shall there be any more pain: for the former things are passed away." (Revelation 21:4)

That is our Hope, and we are thankful with Paul for it!

Then, he reminds us of where this Hope came from; of how it got into their minds and lives. At the end of Verse 5 he says that they heard of this Hope,

> "...in the word of the truth of the Gospel, which, coming to you as it has to all the world, is bearing fruit and is growing, since the day you heard it!"

So, we have to again remind ourselves that it is hearing, and then accepting "the word of the Gospel" that changes barbarians into gracious and productive Christians.

It would seem that this underscores the thought that the "barbarians" around us are not going to be changed into gracious and productive citizens by our providing "better schools," broader curricula, or bigger and better jails, or a stronger world government that our politicians, almost to a person, are urging on us! What will change them is "the word of the Gospel!"

What Paul Sees Our Need to Be

Now this "Word of the truth of the Gospel" IS in all the world and it IS bearing fruit and it IS growing"—in individual lives; but, as we know, it is not going to bring about world peace and world stability. Only our Lord will do this, when He returns to the Earth.

Now, in Verse 9 here in Colossians 1, Paul tells us that from the day that he heard that there was an Assembly of Believers there in the city of Colossae, he has continually prayed for them.

He had a new, additional target for his prayers; a new group of people who had become Believers in our Lord, and who would surely need instruction and encouragement, and so he had added them to his list. Paul would certainly not have run out of "things to do," even though he was confined to a prison situation.

Paul's prayer for them was very similar to his prayer for the Believers at Philippi; the contents of his prayer for them is here in the middle of Verse 9:

> "...that you might be filled with the full knowledge (EPIGNOSIS) of His will, with its wisdom and spiritual understanding." 😊

The purpose for this is so that:

1. "you might walk worthy of the Lord";
2. "being fruitful" (in other words, running your life so that the Holy Spirit can be working in you)
3. "increasing in the full knowledge of God"; and

4. "being strengthened with all might to all endurance and longsuffering; with joy, giving thanks to the Father..."

Do you really want to know what the Lord expects of you? If you're not sure, read these verses 10, 11 and 12 over several times.

Now, having mentioned the Father, to whom we should certainly be giving continual thanks, Paul digresses to set out for us all another series of reasons why we should be giving thanks to the Father. This is the continuation of Verse 12 here:

> "...who has made us qualified to be partakers of the inheritance of the set-apart ones in The Light..." followed by Verse 13, "... who has delivered us from the authority (*EXOUSIA*, "the right to act") of darkness, and has transferred us into the kingdom of the Son of His that He loves."

We Believers are now out of reach of the *control* of Satan; he can no longer *force* us to do anything, as he can other members of the human race. He can still entice us, however, and he can still influence us, but, as this passage tells us in black and white, Satan no longer can touch us without the Lord's permission.

Remember, Satan can "entice" us, but he can't "manipulate" us as he was able to do before our "moment of Salvation!" Here is another tremendous reason to give thanks to our God! Non-believers are at Satan's mercy—under his power. We are not!

And we're not only out from under Satan's control, but we are also now IN the Kingdom of Jesus Christ! Remember what Jesus said about those who have put their trust in Him? Here are his words, in John 10:28-29:

> "And I give unto them eternal life; and they shall never perish, neither shall anyone pluck them out of my hand. My Father, who gave them me, is greater than all, and no one is able to pluck them out or my Father's hand."

Once in, we're locked in! Again, a wonderful source of comfort and certainly, another encouragement to evangelizing children! Another reason for our eternal gratitude to our Father!

A Review of What Christ Has Already Done for Us

All right, having digressed to tell us something about our Heavenly Father and the wonders that He has provided for us, now, having mentioned God the Son, Paul digresses within his digression to tell us some important things about the Son that He loves.

Maybe you can begin to see why I had to outline this chapter; its trail is, as the lawyers say, a bit "convoluted." It "twists and turns" a lot.

Also, if you have a King James Version, you'll notice the length of the sentences; for example, there is a period at the end of Verse 8, then the next period is way down at the end of Verse 17.

Then there's another long sentence that begins with Verse 21, and runs through to the end of the Chapter, Verse 29.

The original Greek Text has no punctuation, of course, but the thought threads are very long, yet they are very interrelated. Paul, in other words, seems to have been, as we say, "on a verbal roll!"

Anyway, starting here in Verse 14, Paul begins to tell us about some of the wonders of this "Son that The Father loves," which is the way the Greek text expresses it. First, Verse 14:

> "…in whom we have redemption, through his blood, the forgiveness of sins."

Notice this verse closely: we tend to slide over its meaning because of the familiarity we have with the words "redemption" and "sins." But the word translated as "sins" means "mark missing," as you know, and involves the way we were alienated from our Creator. He has set standards for His Creations to meet; if we do, we are in a place where He will bless us; if we do not, we are in a place of continual discipline.

Here, by the way, is something that we should be impressing on our children and our grandchildren as we are given the opportunity!

But Jesus Christ "redeemed" the human race from the penalty of their sins, their shortcomings. He paid for our release. But, of course, a person can certainly elect to remain in the stinking prison if he wants to; no one is going to insist that he leave it.

Then the next truth to note is the means by which Christ obtained our redemption; He did it "through His Blood"; in other words, He had to die a physical, human death to accomplish this. He, The Creator of us all, elected to do this in order to buy this redemption, because that is the only way it could be done, since God the Father, long before, had issued an edict that:

"Without the shedding of blood, there is no remission..."

(That, by the way, is a quotation from Hebrews 9:22, which is, itself, a rephrasing of Leviticus 17:11, which is a part of the Law that God gave to Moses.)

Jesus the Christ graciously accepted pain and humility and paid for our shortcomings with a horribly painful, physical, human death, because that is what God required.

That's the first, wonderful thing we need to have constantly in front of us when we think of Jesus; He is loved by God the Father, and, in His love for you and me, He paid this price so that our failures and shortcomings will not stand between us and God the Father!

Who Jesus Really Is

But more than that, Paul wants us to be aware of just who this Jesus really is. As is stated in Colossians 1:15-17:

> "He is the image of the invisible God, the firstborn of every creature; for by Him were all things created, that are in Heaven and that are in Earth, visible and invisible, whether thrones, or dominions, or principalities, or powers; all things were created by Him, and for Him, and He is before all things, and by Him all things consist."

There are many interesting things here in this passage. First of all, the word translated "image." The Greek word is *EIKON*, and to them it meant an exact representation of something or someone.

It's interesting that this word has become an everyday word in our world today—something else that we can thank Bill Gates and Microsoft for. The Windows screens on our computers have little "icons" on them, each one of them representing a different set of programs. When you press one, the Word Processor comes on; when you press another, the Spreadsheet comes on; press another, and your game of Solitaire pops up.

Or, if you get tired of writing a letter on your Word processor, you press another little button, and the Word Processor vanishes, and becomes the same little "icon" that it was before. In other words, the "icon" IS the word processor, only in another form.

Jesus, the Christ, is the exact image of God, who is invisible and intangible; Jesus, the Christ, is God in a visible, tangible form.

What's more, Verse 15 here tells us that He is "the firstborn of every creature." This word "firstborn" was used in a broader sense in that society, broader than just being "born first"; being firstborn endowed that person with special rights and responsibilities; it "put him in charge," or in other words; ahead of everything!

Jesus was not only the first of all creatures to come into existence, He also is superior to all creatures that have come along subsequently because:

> "For by him were all things created, that are in heaven, and that are in Earth." (Col. 1:16)

Everything in the entire Universe. And then Paul covers every possible category: visible and invisible, thrones, dominions, principalities and powers.

He is including in this use of words the legitimate, worldly rulers and their governments, and then, in the words "principalities and powers," he is drawing in what the people in those times thought of as supernatural powers—powers of darkness. So, he is covering literally "everything" that ever is or was or will be. "All things were created by Him and FOR Him!"

And notice: He created all these, not for the benefit of mankind, as the Evolutionists would have us believe; all of this was created FOR Him, and for His Pleasure, and for His Use.

"He is before all things, and by Him all things are held together."

The words "held together," which are translated as "consist" in the King James (*SUNISTEMI*) was a single word used to describe a "tightly knit group of people," or, in another instance, of "sheaves of grain that were tightly bound together."

This concept takes on a broader meaning for us today, since we have learned about atoms and molecules and the composition of what we call "matter." We've learned that this book, for example, is made up of an uncountable number of molecules, each of which is made up of atoms, and the atoms and molecules are held together and in place by a tremendous power that we can't even begin to comprehend.

We (mankind) have proved this, literally, since we have learned how to release that power that holds things together, with the process of Atomic Fission, and if that release were triggered, this book would disappear into thin air, but the explosion that would take place would wipe us out along with the book!

That is the power that Jesus controls! The power that holds the entire universe and all that's in it, together!

And, by the way, He hasn't promised to always hold all of this together; in fact, as we learn from Revelation 21, when His Plan for this earth is completed, He will release this power, and everything as we know it will be totally changed.

So, Jesus Christ is the source of, literally, all the power that there is in the Universe. Think of the power that holds together the molecules that are in just us here in this room, then multiply that by all the people that are on this earth, then by all the buildings that are on the earth, then think of all the stars that are floating out there in space around us! It's His Power that holds them all in place! That is His Power! So, can He take care of us, His People? Well, I would say so!

Verse 18 reminds us that He is not only the power source and guiding director of all physical matter, but He is also our controller, our director. Verse 18 says:

> "He is the head of the body, the *EKKLESIA*, the Assembly of All Believers..."

Just as our head controls the functioning of the other parts of our body, Jesus is in that same position with each one of us who make up His Task Force, His Assembly. He is, Himself, everything that matters in the whole of the Universe!

David, the King of Israel, as we know had been through all of life's upsides and downsides, and one of the great songs that he wrote was the little Psalm 29. Read it when you can. In it he calls attention to the tremendous power of "Jehovah," our Lord Jesus Christ. He says:

> "The Voice of the Lord is powerful.
> The Voice of the Lord is full of majesty.
> The Voice of the Lord breaks the trees.
> The Voice of the Lord divides the flames of fire.
> The Voice of the Lord shakes the wilderness!
> The Voice of the Lord causes the cows to calf.
> The Lord controls the floods—he is King forever!"

But then David adds:

> "The Lord will give strength to His people;
> The Lord will bless His people with peace."

That's Psalm 29! You and I are a part of "His People," so whatever goes on—inside us or outside of us—we keep looking to Him! Everything is under His control, and He is constantly working all things together, for our good!

Lesson 2 Colossians Chapter 1

An Explanation of "Gnosticism"

"**Review" is "good,"** so let's review. Paul wrote four letters (that we know of) during his confinement in the city of Rome while waiting for his trial before the Roman Emperor Nero. The first of the four was the Letter to the Philippians that we have already looked at, and that presented Jesus as the only source for the human race for real inner happiness, inner peace, quietness, and strength.

Now in this letter, the Letter to the Colossians, Paul stresses the fact that this Jesus, even though we think of Him as being "God's Beloved Son," and we remember Him as a man who came and lived on this earth, and who taught us and then ultimately died for us, yet He is truly God. He is the Exact Image *(EIKON)* of God, only in a form that you and I can see and understand.

We are reminded in Verse 16 of this first Chapter that Jesus was actually the Creator of all the physical elements that exist in the entire universe, and He created them for Himself. He created everything, and He, Himself, is the Power that holds all things together.

This is a literal statement of what is really happening, since we now know that every single material, physical thing is in actuality a huge collection of molecules held together by some unknown but miraculous power—a power that man has now learned to actually release, but with terribly devastating results. We call it an "atomic explosion."

But then, Verse 18 tells us that this same Jesus, who is the head, therefore, of all physical things in the Universe, is also the head of a special group of people that He created, called, in the Greek text, the *EKKLESIA*, which meant to them "an assembly of people brought together for a specific purpose." We call that a "task force." The Bible refers to it as "The Body of Christ" and the English translators of the Bible call it "the Church."

And (Verse 19): "It pleased the Father that in Him should all The Fullness dwell."

"The Fullness," aka: the sum-total of everything!

But in this word that is translated "the Fullness," we have a word that had a special meaning in the day that Paul was writing. The Greek word is *PLEROMA* and it comes from a verb that we're familiar with, (*PLERO-O*), that is used to describe, for example, "the filling of the Holy Spirit." The verb meant "to fill or occupy something completely."

The religion of this area we know of as Asia Minor in Paul's time was called GNOSTICISM; it gets its name from the Greek word GNOSIS, which means "knowledge." It was an ingenious development of Satan's that started about the time that Christianity began. It took many of the elements of Christianity, but then, since some of the self-control aspects of Christianity were troublesome to many of the people of that culture, its leaders began to work in a lot of "modifications" and "variations" so that what it wound up to be was a comfortable, watered-down religious system that pacified and satisfied its adherents, who still called themselves "Christians." Very much like what we have in the world around us today.

This is why we say that Paul's letters to these people at Colossae and Ephesus could have been addressed to us; he was up against very much the same thinking that occupies the minds of "civilized" people today.

By the way, this religion called "Gnosticism" lasted up until the end of the third century and then seems to have faded out and disappeared from history. Christianity became the "accepted religion" when the

Roman Emperor Constantine converted to Christianity around 325 AD and had the effect of "purifying" Christianity at that point.

Gnosticism did provide one great (but very indirect) assistance to Christianity, however; a small group of Gnostics, who identified themselves as "Essenes" translated much of the Old Testament into their Coptic language, and not too many years ago, a whole batch of these scrolls were found, including the Book of Daniel, which we know of as the "Dead Sea Scrolls."

These are very valuable to us, because they establish the fact that the Books of the Old Testament were obviously written before 300 AD.

Critics have long tried to establish the fact that the amazing prophecies in the Book of Daniel could not possibly have been written when they were but were actually written AFTER the events they prophesied had actually taken place. The amazing discovery of these Scrolls puts that lie to rest and confirms God's willingness to show us future events.

Many of Daniel's prophecies have already been fulfilled, as we know, and there are still many more that you and I know about that are yet to come!

Well, the Gnostics made fun of the Christians of that day; they called Christians "Faith people" (*PISTICS*, from *PISTIS*, meaning "faith"), while they called themselves "Knowledge people" (*GNOSIS*, meaning "we know"). This is very much like what we have today, of course, with the so-called "scientists" ridiculing anyone who would accept something that can't be "scientifically established."

"Take it by faith? How stupid can you get," they say.

Now, what these Gnostics did to Christian teaching was this: they accepted the Old Testament, which explains why the Essene monks copied the Old Testament that was found among the Dead Sea Scrolls. So, they could say with Christians that "they believed in God".

But then they realized that this "God of the Old Testament" was really quite "unknowable" and distant. However, they reasoned that this "God" must have broken off parts of Himself, one of which was Jesus. So, they could say with the Christians that "they believe in Jesus."

But their reasoning went on, that, over a period of time, there were a great many of these "Emanations" and they built up a complicated mythology to explain the origin of the Universe, and also such things as the expulsion of Adam and Eve from the Garden, the Flood and the destruction of Sodom and Gomorrah.

Jesus Christ Truly IS "The Fullness!"

The sum-total of all these Emanations, they said, consisted of "The *PLEROMA*," or "The Fullness." So, they wound up with many deities, which, together, they called "The *PLEROMA*." This is why Paul stresses here in Colossians 1:19 that:

"…in Christ all 'fullness' (The *PLEROMA*) dwells!"

Jesus, the Christ, the Son of God—He IS the fullness of everything! HE, Himself, is "The *PLEROMA*!" "The Fullness!"

Now, these Gnostics had another interesting side to their religion; they believed, as we do, that a person's soul was supernatural and therefore not a real part of our body; so, to them, it really did not matter to the soul what the body did. This is NOT what Christianity teaches, of course, so Gnosticism became a very convenient "adjustment" for many people.

This concept led some of the Gnostics, who were socially inclined off into all sorts of debauchery—after all, who cares what the body does!

And it led others of them, who were more ascetic, to become monks and to otherwise pull themselves out of the mainstream of the everyday world.

All of this is what the Believers in Colossae and in Ephesus were living in the midst of, just as you and I are living in the midst of it today. This is why these four letters particularly are so applicable to Believers living now!

Paul continues to describe the work and position of this unique person of the Universe, Jesus, the Nazarene, who also is The Christos.

We've seen Him described as the Head of all material matter in the Universe, and the head of His Body—which is the sum total of all those who have trusted both their present lives and their future lives to Him. But He also did something wonderful for each of us, who were, in the past, as Verse 21 expresses it:

> "...we who were before alienated and enemies because of our wicked works, yet now He has reconciled us by His fleshly body through death..."

Can a Believer "Lose His Salvation?"

Our Lord Jesus Christ has done this for us, and to us! Our reconciliation is a settled matter, as the verb tense here in Verse 22 indicates; it's a past, completed action (aorist tense). Also, glance back at Verse 13; there, again, it says:

> "...who has delivered us from the power of darkness, and who has translated us into the kingdom of His dear Son."

These also are "completed action" verbs (aorist tense). We ARE reconciled. We HAVE BEEN delivered. He HAS translated us! It's done! But now look at Verse 23; this says:

> "IF you continue in the faith grounded and settled, and not moved away from the hope of the gospel that you have heard..."

What's this? Doesn't this seem to put a condition on our being "reconciled to God?" Doesn't this say that He will reconcile us IF we continue strong in the faith? Is our Eternal Situation secure or not? Can I lose what

He provided for me? You can hear someone saying: "Oh Dear! Here's another contradiction! See, the Bible is full of contradictions!"

I quoted that verse from the Old King James; the translations in the NIV and the New American Standard Bible are even more a cause for concern; here's how they translate these Verses 22 and 23. Both of them state:

> "But now He has reconciled you by Christ's physical body through death, to present you holy in His sight, without blemish and free from accusation—IF you continue in your faith, established and firm, not moved from the hope held out in the gospel."

So, are we "locked in" to our reconciliation at our moment of salvation, or do we lose out if our faith fails us; if we fail to "continue in our faith?"

Well, I'm sure we agree that the way this passage is translated flies in the face of everything else that the Scriptures teach us! We have just seen here the statement that He "has reconciled us," which is a completed action! Now why would God's Word suddenly place a condition on what God says He has done?

The problem with this translation lies in two areas: punctuation and an understanding of how God works.

Now, at this point, you're probably thinking: "Who does Ed Perry think he is, to criticize the learned men who have spent years studying the Greek Language and worked hard at making these translations?!" And I wouldn't blame you; however, I wouldn't say what I'm going to say, except for the fact that some very learned men that you and I know and respect, have also taken issue with these translations.

Among those who take issue with them are Dr. Lewis Chafer, the founder of Dallas Theological Seminary, one of the great theologians of our times. Also, there is Dr. A. T. Robertson, who is probably the most respected of all Greek scholars of all times. Then there is Dr. Vernon

McGee, who himself was no slouch. And I could go on. So, I can say with confidence what I am about to say.

Our first clue to finding the error in these translations is at the beginning of Verse 23, in that little word "if." We have often spoken of the various "conditional uses" of the word "if" in the Greek Language. There are four of them:

The first says, "If, and it's true." The second carries the meaning of "If, and it's not true." The third is the way we commonly use the word "if," as in, "Maybe it is and maybe it isn't." Our usual "conditional if" usage. The fourth "If" says, "If, I wish it were, but I know it isn't!"

Each of these conditional usages is clearly identified in the Greek Text; no one familiar with the Greek language would misunderstand what the writer intended.

Now, that first conditional use: "If, and it's true," since it IS stating a true situation, we would correctly translate it with our words, "Since that's the way it is, then," or "Seeing that's the way it is, then."

This "if" here at the beginning of Verse 23 is clearly a first-class condition, so anyone reading it would automatically think to word it "Seeing you continue in the faith," or "Since you continue in the faith."

That in itself should stop a person from making the sentence say, as the NIV and the New American Standard have continued to express it, that God's action depends upon man's action.

So, then a translator should begin to look at the sentence structure. In the Old King James, you will note that there is a period at the end of Verse 20 and then there is no period until you get down to the end of the chapter in Verse 29.

On the other hand, if you were to look at the NIV translation, you would see that they have broken this up into nine sentences—they used nine periods.

The point is that the Greeks did not use punctuation as we do; they made the thought itself to make its way through into the hearer's mind.

And the thought here, which is consistent with all the New Testament Scripture, is that in the matter of reconciliation and redemption and salvation, God, through the death of His Son once and for all provided reconciliation for anyone who would avail himself or herself of it. Period.

Then in return for this gracious act, God expects certain attitudes back from men and women in return; attitudes of faith, and obedience, and worship. If God receives those attitudes back from His creation, then the person is blessed and guided and strengthened as he or she goes through this life; if God does not receive them back, then the person misses those benefits.

But God's act in reconciliation is UN-conditional. On the other hand, man has a choice: do things that please God or do not do them.

That's the situation we have here in this passage, and a different English punctuation repairs our passage; put a period after the word "death" in Verse 22 and then these two responsibilities are properly separated. That simple correction makes the passage read like this, in Verse 22:

> "But now He has reconciled you by Christ's physical body through death." (Period)

There is God's gracious provision! Then, here's what will happen as a person responds the way God expects us to respond:

> "He will present you holy in His sight, without blemish and free from accusation, seeing you continue in your faith, established and firm, not moved from the hope field out in the Gospel."

The statement we have in Second Corinthians 5:10 warns us that:

> "We must all appear before the judgment seat of Christ; that everyone may receive the things done in his body, according to that he has done (*PRASSO*—repeatedly done), whether it be good (*AGATHOS*) or bad (*PHAULOS*)."

Paul also described that time of our judgment in his first Letter to the Corinthians:

> "For other foundation can no man lay than that is laid, which is Christ Jesus. Now if any man build upon this foundation, gold, silver, precious stones, or wood, hay stubble;
>
> Every man's work shall be made manifest; for the day shall declare it, because it shall be revealed by fire; and the fire shall try every man's work of what sort it is.
>
> If any man's work abide which he has built thereon, he shall receive a reward;
>
> If any man's work shall be burned, he shall suffer loss, but he himself shall be saved, yet so as by fire." (Cor. 3:11-15)

Our Eternal Future is secure but the maintenance of our daily fellowship and the benefits that go with it, plus our feelings that we will have when we do stand before Our Lord—this part depends on our own decisions as we go along. Will what we habitually do be described as "good" (*AGATHOS*), that which is pleasing to God, or "bad," (*PHAULOS*), which means "worthless"?

Well, we can ask what does God consider "good" or pleasing to Him? What God considers pleasing to Him is Our faith, our obedience, our worship.

And what does God consider "worthless"? The things we do apart from the Holy Spirit's direction and control.

The prophet Samuel told King Saul this in 1 Samuel 15:22:

> "Has the Lord as great delight in burnt offerings and sacrifices, as in obeying the voice of the Lord? Behold, to obey is better than sacrifice, and to listen, than the fat of rams."

And there are also the words that we used to sing. It's too bad that we don't sing them much anymore:

> "Trust and obey, for there's no other way, to be happy in Jesus, but to trust and obey!"

OK: are we clear on the security of our "reconciliation?" I hope we are! Our reconciliation is accomplished; what He wants back from us is our trust, our obedience, and our respect and worship!

Now, what do we do with these modern translations? The Translators of the old King James version we can forgive. In the year 1610, they didn't know much about the common language that the Greeks spoke 1600 years before that. But with the 20th Century translators, it's a different story. Some things they did better, but not always, as we have seen here.

My point is that we must not automatically accept the criticism that God's Word as "inconsistent!" As it was given to us originally, there are no inconsistencies! It's only as man has begun to work with it that the problems have developed.

Paul must have anticipated this, since he prayed for us here in Verse 9 that we grow in full knowledge of God's Word, and in all wisdom and spiritual understanding, so that we do, indeed, "rightly divide the Word of God" for our benefit, as well as for those He puts us in contact with.

And what we have in our Christianity, while it is a simple, very straightforward proposition, it is quite complex when it is applied to the lives of the people of the world, who are very diverse.

It is simple in concept but there are two sides to it: God's side and man's side, and we need to understand them both. God's side is presented to us here in Colossians 1:26:

> "The mystery which has been hid from ages and from generations, but now is made manifest to His saints, to whom God would make known what is the riches of the glory of this

mystery among the Gentiles: which is Christ in you, the hope of glory!"

When we obey God and accept what His Son did for us, we become "set apart ones" and "saints." And at that point Christ is in us; He takes up residence in us. He becomes a part of our life. He does that, and it's "done!"

But then comes man's side: what do we do with this New Entity in our life? Do we welcome Him as our Leader, and look to Him for instruction and guidance and recognize Him for Who He is—God, Himself? Or do we ignore Him and cling to our so-called "independence" and look at Him as an unwelcome "wet blanket?"

Paul recognized this as also being his responsibility. Notice Verse 28:

"...warning every man, and teaching every man in all wisdom, so that we may present every man mature and complete in Christ."

All through this Letter to these Colossians we'll see Paul presenting Christ and His Finished Work for us, and we'll also see his concern that we face up to our responsibility back to Christ, and that we understand clearly of what that responsibility consists of.

In the next chapter, Paul begins to be very specific!

Lesson 3 Colossians Chapter 2

What God Expects Back for What He Did

These people who lived in Colossae and the area surrounding it, including the cities of Ephesus and Laodicea, were all similar in ethnic background, and they all faced very much the same kind of opposition to their Christianity that we face in our civilization today. So, this Letter is very applicable to us!

The opposition they had, as is ours, was an opposition that based its efforts mostly on Ridicule; their opponents called Christians "Faith people" and they said "We are Knowledge People. We KNOW what we're talking about. What you're doing is simply wishful thinking! Our beliefs are based on scientific, logical fact!" Ridicule is their greatest tool!

A few years back, the folks at Campus Crusades thought it would be good to advertise our appreciation of our "New Life" by putting a bumper sticker on our cars, that announced: "We found it!"

So, right away, the opposition came out with a sticker that said: "We lost it!"

Now, there's a different one. Some people want to put the fish symbol that the early Christians used on their cars; then the opposition comes along and puts legs on the fish and Darwin's name inside it! Ridicule!

So, Paul spends a lot of thought and time showing the position that our Lord occupies in the Universe and in the overall scheme of things, and points to information that fully justifies our operating on faith in Him, regardless of what man's feeble thinking might lead them to believe.

Then, as Paul begins to further instruct us, he makes clear to us the twofold aspect of our Christianity: the recognition that God has already accomplished a reconciliation between Himself and mankind, which He did through the death of His Son, and that this reconciliation is free for the taking, by any person who will consciously accept what this Son has done.

That's one part; the other part is what God expects back from those who have accepted this reconciliation; and what He expects is our faith, our obedience, and our respect for Him, which we call "worship."

Therefore, since what we have here in these letters is what God expects back from us, it is very important that we thoroughly understand just what it is He wants us to "obey." And second, what it is that, to God, constitutes our "worship."

Speaking of "worship"; I have an article that Carolyn cut out of the *Oregonian* for me that is headed: "We need to stop trifling with God!" It opens with this statement:

> The sense of awe and mystery that could drop believers to their knees is mostly absent ... Today, many believers have homogenized the Holy One. They conceive of God in ways that don't require their humble obedience or patient trusting in adversity...
>
> One theologian has said: 'Rampant individualism has infected our beliefs. God is shaped to fit our needs, to be no more than a foot taller than ourselves.'
>
> Another theologian has said: 'At one time theologians argued that the chief purpose of humankind was to glorify God. Now it would seem that the logic has been reversed: that the chief purpose of God is to glorify humankind.'

> In modem dress, it sounds like this: if God doesn't fix what's broken in my life, who needs Him?

Then the writer concludes:

> We must face the fact that some of our preconceptions of God are wrong … Only by rediscovering the holiness and majesty of God will we be able to face the sufferings and uncertainties of life with comforting hope. And it must begin on our knees.

Not bad, right?! Thank you, Oregonian! This is "worship"; a deep, honest, reverential respect and gratitude for Who He Is, what He has done, and what He is in the process of doing! It's not just "doing something," it's "thinking something," and that may cause you to do something!

Paul is focusing on what it is that constitutes worship and what it is that God wants from us in return for what He has done for us—so let's be sure we get his message!

When we have learned these things and have molded our life to follow what we know, then our life is one of joy, inner happiness, and peace. And for others, our life is a bright light that leads them to what we have!

Now we keep in mind that, as far as we know, Paul never visited the cities of Colossae and Laodicea, but he did spend about three years teaching in the city of Ephesus, which was about 75 miles away from Colossae. And it is believed that some of his converts started the assemblies there in Colossae and in Laodicea. Paul considers all of them his "children in the Lord" and he says to them now, in this first verse in Chapter 2:

> "For I want you to know what great a struggle I am having for you, and for them at Laodicea, and for as many as have not seen my face."

He has, as we say, a "burden" for them as he realizes what they are facing from the people around them who they live and work with; people that poke fun at them because they operate purely "on faith." Paul, you'll notice, is stressing the importance of what we know to support our faith.

In Verse 2, his prayer for them is:

> "...that their hearts may be encouraged, having been knit together in love, and for all the wealth that comes from the full assurance of understanding, and for a full knowledge (*EPIGNOSIS*) of God's Mystery, of Christ Himself, in whom are hidden all the treasures of wisdom and knowledge."

And our hearts ARE encouraged as we feel the warmth of our fellowship with Him and with His People and as we come to understand all that we have in this Christ, who is the Head of Everything! But then he explains the reason for his concern for them in Verse 4:

> "I say this so that no one deludes you with persuasive but misleading arguments!"

And that, I know, is our "burden" for those in *our* sphere of contact, since the world is full of other ideas! These people were well grounded; they knew that Jesus was a real person. There were people still living who had been eyewitnesses to His crucifixion—even some to his ascension back into Heaven. Also, they were confident because of the many miracles that He had done and the prophecies that He had fulfilled that he truly was the Son of God, the Jews' Messiah!

Further, they knew that Christianity was spreading rapidly through that whole area! So, their "faith" was solid! Notice Verse 5:

> "For even though I am absent in body, nevertheless I am with you in spirit, rejoicing to see your 'order' (your "not breaking ranks

ana letting the Gnostics disturb you," I believe he means)—and your steadfastness in your faith in Christ!"

A Warning Against False Teachers

And then Paul gives them (and us) this great condensation of everything that is involved in Christianity in Colossians 2:6:

> "Therefore, as you have received Christ Jesus the Lord, so walk in Him, having been rooted, and now being built up in Him, and being established in your Faith as you were taught, abounding in thanksgiving."

Then Paul expresses again what it is that concerns him in Verse 8:

> "But beware that no one takes you captive (or "makes a slave of you") through philosophy and empty deceit, according to the tradition of men, according to the elementary principles that the world operates with, rather than according to Christ, for in Him dwells all the fullness of the Godhead, and you have been completely filled in Him!"

So, look at Verse 6 again:

> "As you have received Christ Jesus the Lord, so walk in Him!"

How did you receive Him? You received Him by Faith—then walk that way, in Faith in Him!

There, again, in that sixth verse, he points us to the two sides of Christianity; God's side, and man's side. God's Provision and man's Response. Side One: God made the provision, and we accepted it.

Then, Side Two: Man is to take Him at His Word and respond to Him by following His Instructions!

But let's be sure we know from Him what His Instructions are and not be misled by false teachers!

Persuasive speakers were coming to their meetings. It's interesting how many people there are around that want to be heard, that love to get up in front of a crowd and push their ideas.

For example, they were coming with various ideas of ritual that should be added to their meetings, teaching that those people "needed something more" than simply going to a meeting and singing a few hymns and hearing God's Word. They needed something more "fun" and interesting.

Then some others were teaching that the men must be circumcised, like God had the Jews do.

Others were suggesting that when they sinned or failed God, they should inflict punishment on their bodies or on themselves (by, for example, special gifts to the assembly of time or money), to encourage God to forgive them.

Then some were beginning to say that they should deprive themselves of normal human comforts in order to show God and the world that they were truly Christians, so celibacy was being adopted by some; others were selling their household goods to become more "pauperish" and thereby more "Christ-like." All these are added to what God's Word teaches! Paul is telling them "Don't be misled!" He said in Verse 9:

> "For in Him dwells all the fullness of the Godhead!"

And now he adds, in Verse 10:

> "And you are filled full in Him, who is the head of all principality and power!"

Paul, with this word translated "fullness," is saying that Christ is the *PLEROMA*—the sum total of all the "gods" that the Gnostics (the

"Knowledge people") were talking about. And we Believers are literally "filled full" in Him.

Here Paul uses the word that the Scriptures use to describe "the filling of the Holy Spirit." We are "completely possessed" by the Holy Spirit at our moment of salvation; we become the Temple of the Holy Spirit; a new life is placed inside us. We may resist Him, but He's there, nevertheless!

And the same with our Lord; at our moment of salvation, He also completely possesses us. He moves in with us and we are His. But just like some children rebel against their parents, whose children they truly are, and they go off on their own, many Believers push the Lord away from participating in their life. But we are His, nevertheless!

And we don't need man-devised ritual! Our Lord wants our minds to turn instinctively to Him, not to go through a bunch of motions on a ritual basis to try to impress Him!

Nor do we need the rite of circumcision that God gave to the nation Israel, so that they would be continually conscious of their relationship to Him. That's made clear here in Colossians 11:

> "In Him you were also circumcised with a circumcision made without hands, by the putting off of the body of the flesh, by the circumcision of Christ."

Then Paul tells us what he means by this "circumcision of Christ" in Verse 12:

> "...having been buried with Him in baptism, in which you were also raised up with Him through faith in the working of God, who raised Him from the dead."

We remember our Baptism, I'm sure. It was an act to announce to ourselves and to the world and to the Angels that are up there looking down at us that we believe in what Jesus did. And that we are now identified with Him, with a new life in us!

Then Paul tells us again what Jesus did for us. (He keeps at it, doesn't he! He wants us to thoroughly understand!)

> "And when you were dead as a result of your transgressions and the uncircumcision of your flesh (your open rejection of God and what He stands for, in other words); yet He made you alive together with Him, having forgiven us all our transgressions, having canceled out the decrees that were against us and were hostile to us; and He has taken it out of the way, having nailed it to the cross. Then having put off from Himself the principalities and authorities, He made a public display of them, having triumphed over them through it (through the Cross)." (Col 1:13-15)

The New Testament consistently uses the word that we translate as "principalities" to refer to supernatural beings. I understand Paul to be saying here that in Christ's death on the Cross, and His subsequent resurrection and ascension back into Heaven (all of which was done very publicly) Jesus presented an open and clear victory over all the efforts of both the natural world and the supernatural world, to stop Him. He showed His power over the combined efforts of both the secular world and the religious world.

And remember, you and I are filled, literally, with Him!

Certainly, the position and the authority and the power of Jesus, the Christ, has been established. How any thinking person can view all the evidence and still put Jesus down as "just a good man, many of whose teachings are worth listening to" is more than I can understand.

"Therefore…" And for the rest of the Letter, Paul moves into what "therefore" logically follows, and that is a setting out of Part Two of Christianity—that which God expects back from His People that He has done so much for! He tells us what He wants and what He doesn't want.

Four Areas of Confusion

Among the things He doesn't want are things that originate from four familiar sources and are concepts that have been allowed to get all mixed up with our daily living simply because they are all around us. That was true then with the Christians at Colossae and it is true today.

Paul, through the Holy Spirit, is going to point out these four areas and then he's going to move ahead by setting out for us Chapter 3 what is called "The Christian Ethic," which actually is the basis of Civilized Life. It's the basis for our "Common Law" that, in many cases, still supersedes enacted laws of the various societies that have come and gone. The four areas of confusion are:

1. Philosophy, or man's ideas of how things are and should be;
2. Legalism, or the list of "dos and don'ts" that people have dreamed up, as their idea of what God wants;
3. Mysticism, or man's attempts to draw help from the supernatural, the Occult world; and
4. Asceticism, which is the concept of depriving of ourselves of certain physical pleasures, expecting that somehow God will think we're great for doing this. Monks and monasteries are at the extreme of this but there are all degrees between here and there.

These are four areas of confusion that we face.

Confusion Area number one is Philosophy. Philosophy, of course, is the result of man's ideas of what it takes, mentally, to make it through life. It assumes either that there is no "God," or, if there is, He isn't much interested in people.

So, "Philosophy" is an attempt to fill the place in a person's life that our Creator intended should be filled with a relationship with Him.

Our problem is that we tend to let these reasonings of man get intertwined and mixed in with what we have learned from the Bible.

And this is easy to have happen because most Christians get only a smattering of Bible Teaching as they go through life and, for a great many Christians, what they do hear in many Churches is often wrong or misleading.

Paul made his first clear statement on this back in Verse 8 here in Chapter 2, which we noted earlier:

> "Beware lest any man take you captive (or "make a slave of you") through philosophy and empty deceit, according to the tradition of men, according to the elementary principles that the world operates with, rather than according to Christ..."

Many of the thoughts and ideas that the philosophers have come up with through the ages are good. Confucius taught many great principles. When I was in school, I took a course in Philosophy and I was very much intrigued with the teachings of a man by the name of Marcus Aurelius. He was the Emperor of the Roman Empire from 161 to 180 AD, and he did a lot to lighten the lot of the poor and abused of the land, and that's "good." His "Philosophy" seemed very much right! But then I later found out that he was probably one of the worst abusers of Christians of all the characters of History!

God expects His People to study His Ways, so that we can measure what we hear from well-intentioned people all around us and confine our productive effort as God would have it directed!

Confusion Area number two that Paul calls our attention to is what we refer to as "Legalism." This is the effort of man, including our own nature, to put us under "dos and don'ts" that appeal to us, and then judging one another as we compare them to the list that we have compiled, or that has been ingrained in us as we've gone along.

How many times have you heard someone say to someone else: "No Christian does that!"

Maybe it's bouncing the ball on Sunday or looking askance at you if you don't attend as many religious gatherings as they do.

I even ran into a Christian group up in the La Grande area that considered it wrong to use a comb, because it was a method of outward adornment.

And I can well remember the criticism we took because we allowed our children to go to the high school dances! People building their theology on "dos and don'ts."

Paul talks about this here in Verse 16 of Chapter 2:

> "Therefore, let no one act as your judge in regard to food or drink or in respect to a festival or a new moon or a Sabbath day. These things are a mere shadow of what is to come; the real thing is Christ!"

Again, the urging is to look to Jesus Christ for our guidance and not be disturbed by the criticism from other directions.

Focusing criticism on the people we associate with can be very disruptive. What others eat and drink and what they do on the "Sabbath" is between them and God. What others do is not where our focus should be; our focus should be on Christ and His Concerns!

Confusion Area number three is with what we call "Mysticism," or our attempt to intrude ourselves into the realm of the supernatural.

Don't flinch, now, and don't answer … but how many of you regularly look at your horoscope in the daily paper? Many Christians do, as we know.

It's interesting that in an interview on NBC on June 25 this past year, a woman by the name of Jean Houston acknowledged that she was a frequent visitor to the White House. She explained that one of her purposes was to help Hillary Clinton in her communications with the late Eleanor Roosevelt.

Jean Houston is the co-founder of an organization called "The Possible Society." The other founder was Elsa Porter, who was President Carter's Assistant Secretary of Commerce. Their principal slogan is:

> "You are simply God in hiding. You must achieve your potential Godhood!"

King Saul turned to the Witch of Endor to try to contact Samuel, to get some good advice when he sorely needed it. Isaiah had this to say about that venture:

> "And when they shall say to you: 'Seek unto them that have familiar spirits', should not a people seek unto their God? And they shall look unto the earth, and behold trouble and darkness, dimness of anguish; and they shall be driven to darkness." (Isaiah 8:19, 22)

Paul commented on that source of confusion here in Verse 18 of Chapter 2:

> "Let no man defraud you from your reward by delighting in a false humility and the worshipping of angels, intruding into those things which he thinks he has seen, in vain being inflated without cause, by his fleshly mind."

Notice the first line of Verse 18 where it says, "Let no man defraud you from your reward..." There's not a lot said about our "rewards," but there is enough said to make it clear that at the Judgment Seat of Christ, we Believers will be examined by Christ and the things that we have done in the power of the flesh will be destroyed by fire. They will be shown to be "worthless." But the things we have done in the power of the Holy Spirit will earn us a "reward."

And intruding into the area of the Angels, looking to them and to the other supernatural sources for our guidance, rather than to our Heavenly Father, will rob us of what would otherwise be a wonderful experience!

Then Confusion Area number four that Paul points us to is what we call Asceticism. In Colossians 2:20-23 it says:

> "Seeing you are dead with Christ from the rudiments of the world system, why, as though you are a part of the world, are you subjecting yourself to ordinances, after the commandments and teachings of men such as: 'Do not handle!' 'Do not taste!' 'Do not touch!'?
>
> These things are all to perish with the using. They have indeed a show of wisdom in will-worship and humility, and severe treatment of the body, but are of no value…"

The Greek word translated as "do not handle" was used in the Greek-speaking world to identify handling in a sexual sense. The people at Colossae would have understood what Paul was getting at here. This concept is behind the celibacy attitude of many religious groups.

"Taste not" applied to certain foods and is a taboo followed by many groups even today, as we know.

The Greek word translated "handle not" is *THIGGANO* and it was used then in a hostile sense; the admonition was "to kill nothing."

The people of India have carried this to the extreme, of course, but so have the conscientious objectors, who have also used the Commandment that says, in English: "Thou shalt not kill." But the Hebrew word correctly translates: "Thou shalt not murder."

As Paul warns us here in Verse 23, these activities on our part that are purely the results of man's conjecture of what should please God—these things are a total waste. Instead, as Paul's next words tell us:

> "Seeing you are risen with Christ, be continually seeking those things which are above, where Christ sits on the right hand of God!"

So, from God's Viewpoint, a study of Philosophy is no substitute and gets us nowhere. The blind adherence to ritual has no value with God. Looking to angels and gazing at crystals is actually contrary to God's instructions for us and rejecting the enjoyment of the physical pleasures that God has so graciously made available to us is a rejection of God's grace offered to us. God's Word tells us that:

> "...He has given us richly, all things to enjoy." (1 Timothy 1:6)

Four concepts man's thinking has created for us that can bring confusion and frustration into our lives and rob us of our rewards: Philosophy; Legalism; Mysticism, the Occult and Asceticism. Forewarned is forearmed!

Lesson 4 Colossians Chapter 3

Our "Place of Service"

At our Church we have been exposed to some Missionaries, most of whom have spent many years out in foreign and often strange countries, answering the call to represent our Lord Jesus Christ to those people.

We appreciate them and what they are doing, especially as we realize the difficult living conditions some of them have to cope with, the absence of friends and family and, in some cases, actual physical danger that they have to face.

It's good that we are given the opportunity to be made aware of these people and situations that we are supporting, and are therefore, at least a small part of.

I'm sure that hearing them, if you're at all like I am, causes us to pause for a few fleeting minutes at least to either consciously or subconsciously measure the productivity of our lives for the Lord, against what these Missionaries seem to be doing. The result of that brief analysis probably makes us feel a little depressed.

But I'd like you to think of a couple of things here as we are studying together at this point God's Idea of "the Christian Way of Life."

One thing is that, in all my recollection over the years, I have never seen or heard a bona fide Missionary that was not a happy person and who was not raring to get back to his or her field.

So, they need our support because it is a work that God's Word encourages us to support. However, we don't need to feel sorry for them! They're a happy people!

They are a functioning part of this great "Body of Christ" that we are studying about here in the Letters to the Colossians and to the Ephesians.

They are conscious of the fact that they are doing every day what the Lord has set out for them to do that day. They are firmly convinced that that is what He wants them to be doing and that gives them inner happiness and inner peace.

In other words, when they get up in the morning, they KNOW what and where their mission field is. God called them there and they are functioning on a daily basis. And they have inner peace about their life.

Now, you and I also have been called by God, and placed by God, right in the spot we're in. This is our mission field. It may not be spectacular, and there may be some drudgery connected with it, but it is important in God's Scheme of Things or He wouldn't have assigned someone that He has great concern for to this particular task.

My point is: we must not minimize the importance of the position that we find ourselves in at any given point in time!

So, whatever situation we find ourselves in, we must keep reminding ourselves:

> "This is my Mission Field! I am His Ambassador; and when people look at me or talk to me, I want them to see His Characteristics in me! Father, give me the strength and guidance to function in a way that will bring praise and honor to your name!"

All right, now I will proceed to follow my calling, which is to help strengthen your Faith and to help you to "have an answer to give to anyone that asks you the reason for the Hope that is in you!" So, let's review a minute and look at Colossians, Chapter 1.

We have noted how Paul has analyzed Christianity for us and pointed out to us that there are basically two sides to it and both sides he has clearly presented. The first is God's side, and Paul has pointed out to us, first, exactly Who Jesus Christ really is and the part that He plays in the world order. He states that for us in Chapter 1, starting in Verse 15:

> "He is the image of the invisible God, the first born of every creature; For by Him were all things created, that are in Heaven and that are in Earth, visible and invisible, whether thrones or dominions or principalities or powers, all things were created by Him, and for Him. And He is before all things, and by Him all things are held together."

That's WHO He is—certainly One to be worshipped and respected!

Then Paul makes it clear what Jesus has offered to the members of the human race that He created. That is a "reconciliation" with God the Father that will cover our shortcomings and failures. Verse 22 of Chapter 1 states it:

> "...in the body of his flesh through His death, to present us holy (set apart) and free from blame before Him."

Paul makes it even clearer in Chapter 2 down in Verse 13:

> "And you, being dead in your sins and the uncircumcision of your flesh, has He made alive together with Him, having forgiven you all trespasses; blotting out the handwriting of ordinances that was against us, which was contrary to us, and took it out of the way, nailing it to His Cross."

That's the provision. The offer is open to all members of the human race: accept what Jesus did, and you will find yourself literally "Raised up with Christ" as Chapter 3, Verse 1 expresses it.

And "being raised up with Christ" has some great benefits. In addition to the removal from God's consideration of all of our failures, we also find ourselves now indwelt by two new personages: Jesus Christ Himself and God's Holy Spirit, who is here to guide and direct and educate and protect us as we move through this thing called "Life," and then to ensure our safe arrival in the Next and most wonderful Life! All of this is what God has done!

What God Really Expects from Us

The second part of what Paul is so urgently presenting to us is what God expects back from man in return.

It is God's wish that we will accept what He has done for each member of the human race and receive Jesus Christ into our life; once we do this, He moves us from the raw state that all common humanity is in, moving us into a revitalized state of what He calls "a Child of God."

We often refer to this first state as "Phase One" of Life and to the "revitalized state" as Phase Two and the Eternal Life state as Phase Three.

Now, at the moment of our acceptance of what Jesus did the "revitalization" takes place and we move from Phase One to Phase Two. At that moment, as Chapter 1, Verse 13 expresses it, we will have been:

> "...delivered from the power of darkness, and we will have been translated into the kingdom of His Son ... including the forgiveness of our sins."

This is a wonderful and amazing transformation! God, however, fully realizes that we are living among people who have ideas that differ—some drastically—from His and so He has Paul warn us of the source of these differing ideas and concepts, so that we can be on our guard against them and the confusion they bring. In the last lesson, we identified four sources from which these confusions come:

1. The Philosophies of man, including man's ideas of creation and basic rules of living;
2. Legalism, which is the interjecting of rituals as an attempt to please God with our actions. The rituals seem to soon take the place of a real focusing on God and so become a kind of substitute Christianity.
3. Mysticism, which includes the attempts of man to delve into the area of the supernatural; Astrology, Angel worship, the use of hypnosis in attempt to communicate with the "other world," etc.
4. Asceticism, which is the depriving of ourselves of certain physical pleasures, somehow feeling that such "sacrifice" will make us more "holy." God's Word, however, tells us that: "He has given to us richly, ALL THINGS to enjoy!" (I Timothy 1:6)

So now, having warned us against accepting what Man's feeble reasoning has come up with as a "way of life" (it was called Gnosticism in Paul's day; today it is known as the "New Age Movement"), Paul now proceeds to lay out our Creator's ideas of what man should do and should not do.

A Presentation of "The Christian Ethic"

What we have here is what has come to be called the "Christian Ethic." Combine what we have here with the "Ten Commandments", and you have what is called the "Judo-Christian Ethic" that has really become the basis for all Civilized Life.

It's the basis for what we know of as "Common Law," and that, as we know, still supersedes many of the Enacted Laws of the various societies that have come and gone.

Recently the Supreme Court of the U.S. voided a law that the citizens of Colorado had easily passed. The majority of the people of Colorado wanted the law but the Supreme Court was in a split decision.

Of the Justices of the Supreme Court that dissented to the majority in the Court's ruling, one of them was Clarence Thomas. Justice Thomas.

One of the things that interested me in this was Clarence Thomas's statement that there is:

> "...a body of natural law that is set above any laws of man; laws that came originally from God and have been revealed to us in the Bible. These are meant for all cultures and society and are the basis of our own Constitution."

A stand that we, of course, hold to. By the way, this conviction of Justice Thomas's was one of the issues that was raised against him at the time of his confirmation.

I also heard an interview on television not too long ago between David Frost and the Microsoft mogul Bill Gates. Gates was asked if he believed in God and his answer was that he really wasn't sure but he certainly did believe in "the Christian ethic."

Here, in the Letter to the Colossians, and also augmented by Paul in the Ephesian letter, we have a statement of this "Christian ethic" that was the basis for our Constitution. But as these principles and concepts, one by one, are being canceled out by new laws and judicial interpretation, our Constitution is being chipped away at and altered and, as we know as a result, our society is crumbling. Law and order are disappearing. Crime, violence, and hatred are fast replacing the "Golden Rule."

So, we're going to look now at what has become known as "the Christian ethic," the Rules by which God expects us, His people particularly, to live.

And since Paul has touched on many of these issues in both the Colossian Letter and in the Ephesian Letter, I am going to blend the two together. We'll be covering the Letter to the Ephesians next, so this should work.

Now, as we start to look at this Code of Ethics as it is given to us in the Colossian Letter, the first matter addressed is how Believers are to handle the strong drives that are built into our human nature. Two of the major drives are the drive to procreation and the second is self-preservation.

God has placed in the members of the human race the same compulsion for procreation that He placed in the members of the animal world. Obviously, the reason He did this was because it was His intention that mankind cover and possess this earth.

Yet God does not expect us to live like the animals do. So, in the Beginning, God established the Marriage Relationship, which he made to be a one-spouse-at-a-time relationship to be of mutual help and companionship to each other. And He cemented this beside the drive for procreation.

As for "self-preservation," this goes beyond the fight to keep alive. And the fight to keep breathing. Uncontrolled, it becomes the trait that we call "selfishness" and goes on to include the desire to have more and more possessions, which includes what we call "greed" and "covetousness."

Now, God also knew that these built-in strong desires needed to have controls, so He gave to mankind the capability of "self-control" which is the "easy way," comparatively speaking, to control these basic human traits.

But God also knew that "self-control" would not be enough, so in addition to that, He arranged for the creation of "rulers" and "leaders" by giving some of His created beings the desire for leadership and the ability to lead others.

And to these "leaders" and "governors" He authorized the use of punishment to the bodies of offenders for violation of the laws that would be established from time to time in order to maintain order in the society.

Punishment to the body—to the "corpus"— as we have come to call "corporal punishment," of which "capital punishment" is, of course, the maximum.

A Comparison to Israel's Laws

Now, in God's Instructions to the nation Israel, God set forth His Plan for the marriage relationship and the family relationship, and also His Plan for restraining greed and covetousness. It was also God's intention that the nation Israel be a "shining light" to the rest of mankind, teaching all mankind God's Ways. But they badly failed in this commission, as we well know:

- They themselves made a joke of the marriage relationship by allowing divorce for the flimsiest of reasons.
- They themselves became famous for their practices of usury and greed.

The result was that the rest of the world soon held the Jews in contempt. They, along with their God that they made such a point of claiming to be serving.

So, while God's Instructions to mankind were out there, the teachers of these instructions had fallen into disrepute, so God's Instructions were largely ignored.

Therefore, the people of the so-called "civilized world" really had no basis for restraint, other than what their "philosophers" had come up with, and the result was that the people mostly were actually living like animals.

Then Jesus came along. Among other things, He refreshed the world's memory on the subject of marriage, fidelity, the family life, the one-spouse-at-a-time concept AND consideration for the rights of others. And He also reminded them that at the heart of an orderly, peaceful civilization IS the marriage relationship and the family relationship AND the control of greed. When these relationships fall apart, society falls apart.

The "Christian Ethic" Begins with Self-Control

So, the first subject that Paul considers here in this statement of "The Christian Ethic" is in the area of self-control of these basic urges. That begins here in Chapter 3, Verse 5 and he uses the strongest of commands, the aorist Imperative verb form that says: "Immediately start doing something you have not been doing!" So here it is in Verse 5, summarized:

> "Put to death your fleshly, animal-type activities:
> Fornication (*PORNEIA*, which was their word for 'illicit sexual intercourse')
> Uncleanness (*A-KATHARTOS*—'impurity')
> Lust (*PATHOS*—'Uncontrolled passion')
> Evil desires (*EPITHUMIA KAKOS*) and
> Covetousness (*PLEONEXIA*—which they described as 'the driving desire to have more'
> and which Paul says is Idolatry. *EIDOLOLATRIA*)."

"Idolatry" is always used in the Bible for "placing things, or other items of worship, ahead of God." And Paul adds in Verse 6:

> "...for which things' sake the wrath of God comes (present tense) on those who disobey; in which things you also walked, when you were a part of that world."

In Ephesians, in Chapter 5, Verse 3, Paul expresses this thought this way:

> "But fornication, and all uncleanness, or greediness, let it not be once named among you, as becoming saints."

And in Verse 5, "For this you know, that no whoremonger, nor unclean person, nor covetous man, an idolater, has any inheritance in the Kingdom of Christ and of God."

So, quickly, he has dealt with two major issues:

1. Illicit sex is out, which, by the way, was commanded to Israel in the Law given to Moses, item number seven; and
2. ...covetousness is out! Which, again by the way, was the last item of the "Ten Commandments."

Then there are some emotional responses that we are to eliminate, and some of these are reflected out through our tongue. This starts in Colossians 3:8:

> "But now also put off all these: Anger, Wrath, Malice, Blasphemy, Filthy communication out of your mouth."

First, notice the command to "put off" these things that he has listed here. He used the word they used to mean "putting away something." Laying it off and away from you, like you'd get out of very dirty clothes.

And if the Lord has commanded us to do something then we have to assume that it is possible for us to obey His command, otherwise He would never have given it to us!

So, we have to say that we Believers DO have it within our power to lay off this bad venting of our emotions. We CAN quit giving way to them! Further, the Holy Spirit is within us to help us IF our volition wants it to. One of the "fruits of the Holy Spirit" is "self-control," so, our job is to keep Him free to operate in us!

Now let's look at the whole passage here that runs from Verse 8 down through Verse 15. What we have here is really a statement of how God really expects His People to get along with the rest of the human race. And you will see that it is a life characterized by forbearance and honest treatment.

It begins (Verse 8) with the command to:

1. Put off anger, the slow-burning kind;
2. Put off wrath, which is the hot-flash kind, the "losing your temper" kind;
3. Put off malice, the malicious effort to do harm to someone;
4. Put off "slandering" someone, which is deliberately speaking inaccuracies against them; and
5. Put off abusive speech against anyone.

Now these last two, I know, we usually think of in a different context: "Blasphemy" we think of in connection with "evil speaking against The Lord," but in Paul's time this word was used as we use the word "slander"; and "Filthy communication" or "language" we think of what we call "swearing" or "foul language"; but again, in Paul's day it was also used simply of abusive speech, such as "chewing someone out with ugly language."

Then the next command to us here, Verse 9, also has to do with personal relationships, "Do not lie to one another"!

Lying, of course, is a deliberate attempt to mislead another person, usually to protect oneself, or to gain some advantage to ourselves.

I had to smile here at the detailed reason that Paul gave to support this command; in those days, it was perfectly acceptable conduct for a Jew to lie to a Gentile, or for a free man to lie to a slave. But Paul reminds us that all are equal before our Creator and our life is now to be lived on a higher level than before our rebirth!

It Continues with Our "Putting on Compassion!"

So, instead, and in view of that, Verse 12:

> "Seeing we are the Elect of God, put on: compassion ('bowels of mercies'), Kindness, humbleness of mind. Meekness, Longsuffering, forbearing one another, forgiving one another, as Christ has forgiven us."

And in Verse 14:

> "...above all of these, put on *AGAPE* ("Divine concern"), which is the bond of "completeness," i.e., that which binds these attitudes together..."

And the result to us will be (Verse 15) that:

> "... we will be allowing the peace of God to rule in our hearts, to which we are called in one body! And be thankful!"

The picture the Holy Spirit, through Paul, is painting for us here is that if and as we curb our anger and wrath and hatred and "shooting off our mouths" as responses to the actions of those around us that aren't what we'd like to see, and instead, we are forbearing in our mental approach to the whole thing adopting an attitude of Concern for them, then the Peace of God will actually fill and control our inner being. For which we will give thanks to Him!

So, we have now seen God's model for our inter-personal relationships:

- Honest and straightforward in our dealings;
- Keeping our temper under control;
- Righteously angry at un-Godly acts, but retaliating in God's Way;
- Longsuffering;

- Forgiving, as Christ treated us; and
- With a mental attitude of Concern for those around us, as God is concerned for His Creations.

And the result: Peace within!

Lesson 5 Colossians Chapter 3

"Let the Word Dwell in Us Richly!"

We recognize that humanity had pretty much gotten away from "self-control" by the time God had set for the arrival of Jesus, so when He arrived here, He had to begin the re-education of humanity, teaching them to act like "people" instead of "animals."

And after He left us, as He promised, the Holy Spirit continued the work through the Apostles; the first instruction from them was to get away from illicit sexual practices and to get away from covetousness, that overpowering, driving desire for more and more things, especially triggered by things that other people around us have.

We've seen that Paul's directive to us is to, first:

- keep these base drives under control; then
- to be honest and straightforward in our dealings with those around us; then
- to be righteously angry at un-Godly acts, but retaliating only in God's way;
- to be Longsuffering—slow to act in the face of provocation;
- to be forgiving, just as our Lord has forgiven us; and, tying the whole business together, is
- to develop a mental attitude of genuine Concern for those around us, just as God is concerned for us.

Then, God has promised that His Peace will be our great reward here in this lifetime while we are being prepared for the next and wonderful life with Him!

The next admonition from the Holy Spirit is given to us here in 3:16, and it is a directive to us to assume a responsibility—a very reasonable responsibility. After all, considering all that He has done for us, should we not willingly do something for Him in return?

> "Let the Word of Christ dwell in you richly; in all wisdom, teaching and admonishing yourselves in psalms and hymns and spiritual songs, singing with grace in your hearts to the Lord."

Now here is a very interesting passage and I want to remind you again that the Greek language did not use punctuation as we do with periods and commas and semi-colons and paragraph breaks, etc. The sentence structure and the thought structure themselves determined the breaks.

So, in this case, there could well be a semicolon after the phrase:

> "…dwell in you richly;"

Then, it continues:

> "…in all wisdom, teaching and admonishing ourselves with psalms and hymns..."

That punctuation as we use it makes sense here; God wants His Word to "dwell in us richly" and THEN, "in all wisdom, we teach and admonish ourselves." That's the first thing to note.

The second thing I want to say is that the New International Version has made this sentence say something that the original text does NOT say; so, if you have a NIV, then shut your eyes as we consider this text. OK? I think you'll see what I'm saying as we go along.

So now, the passage. The main verb is translated "dwell," and it is given to us as a present tense, active voice and imperative mood. In other words, it is first of all a "command," which is the function of the Imperative Mood. We are to see to it that God's Word is "at home" in our brain. WE are to take the initiative, which is obviously to read and study it! WE are to do whatever it takes to have this happen!

Now, think of this word "dwell" (*ENOIKEO*). It is a common word that meant to "be at home"; to "make this place your home."

Jesus said (this is in the Upper Room Discourse, John 14:23):

> "If a man love Me, he will keep my words; and my Father will love him, and We will come unto him, and make Our abode with him."

So how do we arrange things so that God's Word—the information contained in this Book—how do we arrange things so that the contents of this Book are "perfectly at home" in our mind? We listen to it, we read it, but most of all, we study it!

I'm going to put this in the "indirect mode" so nobody has to answer, except to himself or herself, but think a minute: how much time did you spend yesterday reading the newspaper? How much time did you spend reading a news magazine?

How much time did you spend watching the news on TV? Or reading news commentaries that give you some so-called "expert opinion" on what's going on in the world?

Then, against that total, how much time did you spend yesterday carefully reading the Bible?

The Bible gives us God's Views on matters; that is wisdom.

So, if we want our life to be blessed with inner happiness and peace, then in addition to controlling our base drives and treating others as we would like to be treated, we are to do what it takes (and we're all different) to give God's Word a home in our brain.

Now, we continue here with Verse 16, "...in all wisdom."

In other words, with this "wisdom from God" to work from, this "wisdom" that is stored in our brain as the result of our carefully studying His Revelation to mankind that we call "the Bible," what are we to do? We are to be: "...teaching and admonishing ourselves."

HOW?

> "...in (or with) psalms and hymns and spiritual songs, singing with grace in your hearts to the Lord."

Now, I think we need to look at this carefully and I'll read to you the way the NIV has "rendered" this passage. They have it as saying:

> "Let the word of Christ dwell in you richly as you teach and admonish one another with all wisdom, and as you sing psalms, hymns and spiritual songs."

They have moved the phrase "with all wisdom" away from where it is in the Greek text and they have added the words "and as you sing" which are NOT in the original text. By this, they have made the passage say something substantially different from what Paul wrote.

In other words, the translators made it say what they thought it ought to say, rather than what the Holy Spirit wrote down.

God's Arrangement for Workers in the Assembly

Now this is important, as it gets back to the problem that is created when well-meaning but misguided people grab instructions that God gives to one person and run off and try to execute the instructions themselves. To whom were these instructions directed? Can you see the chaos that can come from such presumptive action?

The NIV's approach to this matter of admonishing one another would have everybody feeling that they have to be criticizing and admonishing everyone else. How would you like that? This is NOT God's teaching for this dispensation in which we live.

God set up an orderly arrangement for us. Paul described it in two different passages; one is in First Corinthians 13:27:

> "Now you are the Body of Christ, and members of that body. And God has set some in the Assembly, first Apostles, secondarily Prophets, third, Teachers; after that Miracles, then gifts of healings, helpers, governments, specialists in languages..."

Then he asked the rhetorical question:

> "Are all Apostles? All Prophets? All Teachers? All workers of miracles?"

And from the structure of the text the expected answer is, "No, of course not!" Then, in Ephesians Chapter 4, the Holy Spirit, through Paul, makes this appeal to Believers in Verse 2 of Ephesians Chapter 4:

> "With all humility and meekness, with longsuffering, forbearing one another in *AGAPE*, endeavoring to keep the unity of the Holy Spirit in the bond of peace."

Then, in Verse 7:

> "But unto every one of us is given grace according to the measure of the gift of Christ."

In other words, each of us has been given a gift. Then, in Verse 11:

> "And He gave some Apostles, and some, Prophets; and some Evangelists; and some Pastors and Teachers."

And then he states the purpose of this in Verse 12:

> "For the perfecting of the saints, for the work of the ministry, for the edifying of the Body of Christ."

Each of us has a "sphere of influence" and "area of responsibility." A parent has a responsibility to "teach and admonish" his or her children and at what age that responsibility stops is between you and the Lord. But when we get beyond our own home, then it seems like we should be very sure that the Holy Spirit is calling us to be a pastor or a teacher before we begin an "admonishing" process with someone.

This same caution needs to be applied in the matter of personal evangelism; there are those who urge on their congregation that we Believers are obligated to "speak to our neighbor about the Lord" and they put us on a guilt trip if we aren't habitually doing this.

But are you an "evangelist"? Have you been called to that by the Holy Spirit? And if you are not "commissioned" and you walk up to your neighbor and ask him or her, "Are you saved?" are you not being a busy body? Are you not prying into something that is none of your business?

Now, assuming that you are living a life clean before God and therefore the Holy Spirit is operative in you, the Holy Spirit may very well want you to speak to your neighbor, or someone else, about the Lord; if He does, He will give you that urging. He will also set up the opportunity and will give you the words to say.

Otherwise, unless you have a "calling," God's instructions to us living in this dispensation regarding personal evangelism are limited to a very few, but very clear ones. One is First Peter 3:15 that says:

> "But set apart the Lord God in your hearts, and be ready always to give an answer to every man that asks you a reason for the hope that is in you, and do it with meekness and reverential respect!"

Another statement of our position was written by Paul in 2 Corinthians 3:2 where he told us that:

> "We are his epistle written in his heart, known and read by all men…"

People read us. This does not say that we are to read to them! Also, we have the passage in Second Corinthians 5:19 and 20, where he tells us that:

> "…Christ has committed to us the Word of reconciliation, therefore, on behalf of Christ, we are his ambassadors, as though God did beseech through us, to be reconciled to God."

But we also keep in mind that an "ambassador" is under close control of his Prime Minister; he speaks only what and when he is instructed to do so. And obviously, the Holy Spirit is OUR "prime minister!"

Think of it this way: our Ambassador to England, for example, is there to represent our Country, not to try to persuade every Englishman to become an American!

And then there is this directive in Colossians 3, to make God's Word to be "at home" in our minds so that, in all wisdom, we teach and admonish "ourselves." How? "With psalms and hymns and spiritual songs, singing with grace in our hearts to the Lord."

Did you ever have your father or your mother (or your husband or your wife) "admonish" you over something you did that was not according to the rules and do it without saying a word to you? It's called "the family look," I believe.

In Ephesians 5:8, Paul reminds us that:

> "…we are children of Light in the Lord." Then, he says, "Walk that way … establishing what is well-pleasing to the Lord."

The passage says "walk." It does not say "talk."

It's interesting, too, that in Ephesians Chapter 5 which, in content, is a parallel to our passage here in Colossians, Paul expresses this thought a little differently. He has just commanded us in Verse 18 of Ephesians 5, to "allow the Holy Spirit to control us" ("Be filled with the Spirit"), then he continues with:

> "Speaking to yourselves in psalms and hymns and spiritual songs, singing and making melody in your heart to the Lord."

Now we can well ask: How will singing a hymn within someone's hearing teach that person something? Frankly, I don't know. But I do know that "music" is a Divine Institution; it is the only communicator that is universal, and if God didn't see an application for it in this situation, it certainly would not be appearing in His written Word.

Now, you may say, "I can't sing a note!" Well, notice the last of Verse 16. It says,

> "…singing with grace ... Where? … in your hearts, to the Lord."

I hope you will meditate on this passage; God put it right there, in black and white, and I have never known Him to waste words! In this statement of the "Christian ethic," so far Paul has listed out these points:

1. We are to control our base, natural drives that we are endowed with:
   - The drive for "self-preservation"
   - The drive for "procreation"

   (We are not to live like animals, in other words.)
2. We are to be honest and straightforward in our dealings with those around us.
3. We are to be righteously angry at un-godly acts, but we are to retaliate only in God's way.
4. We are to be Longsuffering (i.e., "slow to act in the face of provocation").
5. We are to be forgiving, as our Lord has forgiven us.

6. We are to develop a mental attitude of genuine concern for those around us.
7. We are to see that God's Word is made to be "at home" in our minds.
8. We are to teach and admonish ourselves (*heoutous*) through the psalms and hymns and spiritual songs that we sing in our hearts to the Lord.

I believe that, in this last one that we have just looked at here, we are touching a deep relationship to our Heavenly Father that we may not have been particularly conscious of; and that is that as we sing praises to Him, and as we think of those within our sphere of influence that we feel need teaching and admonition, there is a prayer link here that will ultimately influence our relationship to that person, and will produce results that will honor our Lord.

And now, Verse 17:

> "And whatever you do in word or deed, do all in the name of the Lord Jesus, giving thanks to God the Father, through Him."

What a different place the world would be if this principle were followed—even by Christians only! Shoddy work is the blight of the world!

When I was quite young and impressionable, my dad hand—fettered a sort of plaque for me and hung it in my room. It said:

If a task is once begun,
Never leave it till it's done.
Be the labor great or small,
Do it well, or not at all.

I know that was his creed, and that little poem has stuck in my mind all these years.

When something comes along that you *HAVE* to do—no escaping it—if we think, *I am doing this for the Lord*! If we will adopt that mental attitude, it will put a totally different look on what we're about to do.

And that is a fact, anyway. We belong to Him. We are His by right of purchase. Plus, we have, of our own volition, placed our life in His Hands.

And, assuming that your life is clean before Him, and the Holy Spirit is therefore freely operating in your life, then whatever comes into your life is God's best for you. So, if you have to stop and change a tire along the freeway, on the way to an important appointment, then:

> "...do it in the name of the Lord Jesus, giving thanks to God the Father, through Him."

What a difference this mental attitude will make in your life—as well as in your general health! I am sure you are seeing where the "Christian ethic" is taking us. It is taking us from the animal existence, characterized by greed, selfishness, covetousness, and hatred, and putting us in an atmosphere of self-control, concern for one another, gentleness, with a desire to do our work well for the sake of our Lord, who has made such a wonderful provision for us.

And as a result, the world will be attracted to the Light that we reflect, and we will enjoy inner happiness and peace, in the midst of the turmoil outside.

Lesson 6 Colossians Chapters 3 and 4

God's First Principle Is "Order"

WELL, WE'RE ABOUT to complete our look at the second of the four letters that Paul wrote from his imprisonment in the city of Rome.

The letter he wrote first was the Letter to the Philippians, the Letter that points us to Jesus, God's Special Son as the source of joy, inner happiness, and peace in the life of those who will trust their lives to Him.

In this letter, written primarily to the Believers in the city of Colossae, we see that Paul is making sure we all understand the reason why Jesus, God's Special Son, *CAN BE* the source of inner happiness and peace—because He, Jesus, is truly Himself Deity. As we read in Chapter 1 Verse 16:

> "For by Him were all things created, that are in Heaven, and that are in Earth, visible and invisible, whether they be thrones, or dominions, or principalities, or powers; all things were created by Him, and for Him; and He is before all things, and by Him all things are held together."

That's a part of the reason why we can and should look to Him as our life support system, but even beyond that, as Verse 13 of Chapter 1 tells us:

> "He, Jesus, has delivered us from the authority of Darkness, and He has translated us into the Kingdom of Christ, in whom we have redemption from our failures and shortcomings, through His Blood."

Whenever I see a TV showing of the astronauts floating around up there in space, all encased in their space suit and connected by their umbilical cord to their spaceship, I see a representation of you and I, as we go through our life. We are living in an environment that is totally adverse to us, and with no more understanding of how to keep alive or how to operate than, as we say, "the man in the moon." Yet, in fact, we are encased and attached to this Jesus, and if we just follow His Rules and do as He instructs us to do, we will live productively, and He will deliver us safely to our destination.

However, if we were to try to take matters into our own hands, or fail to follow the carefully given instructions, we are goners!

In the case of the astronauts the choice is not hard to make—stay attached, follow orders, and live! Yet for us humans, whose true situation is no different, we seem to resent being "connected" to something and required to follow our Creator's instructions. And we think we are so smart!

So, in this letter Paul tries his best to make our situation clear to us, and he includes in this Letter a quick sketch of these basic Instructions. These instructions are enlarged upon in the next Letter, the Letter to the Believers at Ephesus, and, together, they form what is commonly referred to as "the Christian ethic."

This code of conduct was the code that created stability in our world system; it has formed the basis for Western Civilization, as we call it. It was the code carefully followed by the men who established these

United States of America, and it was the background from which came the original Constitution of the United States and the Bill of Rights that went with it.

It is very logical and reasonable that all Mankind should know it thoroughly and follow it carefully. Even Bill Gates, the founder and developer of Microsoft, who is conceded to be the richest man on Earth today, and certainly one of the "smartest" when it comes to Human Knowledge, has publicly stated:

> "I am not sure I 'believe in God,' but I certainly do subscribe to 'The Christian Ethic' as a way of life!"

I heard him make this statement not too long ago in an interview on television with David Frost.

"Wise men" by the world's standard "subscribe" to it but is it taught in our public schools today? No way! Even Aesop's Fables have been ruled out.

Instead, our children have been and are being mostly taught how to operate computers, how to fit into the world system, how to have "safe sex," and how to outwit your neighbors so that they don't "get the best of you" in this "game of life."

So, what are you and I supposed to do, we who "know better?" It's up to us to know these operating instructions, to be ready to impart them when we are asked and when the Holy Spirit sets up opportunities.

Now, so far in this statement of this "Christian ethic" we have already noted several points, and now The Holy Spirit, speaking through Paul, turns next to the two areas of our life where He knew we would be spending most of our waking hours: with our family and in our employment situation.

And He lays out His Way, under which mankind needs to be operating to ensure inner happiness, peace, and personal productivity as we move through this phase of our lives.

God is a God of "order" not "disorder," and the "order" that exists in the Universe is the prime example! The root word that humanity has used to characterize a good life is the word "order." It is our translation of the Greek noun *TAXIS*, which means "a regular arrangement." The verb form is *TASSO*, which means "to arrange things in an orderly manner."

And the Greeks, in their direct way, made a "negative" out of the word simply by putting the letter "A" in front of the word so that gives us "no order" or, as we say, "disorder." Paul used this negative word in his Letter to the Thessalonians, where he wrote:

> "Now we command you, brethren, in the name of our Lord Jesus Christ, that you withdraw yourselves from every brother that walks disorderly, and not after the teaching which he received of us" (3:6)

"Order" makes life pleasant, as we know. It's a part of God's "intended way" for mankind.

Think, for a moment, of what God has endowed us humans with; first, and basic to it all, is our volition—our right to choose. That's the first "Divine Institution." Animals, in their natural state, also have that ability.

But then God quickly directed mankind to elect to "control" his "animal instincts" for his good and for the good of society in general.

And, as a part of that "controlled environment" God set up the Marriage Relationship—His second "Divine Institution." The concept of one-spouse-at-a-time. Paul, by the way, covers this relationship next, here.

Then, intending that the human race expand to cover the Earth and still live at peace, God established the Family Relationship—Divine Institution number three. Parents and their children. Paul sets out the rules for that relationship here.

Then, knowing that the family units would be drawn together for fellowship and for mutual protection against the world around them that will not follow God's instructions, God established the National

Entity—Divine Institution number four, and God set up rules for the Nations to follow.

The "One World" Concept is Not God's Way

We have to recognize that the one-world concept is not God's way. He well knew that when given any power, men and women would soon be "lording it over" their weaker, less aggressive neighbors.

We recall how mankind tried to set up a one-world system back in the early days at the Tower of Babel. God put a stop to that in a hurry, didn't He! In fact, God was so definite about it that it was at that point that He separated the people into groups that would be at odds with one another because of a language barrier. When people can't communicate verbally, they immediately become "at odds" with one another!

So, since God established the concept of National Entities, then we know that a one-world system will never work, because it is not "God-ordained."

But the basis of God's Plan for the human race begins with the Marriage Relationship and is closely entwined with the Family Relationship. And the word that is the binding and determining factor in these very important relationships is our word "ORDER." And this, naturally, as we would expect, is Paul's next subject.

In the letter Paul wrote next, the one to the Ephesians, Paul discusses this relationship in a little more detail, so we'll look at that, too. Back up a few pages to Ephesians, Chapter 5. In this Ephesian Letter, Paul will be illustrating some of his points by giving us the example of the relationship between our Lord Jesus Christ and the great Body of Believers that will be accumulated through the years since His time here on Earth.

Look at Ephesians 5:18. Here is the "starter" and a command:

> "And be not drunk with wine—instead, be filled with ("controlled by") the Holy Spirit..."

Then here is a statement similar to the one we considered in Colossians in Verse 20:

> "Speaking to yourselves in psalms and hymns and spiritual songs, singing and making melody in your heart to the Lord; giving thanks always for all things unto God the Father, in the name of our Lord Jesus Christ, placing yourselves in subjection to one another, in the fear of God."

Now here, in this word that is translated "in subjection to" or "subject to," we have our word "TASSO" that means "order," only now it has a preposition hooked in front of it (*UPO*) that we translate as "under."

Actually, this word was a military word that meant "under orders" or "subject to." It meant "you get in line and move as a unit."

"Order" is everything in life, as we well know. We know what happens at a busy intersection when the signal lights go out; the "controlling authority" is gone and chaos quickly takes over. We have to have "order" and "order" means that there is a chain of command, with people respecting that "chain of command!"

In this passage here, in Ephesians 5:18, the verb is at the end of the sentence, "...be *controlled* by the Holy Spirit." And then follows a string of participles:

> *"...speaking to ourselves in psalms and hymns," and "making melody in our hearts to the Lord," and "giving thanks always to God," and "submitting ourselves to one another, in the fear of God."*

God's "Chain of Command"

Placing ourselves voluntarily, in the "chain of command!" Then, the next verse: "...wives to your own husbands, as unto the Lord."

Then he quickly explains this statement (and I'm sure Paul knew he'd better hurry with his explanation). The explanation is a comparison of the Marriage Relationship to the relationship that Christ has with the entire Body of Believers, and he says in Ephesians 5:23:

> "For the husband is the head of the wife, as Christ is the head of the *EKKLESIA*, and He is the Savior (the "protector and deliverer") of the Body.
>
> Therefore, as the *EKKLESIA* is subject to Christ, so the wives to their own husbands in everything" (Eph. 5:24)

And then the Holy Spirit is quick to add in Ephesians 5:25:

> "Husbands, love your wives, even as Christ also loved the *EKKLESIA*, and gave Himself for it..."

As Dr. Robertson commented at this point:

> "Wives have rights and privileges, but recognition of the husband's leadership is essential to a well-ordered home; only the assumption is that the husband has a head, and a wise one."

Colossians 3:19 has an interesting way of putting it: "Husbands, love your wives, and do not be embittered against them."

The Greek word that is translated as "embittered" is used in other places in the New Testament. For example, it speaks of "water that is bitter, as though poisoned". Also, the Greeks used it as we would say, "being bitter against someone," or, as we also say, "It's all you can do to stand them!"

Personally, I believe that Paul had been married, simply because his insight into life in general would have to have come from that background. And what I see here, in this addendum he has hung onto this Command, in Verse 19, is this: there is a tendency for men to be impatient with what we look upon as our "wife's frailties." We tend to think, "Well, why CAN'T you do that?" or "Why can't you understand that?" or "Why is that so important?" etc.

But we have to recognize that the woman is both physically AND psychologically different from the male of the species. And Husbands need to recognize this fact and operate accordingly.

The Apostle Peter had this information given to him by the Holy Spirit, and he passed it along to us in First Peter 3:7. Here he warns us husbands:

> "You husbands, likewise live with your wives in an understanding way, as with a weaker vessel, since she is a woman, and grant her honor as a fellow heir of the grace of life!"

Then Peter also added this bit of information that may startle some of you men:

> "[Do this] so that your prayers may not be hindered"!

In other words, he recognizes that our failing to live with them in an understanding way "according to knowledge" AND if we fail to give honor to her, as unto the weaker vessel, then we are missing God's Mark, which is what we call "sin," and our fellowship with the Lord is broken and our prayers are definitely "hindered!"

We need to continually remind ourselves that God considers the Marriage Relationship to be on the same level as is Christ's relationship to the great Body of Believers. And Paul, in the passage in Ephesians Chapter 5, said this:

> "Let each man among you also have the highest concern for his own wife, even as for himself; and let the wife see to it that she respects (*PHOBIA*) her husband." (Eph. 5:33)

The husband is responsible for and is to have a deep concern for his wife; the wife is to encourage her husband to fulfill his role by respecting his position AND his responsibility.

All right, continuing in the Book of Ephesians. The next step in the matter of "order" in the world, has to do with the children in the family. Ephesians 6 begins:

> "Children, obey your parents in the Lord, for this is right. Honor your father and mother, which is the first commandment with a promise..."

The word translated "obey" here for the children is not the word that was used to describe the relationship of the wife toward the husband; THAT word meant to understand and respect the "order" of responsibility. THIS word, "obey," meant "to obey!" To follow instructions to the letter! For, as the passage says, "This is right in God's eyes."

And then he states the "promise" that went with this instruction. Actually, it was a part of Commandment number five of the ten given to Moses. The promise is:

> "...so that your days may be long upon the land which the Lord has given you."

Now while this was a promise to the Nation of Israel, the fact that it is restated in the Epistles makes it a promise applicable to people living in this dispensation. We will do well to remind our grandchildren of that one!

> "Honor your father and mother, SO THAT it may be well with you, and you may live long on the earth."

Then a special word to fathers, in dealing with your children in Verse 4:

> "And fathers, do not provoke your children to wrath, but bring them up in the nurture and admonition of the Lord."

In the Colossian Letter, Paul says it this way:

> "Fathers, do not provoke your children, lest they be discouraged" (or, literally, "without spirit"). (Colossians 3:21)

If discipline is meted out unjustly, or excessively harsh, that, as we know, can be spirit-breaking. Also, a failure to forgive the child upon his acknowledgement of his wrong-doing can be just as spirit-breaking. The illustration we have of that is in the account of David and his son Absolom. It begins in Second Samuel 13. If "forgiving someone after their acknowledgement" is a problem for you, it would do you good to see the results of this failure by reading this account again.

All right—continuing the reaching out for "order" in our society and the benefits from "order," Paul moves from the "Don't act like animals" command through "Don't covet what isn't yours,"

through the husband-wife "order of responsibility," and through the child-parent relationship to the work relationship.

Still in Ephesians 6, notice Verse 5:

> "Workers, be obedient to those who are your master according to the flesh, with fear and trembling, in the sincerity of your heart, as to Christ; not by way of eyeservice, as men-pleasers, but as slaves of Christ, doing the will of God from the heart.
>
> With good will render service, as to the Lord, and not to men, knowing that whatever good thing each one does, this he will receive back from the Lord, whether slave or free."

Now, I know it starts out with the word "slaves," but the Greek word here is *DOULOS*, and in Paul's day the "Master-Slave" relationship was very similar to the "Employer-Employee" relationship of our day. Some, then, were truly "slaves," but many more were paid for their work, and many more had voluntarily indentured themselves to someone as a way to eat regularly.

Also, you will note there at the end of Verse 8 that he states that what he has just said applies to "either slave or free."

In the Letter to the Colossians, in Chapter 3, Verse 23, Paul adds these words,

> "And whatever you do, do heartily, as to the Lord, and not unto men; knowing that of the Lord you shall receive the reward of the Inheritance. You serve the Lord Christ!"

People who are still in the "work world" need to continually remind themselves that we are here, first and foremost, to serve the Lord, being concerned primarily for Him and for His Aims and Goals.

And, as he has instructed us here, we, in a like manner, owe our "superior" a true "concern" for his aims and goals. And that means no shoddy work!

And, further, the Lord has promised to reward us even if our employer doesn't. Remember that we are working, primarily, for the Lord!

And the last word is to those at the "top of the economic ladder," the "Masters." Paul has this word for them, in Ephesians 6:9:

> "Masters, do the same things to them, and give up threatening, knowing that both their Master and yours is in Heaven, and there is no partiality with Him."

So here we are! We have gone from the basis of our society to the top of our society, and the by-word is "order."

Paul's Final Word: "Pray, Walk in Wisdom, Guard Your Time!"

Now, back to Colossians 4 to get Paul's final words to these people at Colossae. The first of his "last words" are in Verse 2: "Continue in prayer, and watch in the same with thanksgiving." Then, in Verse 5, "Walk in wisdom toward them that are outsiders, redeeming the time..."

In other words, "Not wasting time—it's precious; it's all you have to work with!" And then the last one, here in Verse 6, is one to ponder over:

> "Let your speech be always with grace, seasoned with salt, so that you may know how you ought to answer every man."

Paul knew that our speech must be "gracious," up-building and not down-tearing. He also knew the benefit of a "sprinkling of salt" to liven things up. In other words, try not to be a bore!

But the "grace" part of this statement seems to me to be the key; God, in His Grace, gave Believers the Holy Spirit, to guide and direct us, if we will allow Him to do so. You and I DO NOT know how to answer every man that asks, but God does know what that person should hear, and, in grace, God will provide us with the words, as we look to Him for that help.

And, finally, Paul's prayer of them, stated in Verse 12 of Chapter 4:

> "...that you may be made to stand (passive voice) MATURE and FULLY ASSURED in all the Will of God."

When the Holy Spirit is in control, we ARE in the will of God. And the Holy Spirit will make us stand "fully assured!" There's the source of inner happiness and the peace that we all so much want to have!

THE LETTER TO PHILEMON

An Application of Christian Doctrine

The Letter to Philemon—
An Application of Christian Doctrine

THIS VERY SHORT letter is right after Paul's Letters to Timothy and Titus and just before the Book of Hebrews. I hope you can find it in your Bible.

It's only one chapter and only 25 verses, as we have it divided, and it is generally thought to have been written in Paul's own handwriting. It was written about the time that the Colossian and the Ephesian Letters were written, which was during Paul's two-year imprisonment in Rome.

A person can easily wonder why the Holy Spirit would cause it to be included in the Canon of Holy Scripture, but here it is. However, as we will see, it is a practical application of Christ's Teachings. First of all, it is certainly an expression of AGAPE, our word for "Love," in its highest form. In my mind, I think of that Greek word AGAPE as expressing "Divine-type concern," the kind of concern that God has for you and me!

Then the second thing this little letter gives us is a very graphic illustration and playing out of the Doctrine of Substitution, and of Christ's intervention before God on your and my behalf. This is what Paul is doing in this Letter—he is offering himself as a substitute for this former slave, Onesimus, and it's what Jesus did for you and me.

Now, while the letter concerns a man who was a slave-owner and a man who was formerly his slave, still the letter does not deal directly with the subject of Slavery. However, the fact that it is a part of the Scriptures and that it discusses Human Relationships as it does, has been thought by many to have strongly influenced the abolishing of Slavery in many of the countries of the world, including our own. The Bible, we know, used to be widely read throughout the world!

Dr. A. T. Robertson put it this way, "Paul applies the spirit of Christianity to the problem of slavery in words that have ultimately set the slaves free from bondage to men."

So, we can begin to understand why God preserved this little Letter in His Instruction Book. Slavery, as it has been practiced, is not in God's thinking and its inclusion in His Word has apparently had its effect in removing this plague from parts of our society, at least.

Now, naturally, I have to begin by refreshing your mind on the story that is behind the Letter Paul wrote to Philemon.

Philemon was a wealthy man who lived in the city of Colossae and he apparently had a number of slaves, among whom was one by the name of Onesimus.

Slaves were an important part of the way of life of the people in the Roman Empire. Every time the Roman armies went out on a conquering mission, which was frequently, they always brought back a bunch of men, women, and children as captives—brought back with the intention of making them slaves to the people who were identified as "citizens" in the Roman Empire.

It is generally understood that in Paul's time, approximately half of the population of the Roman Empire consisted of slaves. 60 million slaves out of a total population of 120 million people.

And, as you can imagine, there were all kinds of relationships that existed; some horrible for the slave, some not so bad, depending, of course, on the dispositions of the masters and the slaves, and the work, etc. But the "master" had full control over the life of his slaves. And, as far as the slave was concerned, the "master" was accountable to no one for the way the slave was treated.

This particular slave, Onesimus, had run away from his master, and by what we sometimes refer to as "a stroke of fate," he had come under the sound of Paul's teaching and had accepted Paul's message and had placed his life in the hands of our Lord Jesus Christ.

Further than that, he had become very useful to Paul there in Colossae. In the last Chapter of Paul's Letter to the Colossians, in Verse 9, Paul mentions Onesimus as "a faithful and beloved brother." And, at the end of the letter, there is a final note that states that the letter was actually "written from Rome to the Colossians by Tychicus and Onesimus."

But Onesimus had obviously told Paul of his former life and it came out that his former "master" was Philemon, and Philemon had, in the meantime, also become a Believer. So, it also follows that Onesimus should return to Philemon, whose property he was.

However, now the relationship between these two men has had a new dimension added—both are now Christians. Now Jesus has become the Master of them both!

Paul wants to make sure that Philemon completely understands and appreciates the situation and the new relationship, and so Paul handwrites this very short but very expressive letter to his convert and friend, Philemon.

Paul begins the letter as he has the others,

> "Paul, a prisoner of Christ Jesus, and Timothy our brother, to Philemon, our beloved and fellow worker, and to beloved Apphia, and Archippus, our fellow-soldier, and to the *EKKLESIA* (the "assembly") in your house; grace to you and peace from God our Father, and the Lord Jesus Christ." (Phil. 1:1-3)

First, we note that Paul describes himself as "a prisoner of Christ Jesus," not of the emperor. Totally under the control of Christ Jesus. For that matter, just as is every Believer; our life depends on Him, our food depends on Him, what we are able to do or not do depends entirely on Him!

And Paul was entirely happy with this situation. He was not the kind of prisoner that bangs his cup on the bars to be obnoxious, nor was he fighting his situation. He was fully aware of his situation and happy to be in it!

You'll also note that the "assembly" met in Philemon's home. The "assemblies" met in their members' homes for the first 200 or more years until Constantine, the then-Roman Emperor himself became a Christian and got the idea that God needed a "better meeting place," one to outstrip the temples that the people had erected to their man-made "gods."

I smiled at Dr. Vernon McGee's comment on this, "Let's think about this for a minute: the church building has become so all-important to people today that it is all out of relationship to the real purpose of the local church."

Then he added this interesting information:

> The great cathedrals of the past were actually never meant for public meetings. Westminster Abbey, in England, for example, was never intended for public services. It was built in the shape of a cross as a monument to Jesus Christ.
>
> Although I think they had the wrong idea (he added)—instead of spending all that money on a cathedral, they should have used it to send out missionaries—that was their way of expressing their devotion. The idea of putting the emphasis on a building and on a building program is a little out of line with the example of the early church.

So says Dr. McGee. Then, to Philemon, Paul says:

> "I thank my God always, making mention of you in my prayers, because I hear of your love, and of the faith which you have toward the Lord Jesus, and toward all the saints; and I pray that the fellowship of your faith may become effective through the knowledge of every good thing which is in you for Christ's sake.
>
> I have come to have much joy and comfort in your love, because the hearts of the saints have been refreshed through you, brother." (Phil. 1:4-7)

If you're looking at a King James version, you'll see the word "bowels" used there in Verse 7:

> "...because the bowels of the saints are refreshed by you."

The Greek word is *SPLANCHNON*. Technically it meant "intestines," and it's used this way in Acts 1:18, but it was also commonly used to indicate the center of a person's emotional system. You know, if something stirs you real hard, you feel it "right here" first.

Paul had learned of Philemon's habit of "refreshing emotionally" the Believers there in Colossae. That's a wonderful gift. It's great to have our minds fed and refreshed, but to have our "spirits lifted" is a wonderful thing! As some wise man once said, "A reasoned 'No!' from a friend is a great gift; but a joyful 'Yes!' at the right time, is wonderful!"

And now Paul gets to the point of his letter in Verse 8:

> "Therefore (knowing you as I do) in Christ I could order you to do that which is proper, yet for love's sake I rather appeal to you, since I am such a person as Paul, the aged (he was then about sixty), and now also a prisoner of Christ Jesus—I appeal to you for my child, whom I have begotten in my imprisonment,

> Onesimus, who formerly was useless to you, but now is useful both to you and to me." (Phil. 1:8-11)

Paul was a real master of the "tactful approach" wasn't he! And he also had a sense of humor; the name "Onesimus" actually meant "useful" or "profitable," and now Paul makes a play on words here. Onesimus was "useless" but now he is "useful," he's saying, both to you and to me!

Then Paul continues:

> "And I have sent him back to you in person, with my very heart, whom I wished to keep with me, that, in your behalf, he might minister to me in my imprisonment for the gospel.
>
> However, without your consent, I would not want to do this. For perhaps it was for this reason that he parted from you for a while, so that you should have him back forever—no longer as a slave, but more than a slave—a beloved brother, especially to me, but how much more to you, both in the flesh, and in the Lord.
>
> If you then regard me as a partner, accept him as you would me." (Phil. 1:12-17)

Here begins the substitution! Paul continues in Verse 18:

> "If he has wronged you in any way, or owes you anything, charge that to my account. I, Paul, am writing this with my own hand, I will repay it."

Here is Paul's promissory note. And this is a replay of the many conversations that have gone on in Heaven through the years. Up for discussion many years ago came the name of Ed Perry. "Ed would like to become a part of Our Kingdom," the Official of the Royal Court states.

God's mind reviews, for about one-tenth of a second, the good things Ed Perry had done, and then He begins to look at the thoughtless and bad things he had done (this takes quite a few minutes), and then God says:

"I'm afraid Ed Perry is not fit for admission into our Kingdom."

But then, Jesus, who is at God's right hand during this Court Hearing, says, "I had Ed Perry in mind when I went to the Cross, so seeing you have Me as a partner, then receive him to Yourself, as You have Me." Then our Heavenly Father smiles, and says, "We are happy to welcome Ed into the Kingdom!"

How thankful we can be that we have an intercessor seated at God's Right hand! And not only that we HAVE Him there, but that we KNOW that we have Him there!

And reminding us, once again, of this fact, is the reason why God's Holy Spirit caused this little Letter to be included in the Holy Scriptures. And, interestingly, it was among the letters included in the Canon of Scriptures, right from the very beginning! No one ever questioned its right to be there!

Well, Paul apparently wasn't totally sure what Philemon's reaction to all this would be. At least Paul wasn't taking any chances, so he added a little clincher, which starts there at the end of Verse 19. He says,

> "Now I'm not going to mention how you owe to me even your own life, as well; instead, I'm just going to speak of the way my heart is refreshed, as I think of how you will be doing even beyond what I have said!
>
> And (Paul adds) make a reservation there for me, for I am relying on the fact that through your prayers, I will be visiting you soon!" (Phil 1:19-22)

An additional lesson I see here is: Don't leave anything to chance. Cover all the bases. Be thorough in what you do! Then Paul concludes his letter:

> "We, here, send our greetings to you, there—to you, our fellow-laborers. The grace of our Lord Jesus Christ be with your spirit!"

The End. A sweet story, right?

THE LETTER
TO THE EPHESIANS

"The Body of Christ"

Lesson 1 Dispensations

A Discussion of "Dispensational Truth"

We have now begun our look into the Great Revelation of the Great God, to the Created Beings of this earth.

I heard Dr. Stanley say, a few weeks ago, that if a person who is a new Believer wants to know where to begin his or her study of the Bible, the best place to suggest they begin is with these three letters that the Apostle Paul wrote from Rome—Philippians, Colossians, and Ephesians, saving Ephesians for the last! They, together, very clearly present the whole, wonderful picture, and the life that God says is Christianity.

Philippians shows us how to have peace and inner happiness, and it is found in our relationship to Jesus, God's Special Son. Deity that became Humanity, so that He could tell us humans about divine things, and open the door for us, to it all!

Colossians tells us just who this Jesus really is and why we should reverence Him and pay attention to what He has to say.

Ephesians paints for us the great future that is in store for Believers, both here on this earth and in the Life to come; PLUS, it opens to our eyes the Plan of God for the human race! It lets us see what God sees, and what was never seen before in the history of mankind.

I don't know if you've ever stopped to think about it, but in the days before Moses and the Giving of the Law, mankind didn't know very much about God; they felt that He (whoever "He" was) was much to be feared, and to be placated, if possible. As a result, many different approaches to God were invented by men.

Some people had the benefit of coming into contact with a few men like Abraham and Isaac and Jacob and Moses, to whom God had spoken, and to whom God had made certain promises.

These people had learned that if a person obeyed God's instructions, he or she was the beneficiary of blessings. And, likewise, if one disobeyed God's instructions, discipline and cursing was sure to follow.

This was the first and basic lesson from God for the human race. Many people don't believe that today, no matter how obvious a truth it is.

The fact of the availability of this knowledge of God to those people is confirmed by what we read in the oldest Book in the Bible, the Book of Job. Job is believed to have been a contemporary of Jacob's, and from the things that Job's friend, Elihu has to say to Job, in Chapters 35 and 36 of the Book of Job, we know that some, at least, had quite a knowledge of God and His Ways.

To illustrate, let me read you what Elihu had to say to Job at the end of his "counseling session" with this man Job who was, mentally, about as low as anyone can get, at that point in time. This begins at Verse 23 of Job:

> "Regarding the Almighty, we cannot find Him; He is exalted in power, and He will not do violence to justice and abundant righteousness.
>
> Therefore men Fear Him; He does not regard any who are wise of heart" (Job 37:23-24) (Or wise in their own eyes, in other words)

Those people also understood that God lived in a place they referred to as *SHAW-MEH*, which we translate as "Heaven." But the Hebrew word

SHAW-MEH just meant to them like we would say "up there." It was simply, "some lofty place."

Also, in the Book of Job in Chapter 38, where God, Himself, is speaking directly to Job, we hear God saying these rather remarkable words (this begins at Verse 28):

> "Has the rain a father? Or who has begotten the drops of dew?
>
> From whose womb has come the ice? And the frost of heaven, who has given it birth?
>
> Water becomes hard like stone, and the surface of the deep is imprisoned." (Job 38:28-30)

Then notice here in Verse 31-33:

> "Can you bind the chains of the Pleiades, or loose the cords of Orion?
>
> Can you lead forth a constellation in its season, and guide the bear with her satellites?
>
> Do you know the ordinances of the heavens, or fix their rule over the earth?"

(Please note that Astronomy is a very old science). Then on in Chapter 41, starting in Verse 10, God had this to say:

> "None is so fierce that dare stir him up: who then is able to stand before me?
> Who hath prevented me, that I should repay him? Whatsoever is under the whole heaven is mine." (Job 41:10-11)

Somehow these people understood that God is in "The Heaven" and that He controls everything under "The Heaven."

Then, further, somehow these people also understood that there was a place where the dead went, which, they called in the Hebrew language, SHEOL. The Old King James always translates that word as "Hell".

For example, in Job, Chapter 11, another of Job's "friends" was talking with Job about his great problems; this man's name is Zophar, and he wasn't very kind to Job. His words to Job went this way:

> "You say you are pure before God, and you wish that God would just talk with you and tell you where you erred, and how to get back in God's good graces."

Then he said to Job, and this is Verse 7 of Job Chapter 11,

> "Can you by searching, find out God? Can you discover the limits of the Almighty? They are as high as Heaven, what can you do? They are deeper than Sheol; what can you know?"

So, we know the people of Abraham's time and Jacob's time were also aware of this place called *SHEOL* that we call "hell."

Later, Moses refers to it in his great Song of Praise that he sang to God in Deuteronomy 32:21.

But they didn't seem to have much of an understanding of it, except that it was a place where the souls of the dead went.

King David first began to express an understanding of what went on in Sheol, not only as a place where all the dead went, but also as a place of punishment for those who disregarded God and were doers of evil things. Here's what he said:

> "The Lord is known by the judgment that He executes, the wicked is snared in the work of his own hands.

> The wicked shall be turned into Sheol, along with all the nations that forget God." (Psalm 9:16-17)

That's a thought-provoking statement, isn't it! Then there also was a confidence on the part of some, in a resurrection, an opportunity to escape from this place of death that they called Sheol. The passage that we often hear from the Book of Job, words that he spoke from the depths of his despair. In Job 19, starting in Verse 25, he gave us these familiar words:

> "I know that my redeemed lives, and that He shall stand at the latter day, upon the earth; and though worms destroy my body, yet in my flesh shall I see God" (Job 19:25-26)

David also had been given an insight concerning a resurrection of some sort. In Psalm 16, he referred to the Lord Jehovah as "his inheritance," and David went on to say:

> "I will bless the Lord, who has given me counsel, my mind also instructs me in the night.
>
> I have set the Lord always before me, because He is at my right hand, I shall not be moved.
>
> Therefore my heart is glad, and my glory rejoices, my flesh also shall rest in hope." (Psalm 16:7-9)

NOW note, verse 10, "For You will not leave my soul in Sheol; neither will You suffer your holy one to see corruption."

This same vagueness of information existed at the time that Jesus arrived on the earth; for example, we are told in the Gospels that the Pharisees believed in a resurrection from the dead, but the Sadducees, who were also learned Jews, did not accept that idea.

There is the conversation that took place between Martha and Jesus at the time of Lazarus' death. Lazarus was Martha's brother, and a close friend of Jesus, and she had gone to meet Jesus, to tell him the sad news. Jesus said to her (this is recorded in John Chapter 11, starting in Verse 23):

> "Jesus said to her: 'Your brother shall rise again!'
>
> Martha said to Him: 'I know that he shall rise again in the resurrection at the last day.'" (John 11:23-24)

Martha knew of "a resurrection," but that was about all. So, we realize that in the Old Testament times, there only was a vague knowledge about God. Most people considered Him to be:

- "Unknowable" and remote.
- That He lived "up there" in "The Heavens, someplace."
- That there was a place of darkness called Sheol (or "Hell") where the souls of the dead went, and which was also a place of punishment for those who do "evil."
- Also, that God is really interested only in the Sons of Jacob, the Jews.
- That there probably was some sort of a "resurrection."

But of the wonderful things WE know about, they knew nothing about! Things like:

- The wonders of Heaven
- The guarantee of a Resurrection
- An Eternal Life face to face with our Lord
- The forgiveness of our shortcomings and failures
- The wonder of Divine Guidance
- The Holy Spirit, to protect us and teach us

- The fact that we have direct access to God's Throne of Grace; we don't need a priest, we ARE a priest, with all the privileges!

All these things and more, were all unknown to the Old Testament Believers. A "*MUSTERION*," the Greeks called it. A "mystery"; one that was to be revealed at the Coming of Jesus to the earth.

So, when Jesus was talking to Martha about her brother Lazarus, he said this to her, after she had said, "Yes, I know that my brother will be raised in the last day" (John 11:24).

> "Jesus said to her. 'I am the resurrection, and the life; he that relies on Me, though he were dead, yet shall he live. And whosoever lives and believes in Me, shall never die.'" (John 11:25-26)

And that began the revelation to the members of the New Dispensation that was about to begin, the revelation of all of the wonders that come from a trust in God's Special Son, Jesus—that institution that came to be called "Christianity!"

It wasn't long after that that Jesus gave a great amount of additional information to the special group of twelve men that He had assembled—information that began to unfold the wonders that were to become available. This information was given during that meeting there in the famous "Upper Room" where they met for a last meal together, just before His Crucifixion. This information is recorded in John's Gospel, beginning with Chapter 13 and continues through Chapter 16.

In Chapter 14, He tells us about our future home:

> "In my Father's house are many 'dwelling places.' I go to prepare a place for you." (John 14:3)

Then about the transfer there of our Spirit, at the time of our death:

> "...I will come again, and receive you unto Myself." (John 14:3)

Then He told them about the new relationship that will exist:

> "If a man loves Me, he will keep My words; and My Father will love him, and We will come unto him, and make Our abode with him." (John 14:23)

Then He told them about the Holy Spirit, that was to come in Verse 26:

> "But the (*PARAKLETOS*), the Holy Ghost, whom the Father will send in My Name, He shall teach you all things, and bring all things to your remembrance, whatsoever I have said unto you." (John 14:26)

There was the beginning! But obviously, there was much more to be said, details and applications to be provided. Then, also, there was the need for writing these things down, and broadcasting them to the Gentile Nations that are now to be included.

So, the Apostles were commissioned, filled with the Holy Spirit, and sent out. Then Paul was added to the group, and his education and gift with words and his knowledge of the common Greek Language were put to use. And the culmination of his writings we have here in this Letter to the Ephesians. Look, for a moment, at Ephesians 3. Here he explains his work:

> "For this cause, I, Paul, the prisoner of Christ Jesus for you Gentiles, seeing you have heard of the Dispensation of the grace of God which is given me to you-ward:
>
> ...how that by revelation He made known to me the Mystery which in other generations was not made known unto the sons of men, but is now revealed to His holy apostles and prophets by the Spirit..." (Eph. 3:3,5)

And now we have it: the revelation of everything that was not known before—everything, that is, except the actual description of "Heaven." That was given to us by the Apostle John a few years later, when he was given the information that is contained in the Book of Revelation!

So, I'm sure you and I agree that it's important that you and I fully understand all that's involved. That's the first thing we must understand (all that's involved). The second thing that we must have, is a full and complete and absolute confidence in this Book as being the bona fide Word of God. The third thing that's important is that we, therefore, have enough faith to apply what is written here to our own lives, and the fourth thing is that we have it sufficiently in our minds so that we can, as Peter directed us, that we can:

> "…give an answer to anyone that asks us the reason for the Hope that is in us!" (1 Peter 3:15)

That must be our goal. I hope you can be serious about it being your goal! Now, then, we recognize the fact that God started what we can call a "special arrangement" with Mankind, when He called Abraham out from his relatives, and asked him to go out to a new land and become a "special people" for Him.

That was a new "economy." It was to become a new "stewardship." Abraham and his people were to become God's Representatives to the world. God put in their hands—He "dispensed to them"—the custodianship of His Affairs here on Earth.

But then we know that they failed God; they did not accurately represent Him and His Ways. And so, after 2,000 years of working with them without success, God sent His Son to the earth to appeal to them.

The appeal failed, as we know. In fact, they even killed Him as an Impostor. So, at that time, God started a new "stewardship." A new "economy." An "economy" in which God dispensed the custodianship of His Affairs to a new group of people that He called "The Body of Christ."

God even gave this new period of "stewardship" an identifying name to separate it in people's thinking from the Nation of Israel. God referred to this new "stewardship" as "the Times of the Gentiles."

This new group of people are to represent His Affairs until a certain point in time arrives, when God decides that "the times of the Gentiles has been fulfilled." Luke tells us of this point in time, in Luke 21:24, by the way.

Now we know, from prophecies such as Daniel's, that the Gentile Nations are also going to fail to perform. You and I are witnessing this fact right today. And, as we might expect, once again God is going to change Administrators.

That's what we have laid out for us here in Ephesians Chapter 1 and Verse 10. But notice first Verse 9 of Chapter 1:

> "Having made known unto us the 'Mystery' (*MUSTERION*) of His Will, according to His good pleasure which He has purposed in Himself."

That is what we have been talking about here all through this lesson—the New Revelation of God's Plan for Mankind. Now note verse 10—and here is how the King James version has it:

> "...that in the dispensation of the fullness of times, He might gather together in one, all things in Christ, both which are in Heaven, and which are on Earth; even in Him!" (Eph. 1:10)

Here comes another new "economy," a new "stewardship," a New Administrator; it will be Jesus Himself, and He will rule all and control all. Principalities and Powers of the earth will all bow before Him; He will rule with a literal "rod of iron."

So, we have outlined here three eras of "stewardship." I didn't talk about the first era, which began with Adam and lasted for 2,000 years or so, during which time God dealt with certain people of the earth on a direct basis—men like Adam, and Enoch, and Methuselah, and Noah.

Next will come the period that Paul calls the "fullness of times," when Jesus Christ is in control, and which will last for 1,000 years (The "Millennium").

Then, we move into what God's Word calls, simply, "The Eternal State," which is sketched out for us in the Book of Revelation.

My point in making a point of these periods of stewardship is to help you become comfortable with this word "dispensation" that we have in Verse 10, in the King James translation.

The word "dispensation" is a good word; it is a translation of the word *OIKONOMIA* that the Greeks used to identify, for instance, the management of the affairs of a household, or a government. Our word "economy" comes from this. And, as you know, we do have changes in our "economy" from time to time, as new administrators come and go.

But it's vital to a person's understanding of the Bible to realize that there were these various "economies" existing in the history of mankind. And each period had its own rules for operation.

God dealt one way with the people from the time of Adam, up until He set up a new arrangement with Abraham. Then He set up a new arrangement for Abraham's people, when He gave His Law to Moses. Then he set up a new arrangement for this new "Body of Christ" called "Christianity," and they had new rules for operating, as we have been examining here in Colossians, and with more to come in the Letter to the Ephesians.

So, we must not put ourselves in the wrong dispensation, or "period of stewardship," when we go to the Bible for our Instruction. We must not take God's instructions to the Jews and try to make them our own. We must go to God's Instructions for us living in the Times of the Gentiles, which we are!

In the Letter to the Galatians, Paul talks about this; in Galatians 3 starting in Verse 10. Here are a couple of verses from there:

> "For as many are of the works of the Law are under the curse; for it is written, 'Cursed is everyone that continues not in all things that are written in the Book of the Law, to do them.'" (Gal. 3:10)

That is a quotation from Deuteronomy 27, Verse 26, and there God was telling them that if they failed to keep one jot or tittle of the Law that He had given to them, they were as guilty as if they had broken every one of the laws! Then Paul continues, in the Galatian Letter in Verse 11 of Chapter 3:

> "But that no man is justified by the law in the sight of God, it is evident: for, 'The Just shall live by faith…'"

That, by the way, is a quotation from another Old Testament prophet whose name was Habakkuk, Verse 2 of Chapter 2. Then Paul continued, in Verse 12 of Galatians 3:

> "And the Law is not out from faith: but, the man that does them, shall live in them."

And then he gives us these wonderful words in Verse 13:

> "Christ has redeemed us from the curse of the Law, being made a curse for us: for it is written (as in Deut. 21:23), 'Cursed is every one that hangs on a tree!' (SO) THAT the blessing of Abraham might come on the Gentiles through Jesus Christ; that we might receive the promise of the Spirit, through faith." (Gal. 3:13-14)

You and I are not under the Law that governed Israel; we are under the Instructions that God gave to this new "Body of Christ" and that are given to us so clearly and simply by the Apostle Paul, here in these Letters to the Colossians and the Ephesians.

Now, you might ask: where is the cut-off point between the Law of Israel and the Instructions for the Body of Christ?

The cut-off point for us, living after the Apostolic period, begins with the presentation of the first of the letters from Paul, which were the two Letters to the Thessalonians. They were followed by:

- the Letters to the Corinthians,
- then the Letter to the Galatians,
- then the Letter to the Romans,
- then the Letters to the Philippians,
- the Colossians, and
- then to the Ephesians.

The Letter of James was written earlier than any of Paul's letters, and James knew a lot, but as he makes no reference to the work of the Holy Spirit, we have to conclude that he did not have the full revelation of "The Mystery."

So, what, you ask, about the words of Jesus that are contained in the Gospel accounts?

Well, to whom was Jesus talking during this time? He was talking to the Jews. He was trying to get them to see and understand God's Truth, as God had presented it to them. And that He had come, now, to fulfill the requirements of the Law, including the symbolism that the Temple worship contained, the sacrifice system, and the functions of the priests and the High Priest.

The exception to His working with His People Israel is in the Information that Jesus gave to His Disciples that last night, in the Upper Room—that which is recorded for us in John Chapters 13 through 16. There Jesus is clearly telling them of what will come after His Return to Heaven; all of which will involve those of us who are to come on the scene later.

So, it's important that we realize that while, as Timothy said, in First Timothy 3:16, that "All Scripture is profitable for doctrine, for reproof, for correction, for instruction in righteousness," he also cautioned us, in First Timothy 2:15, to "Study to show thyself approved unto God, a workman that needs not to be ashamed, handling accurately the Word of Truth."

So here we are, as Ephesians 1:10 makes clear, in the "Times of the Gentiles" looking forward to the dispensation of the fullness of times, when "...all things are gathered together in one, in Christ."

Then we have these wonderful words, in Verse 11, "In Whom also we have obtained an Inheritance."

The inheritance that Peter told us would be:

> "...incorruptible, and undefiled, and that fades not away, reserved in Heaven for you, who are kept by the power of God, through faith unto salvation, ready to be revealed in the last time." (1 Peter 1:4,5)

What God has provided, and what the Old Testament Believers did not know—the MUSTERION—the "mystery," included:

1. The wonders of Heaven;
2. The guarantee of a Resurrection, and then an Eternal Life, face to face with our Lord;
3. The forgiveness of our shortcomings and failures;
4. The wonder of Divine Guidance;
5. The Holy Spirit, to protect and teach us;
6. The fact of a personal relationship to God; a Direct Access to Him! Result: we don't need a Priest, we ARE a Priest, with all the privileges!

Our only reasonable response:

1. We must know the above—what was "The Mystery";

2. We must study until we have absolute confidence that the Bible is truly God's Word to Mankind;
3. We must have enough faith, then, to apply to our lives that which is written in God's Instructions to us; and
4. We must have God's Word sufficiently in our minds, so that we can "give an answer to anyone that asks us the reason for the Hope that is in us!"

Lesson 2 Ephesians Chapter 1

Introduction to God's "Task Force"

We have arrived, now, at the fourth of the four letters we have of Paul's that he wrote during his imprisonment in the city of Rome while he was waiting for his hearing before the Roman Emperor Nero.

We have talked, as we have gone along here, about the fact that these four letters together constitute the great setting forth of the Doctrines of Christianity—the statement of "What God's Word teaches about Christianity," or, better, "What God's Word says Christianity is."

Now I *should* say it's "What we believe," because that is the meaning of our word "doctrine." But then I would have to really say, "It's what we should be believing, according to God." Because of what an awful lot of Christians "believe" about Christianity (or believe Christianity to be) is not what God's Word teaches.

And that's too bad. But, as we know, that's the way it is.

The problem is, as we talked about when we were considering the Letter to the Colossians, Satan and Man's own human nature have brought four confusions into the picture:

- The first is the confusion brought in through the teachings of those we call "Philosophers," men and women who have introduced their ways of getting through this life, rejecting the

Fact that there is a God, or trying to work around Him and His Principles; all well-meaning, of course, but very confusing!

- The second is the confusion brought in by lists of "dos and don'ts" that various people have devised that often have no basis or confirmation from God's Word Itself. And we know all about these don't we!
- Third, confusion about Christianity has been introduced by those who delve into the world of the supernatural; for example, such things as seeking guidance and help from the Dead or the reliance on the many systems of Astrology for daily guidance. Or Dreams.

And the fourth source of confusion that has been mixed into Christianity is the concept of Asceticism, which is the idea of depriving ourselves of certain physical pleasures, expecting that somehow God will think we're great for doing this or that. Or, by our doing this, we somehow can come closer to God.

Adding to this particular confusion is a misunderstanding of the Old English word "humility" that the Old King James frequently uses. Some think that the "humble" or "pious" look somehow pleases God. God, however, wants us to find pleasure! His Word teaches us that: "God has given us richly all things to enjoy" (1 Timothy 1:6).

Now, when you stop to think about it, I'm sure that for most of us we have acquired our knowledge of Christianity over the span of quite a few years, and in a fairly disorganized fashion. So often one Sunday we would hear the pastor "take a text" from one Book of the Bible, then very likely the following Sunday, his text was from another part of the Bible.

Then, during the intervening week, we picked up some human philosophy, which we may have also read in a book and, from it, we got some more "practical ideas about living." So, all of this winds up in our brain as a sort of "blend."

Now, you and I have been blessed specially, more than many other Christians, in that we have been exposed through the years to some verse-by-verse, rather in-depth study of God's Word. But because we are the exception rather than the rule, Christianity languishes because it is not understood and, as a result, it has very little impact on society. In fact, its efforts are often seriously challenged.

For example, this article appeared in the August 28, 1996 issue of *USA Today*:

> CHILD BAPTISMS PROBED
>
> Massachusetts state prosecutors and police are investigating claims that the Anchor Baptist Church in Woburn, Mass. used promises of pizza and basketball games to lure hundreds of children to the church. The youths sat through services before some were baptized in a tank of water. The State Dept. of Social Services is investigating claims that an 8-year-old boy was emotionally harmed. Church officials have not commented.

This is an example of what the world thinks of Christianity and the way we operate!

Now, frankly, our goal here is to know what God wants us to know, and to have the discernment to separate God's Ideas from Man's ideas and then encourage us to adhere to God's thoughts and directives! And in these four letters, we have it all!

I hope you are fixing in your mind the central theme of these various Books of the Bible as we are going through them. Let me tell you again.

The first one written of these four so-called "Prison Epistles" was the Letter to the Philippians; its identifying title is, "Jesus Christ, the source of joy and inner happiness, no matter what!"

The second Letter he wrote is the Letter to the Colossians; it tells us quite graphically just WHY this Jesus is worthy of being trusted with our very life and that's because He IS God, the very IMAGE of God! He is our Creator, our Designer. It's only logical that we should trust Him and listen to these words of advice that His representative, Paul, placed here in this Letter! Listen to these words, above all else!

The third Letter, which we have just considered, was Paul's Letter to his friend and convert, Philemon, asking him to take back to his heart his former slave Onesimus, who also has become a Christian.

And in this short Letter, we have had demonstrated for us the principles that Christ wants to teach us—the Doctrine of Substitution that enables one person to pay for the sins and failures of another person, which is what Jesus did for you and for me when He gave up His Life on the Cross.

That's a part of it. The other part is demonstrating the meaning of the Greek word AGAPE that we translate as "Love" or "Divine Concern," which is really the motivation that lies behind the application of the Doctrine of Substitution!

So, we have had presented to us:

- Jesus Christ, as the source of inner joy and inner happiness.
- Jesus Christ, as our Creator and the very Image of God, and, therefore, entitled to our trust and our worship.
- Now we come to the Letter to the Ephesians, which presents to us Jesus Christ as the head of not only all physical matter, but He also is the head of a great supernatural organization of people!

This is an organization to which everyone who believes in Him belongs, which, in the Greek is called "The *EKKLESIA*" that we could best describe, in the language of our time, as a "Task Force"— "a group of people especially selected to perform a specific task."

The Bible itself describes the *EKKLESIA* as "The Body of Christ" and speaks of it as having a "Head" which is Christ and having arms and legs and fingers and eyes and a voice, which is You and Me—all under the control of The Head.

So, in the presentation of the material in this Letter to the Ephesians, Paul has done these things:

- he has stated Christ's Position in this vast Universe system;
- he has stated the real relationship between Christ and those people who have put their trust in Him;
- he has laid out for us the way that our Leader, our "Head" wants us to live our life; and
- he explains to us the equipment that Christ has so wonderfully provided to us to live that life!

And now, before we really get started with our look at the Letter to the Ephesians, let me point out to you where God, our Father, sees you and me to be in all of this. Here's what's at the end of Verse 3:

> "He (God) has blessed us with every spiritual blessing IN the Heavenlies, IN Christ Jesus!"

First, it is telling us that God has blessed us "with everything that comes from God, through the Holy Spirit." That's what we have available to us because of our relationship to His Son!

It's not, "we will get these blessings." We HAVE them!

There are stories told, as we know, about people who were living in great poverty, and yet there were great inheritances out there just waiting for them to hear about them and claim them. And in the same way, there are many Christians out there who are struggling to get their lives together, yet they are either not aware that there is spiritual guidance available to them, if they would just seek after it, or they are too proud to look upward for help!

Then the next phrase here at the end of Verse 3 states for Believers, our present position,

> "[We are] IN the Heavenlies, [and] IN Christ Jesus!"

The little Greek Preposition EN is the preposition of "location." For example, we say of something: "It is within that"; that's the preposition EN. Or "it's an integral part of something."

Believers are "an integral part of" the Heavenlies and "an integral part of" the Lord Jesus Christ! We are "citizens" of Heaven—that's why the earth has no real hold on us, nor claim on us.

And we are with Christ, where He now is! Look on here in Chapter 1, to Verse 20 (Paul is speaking of God's great power):

> "...which He wrought in Christ, when He raised Him from the dead, and set him at His own right hand IN THE HEAVENLIES!"

Then look on in Chapter 2, to Verse 6:

> "And He has raised us up together, and made us sit together IN THE HEAVENLIES, in Christ Jesus!"

There we are—in the highest of all places! And that is our Home!

I was talking with a young lawyer the other day, who had not too long ago been taken into one of Portland's leading law firms. He was saying that he really appreciated being where he was. He said, "If I have a problem I don't know quite how to tackle, I can quickly talk to one of the old hands—the 'Experts'—and get immediate guidance!"

You and I are in that position; we have immediate access to The Best, who really is concerned for us, and loves to be called on!

> "Blessed be the God and Father of our Lord Jesus Christ, who has blessed us with every spiritual blessing, IN The Heavenlies, and IN Christ Jesus!"

So, there we are—in the Heavenlies—in the Lord Jesus Christ!

Lesson 3 Ephesians Chapter 1

How "The Body" is to Walk

In our last lesson we took a look at the opening verses of Paul's fourth Letter that he wrote from Rome while he was a prisoner, waiting for his hearing before Nero, the then-Caesar of the Roman Empire.

This letter has been called such things as, "The highest peak of Scriptural Truth, the very apex of Bible Revelation." I smiled at Dr. Vernon McGee's comment that, "...some have even suggested that Ephesians is so profound that none but the very elect (in other words, the chosen few) can understand it." Then he added, "But I have always noticed that the folk who say this, include themselves in that inner circle…"

Obviously, you and I are not in that group, but we are counting on Divine Revelation to make clear to our minds just what God wants us to know!

As we have already commented (on several occasions), the first three of these "Prison Epistles" have clearly described Jesus Christ's position in God's Scheme of Things. and His Position in the material universe. Now, here in the Letter to the Ephesians, the world is made aware of His position as the head of a great supernatural yet very "human" organization! This great organization is called, in the Greek, The *EKKLESIA*.

This is described in the scriptures as "The Body of Christ," which, the Bible tells us is made up of every person through all the ages who has put his or her trust in the hands of Jesus Christ, God's Special Son. In this sense, we refer to it as the "Universal Church."

This Greek word *EKKLESIA* is also used in the Scriptures to identify the individual, local groups of Believers, which we would call "Assemblies."

Now, in this Letter we are going to see Paul explain this "Body of Christ" so that we will know that it is "a Body" in the same sense that our "body" is a "body" (that is in Chapter 1).

Then, in Chapter 2, we will see that it is also a "temple"—a "temple of the Living God!" Lots of people don't treat it that way but that's what it is!

Then, in Chapter 3, we are going to see that this *EKKLESIA* is also a "Mystery," which, by definition, means "something known only to insiders," and it is something that was not made known to the Spiritual men and women of the past ages, but has now been revealed to us!

Then, following that, Paul is going to talk about how God expects the members of this "Task Force" to conduct themselves here on this earth while we are here doing our assigned work, and then He is going to detail out for us the special equipment that He has provided to enable us to successfully accomplish what He has assigned us to do and to "make it through" to the completion! So, hang on!

And Paul begins, with his usual "inside address":

> "Paul, an Apostle of Christ Jesus by the will of God, to the saints which are at Ephesus, and to the faithful in Christ Jesus..."

This was a letter intended for general circulation. It is known that the members of the Assembly in Laodicea and others in the area had copies of it. Also, the Greek Text definitely has the word "and" in it there where it reads "AND to the faithful in Christ Jesus." So, since you and I are definitely "full of faith" and we are, therefore, "in" Christ Jesus, this is specifically for us, including Paul's salutation in Verse 2:

> "Grace to you, and peace, from God our Father, and from the Lord Jesus Christ."

Then, in the last lesson, we looked briefly at Verse 3, where Paul pronounces a "benediction" on our Heavenly Father, and also reminds us that we have been blessed with all "blessings connected with the Holy Spirit" and that our position is "in the Heavenlies" and that we are "IN Christ." We are situated "in Him." We are, technically, "an integral part" of Him!

I have to pass along one more comment of Dr. McGee's; he points out that this Epistle is very practical, in that we are being told, first, that, "…this "Body of Christ" has a "head"; the "head" of the Body is Christ, and He is in Heaven. Also, we are identified with Him. However, the "feet" of the Body are down here on Earth. Paul won't leave us sitting up there in the Heavenlies; he says: walk worthy of the vocation wherewith you are called!" (a reference to Eph. 4:1)

Then Dr. McGee continues, "In other words, Christian, it's nice to sit up there in the Heavenlies and boast of your position in Christ, but, for goodness' sake, get down out of your high chair and start walking!"

After reading Dr. McGee's comment about "walking," I thought I'd better find out what Paul included in this "walking," so I turned to Ephesians 4:1 that he quoted to see what comes next. So, I am going to divert a bit to look at this, as I'd hate to have you not understand what Paul had in mind when he talked about "the Christian walk."

Definitions of "Lowliness" and "Meekness"

Here it is, in Ephesians 4:2:

> "With all lowliness and meekness, with longsuffering, forbearing one another in love; endeavoring to keep the unity of the Spirit in the bond of peace."

Now, I ask you—but don't answer out loud—is that what came to your mind when I mentioned the words "the Christian walk?" I frankly doubt it.

So then, it's interesting what the words "lowliness" and "meekness" really meant, in Scriptural terms.

Dr. Richard Trench is one of the most respected of the Greek Scholars of the last couple of hundred years. His book, called "Synonyms of the New Testament" is, I'm sure, a part of the reference library of a high percentage of serious Bible students.

By the way, let me recite for you his credentials. From 1866, and for 20 years up until the time of his death, he was Honorary Archbishop of the Dublin Church of Ireland. He was also Professor of Divinity and Professor of Exegesis of the New Testament at King's College at Oxford for many years. Prior to that, he was Dean of Westminster. Certainly, a great scholar!

Here is Dr. Trench's definition of these two words, "lowliness" and "meekness," Since they constitute the principal ingredients of God's idea of "The Christian Walk," we'd better understand what they mean. Of the word "lowliness," he says,

> "The Christian lowliness is no mere modesty or absence of pretension, nor is it a self-made grace. The making of ourselves as 'small' is simply pride in a disguise of humility. But the esteeming of ourselves as small, since we are so, is thinking truly of ourselves."

Of the word "meekness," he says,

> "It is an inwrought grace of the soul, and it moves first and chiefly toward God. It is that kind of spirit in which we accept His dealings with us as good, and therefore without disputing."

In other words, we accept Him and His Choices as being the best for us, in accordance with His Promises to us!

Then our word "longsuffering" is just that, "slowness to anger in the face of provocation."

And the word "forbearing" is interesting. The Greek word is a compound word, as a great many Greek words are, and it translates literally as "to hold yourself up from someone." To put this in our everyday words, it means that, "because of our concern for the other person, we go along patiently with what appear to us to be his or her shortcomings."

And finally, in Verse 3, God expects us to "work at keeping the unity (the 'one-ness') of the Spirit and do it in the binding influence of this peace that our position gives us."

Then he explains what he means by "one-ness" in Verse 4-6: "…one body, one Holy Spirit."

We all have the same "Hope"; we all have the same Lord, the same faith, the same baptism," (which, by the way, is the Baptism of the Holy Spirit, which we receive at our Moment of Salvation).

> *"[We all have] one God and Father of all, who is above all, and through all, and in you all."*

That is the "unity" that He wants us to "work at" maintaining. So, if you want to please the Lord with your daily life, then here is the area to concentrate on! Ephesians 4:1-6!

And, since the Holy Spirit is the One who leads us into all Truth, it is important that we keep our relationship with Him so that He can do His work of leading us!

There is God's idea of "the Christian walk," which is how God wants us to live and operate! Our position is "in the Heavenlies." Our citizenship is there but our work, for now, is here on this earth, where we are Ambassadors of our Lord Jesus Christ.

Now, as "ambassadors," we are to reflect Him and His Concepts. So, we are to say what He instructs us to say, where and when He sets it up. And He will give us the words, the strength, and the opportunity. We are not to go running off on our own, nor trying to master-mind His work.

We're here as a part of His "Task Force" and each of us has an assignment, a place of usefulness to Him—each a little different, each equally important!

Alright, back to Chapter 1, and now Verse 4, where we learn more about what He has done for you and me as individuals.

The "Choosing"—"Predestination"

And the little conjunction here at the start of Verse 4 links what comes next here, with the "blessings" that our position IN Christ involves, and it begins:

> "...He chose us in Christ, before the foundation of the Universe System (the *KOSMOS*)."

And I have to stop right here, because there's too much wonderful stuff just to slide over it. He chose us—a past, completed action. Also, it is in the middle voice, which says that the subject, "He," (which is God) took this action for His Benefit. Isn't that amazing—that my selection would be important to God!

This really shouldn't surprise us, however. When an employer hires a person to do a job, it's normally done for the employer's benefit. Now if I am the person hired, and I've been out of work for a while, I may think that I am the one who is benefited but the employer has a very definite gain in mind for himself. God, when he selected you out, had great hopes that you would be a benefit and a source of satisfaction to Him!

And Paul even expresses that hope of God's here, at the end of Verse 4:

> "...that we should be set apart—dedicated to God who has selected us out, and that, in our concern for Him, we be above all criticism and without fault; that we operate "flawlessly" for Him!"

God had that hope for you and for me when He selected us out to do our special assignment in His "Task Force!" We need to keep that in mind when we think, as I'm sure most of us do from time to time, that our life is pretty dull and pointless!

Then I want to call your attention to this word that is translated "chose," there at the beginning of Verse 4. I know that this passage opens the door on the much chewed-over subject of "predestination," and it's important that you and I are comfortable with our own understanding of this concept.

This word that is translated "chose" is the same word that, in other passages, the Holy Spirit used to describe God's Selection of the Nation of Israel. A Greek Scholar by the name of Dr. Hermann Cremer, who spent many years gathering together the material in his "Lexicon of the Greek New Testament," which is another masterpiece that scholars regularly refer to, makes this point:

> This choosing out of Israel from among the nations does not imply that those nations not chosen are rejected or refused salvation. Indeed, the salvation of Israel was for the purpose of making salvation possible to the other nations. The same usage applies in the case of individuals, selected out from among mankind. These are selected to be channels through which the knowledge of salvation might be brought to the rest of mankind!

You and I were chosen by God to fill a place in His Plan. But there are a couple of things that this fact does NOT mean; one is that it does not mean that we will perform as He hoped we would; and two, it doesn't mean that those not chosen for this particular function are going to be denied Salvation. The verse in Second Peter 3 that we're so familiar with is important right here! It says,

> "The Lord is not slack concerning his promise, as some men count slackness; but is longsuffering to us-ward, not willing that any should perish, but that all should come to a place of changing their mind about Him and His Son!"

As Dr. Dwight Moody put it, "The whosoever wills are the Elect, and the whosoever won'ts are the Non-elect!"

So, you and I were chosen just as the Nation of Israel was chosen!

It's also very interesting that this "choosing" took place before God even created this earth that we live on. Verse 4 also says that He chose us "...before the foundation of the *KOSMOS*."

Which, to the Greek of Paul's day, meant the entire Universe system. That is a long time ago!

Then Dr. Charles Spurgeon once said, "God chose me before I came into the world, because if He'd waited until I got here, He never would have chosen me!"

Now, in Verse 5, we have that frightening word: "Having predestinated us," (or "He predestined us," in the modern versions).

Now we have this same word back in the Book of Acts, Chapter 4, and in Verse 28, but there it's translated a little differently.

There we have this great prayer that someone prayed with these early Christians, right after Peter and John were delivered from the mob. Their prayer to God went like this (I'm starting in Verse 26 of Acts 4):

> "The kings of the earth stood up, and the rulers were gathered together against the Lord, and against His Christ. Actually,

> against Thy holy child Jesus, whom you have anointed, both Herod and Pontius Pilate, with the Gentiles, and the people of Israel, were gathered together … for to do whatsoever your Hand and Your counsel (and here's our word) had determined before to be done."

Way back when, God made a determination! And with us it was, as Ephesians 1:5 expresses it, that we would be adopted by Jesus Christ to Himself, and that was for a specific purpose—that we would be (Verse 6), "…to the praise of the glory of His grace!"

He put us on His team. But how we perform, of course, is up to us, just as it is with every member of any team! And we need most of all, to see what He is saying here, that the purpose of all of this is that we will be, "…to the praise of the glory of His grace!"

This is a little hard for us to grasp and really understand; it may seem like God is selfish, that He's doing all this for Himself, so we sort of back off from it. After all, we humans like to think that God is doing these wonderful things for us so that we can have a great place to spend Eternity.

But God is very wise. He knows that self-centered people are not going to create a society that is mutually beneficial. That takes a properly functioning "body"; one in which all parts function well and together, for things to be right.

And that "body" that God visualized has a "Head," which is Christ, and we, the parts of that body, are to look to Him and be controlled by Him. Here is what Jesus had to say about this. It's in John 15:5:

> "I am the vine, you are the branches. He that abides in Me, and I in him, the same brings forth much fruit; for without Me, you can do nothing!"

And the fruit will be an acknowledgement of our God and His Greatness! But now, having put the focus on our Creator, he begins to tell us of the advantages that will accrue to "whosoever" will fit themselves into His Plan. It begins there at the end of Verse 6, "He made us to be accepted in the Beloved," ... which means (Verse 7) we have Redemption, as a result of the shedding of His Blood and "Redemption" means that we have "the forgiveness of sins!"

And along with it (Verse 9) we actually are told what His Will is—this knowledge and information that has been a mystery all these years!

What is meant by the expression "The Beloved"? The very word "beloved" in the Greek is not a noun, but actually a participle—a verb form— "To be one very much loved!" And it's stated in the perfect tense! And Jesus is said to be "The Beloved of God."

But we, also, are the beneficiaries of something else that God said, and that is that Jesus was to be, "The Firstborn among many brethren" (Romans 8:29). So, by attaching ourselves to Jesus, God pronounces us to be a part of "The Brethren," and therefore, a part of "The Beloved."

Discussion of "Redemption"

We're the Object of God's Concern, and it is an action that is totally complete, with results that go on and on and on! When I think of the Greek perfect tense, I think of what happens when you throw a rock out into the middle of a still pond of water; the waves just seem to go on and on and on! That's the way God expresses His Concern for us—on and on and on!

Now, what is Redemption?

Dr. McGee told this story about a young black man down in Memphis, Tennessee, who wanted to join a Baptist Church down there, and the deacons were examining him. They asked him, "How did you get saved?" He answered, "I did my part, and God did His part."

The deacons thought they had him, so they asked him what was his part, and what was God's part? He said, "My part was the sinning. I ran from God as fast as these legs would take me and my sinful heart would lead me. I ran from Him. But, you know, He done took out after me 'til He done run me down."

Our part is the "sinning," and for this, somebody has to pay, sooner or later. But Verse 7 again here:

> "In Jesus we have redemption through His blood, which is the forgiveness of sins, according to the riches of His grace!"

That's what "Redemption" is—it's getting out from under our sins!

But then, along with this getting us out from under the penalty of our failures—which, in itself, is a wonderful gift—in addition to that, He made it possible for us "to be on the Inside," not "outsiders!"

It's a terrible feeling to be an "outsider." I'm sure that most of us have felt that way at some point in our life. It's not good!

God very much wants us to be "an insider," with intimate knowledge of what His Plans are and what He is up to. That's why He gave us this amazing and wonderful Book, so we can know His Plans and His Purposes.

There is no longer a need for us to ask when something strange moves across our path, "Why is this happening to me, Lord?" Now we know that answer; He is getting ready to bless us! (Romans 8:28, and Philippians 4:13 and 19)

Verse 8 of Chapter 1 here begins the thought. Paul says (and I'll streamline the translation a little bit):

> "...in all wisdom and understanding, he made known to us the Mystery of His Will, as it was His Good Pleasure to do," (and here it is) that in the period called "The Fullness of Times," He might gather together in one, all things in Christ, both things that are in heaven, and on earth, all in Him!"

In other words, when God determines that this present age is complete, everything is going to be centered in and around Our Lord Jesus Christ! Everything!

The "Inheritance" Reserved for Members

In Chapter 3, Paul adds to our information about this "mystery." In this Chapter, Paul begins by saying to us that this mystery was given to him, and others, and his special task is to give it on to us. He says,

> "...which, in other generations was not made known unto the sons of men as it has now been revealed to His holy Apostles and prophets by the Spirit" (Eph. 3:5)

And here it is: "That the Gentiles should be fellow heirs, and of the same body, and partakers of His Promise in Christ by the gospel" (Eph. 3:6) Then there is one more part to it, and that's given to us on in Verse 10 of Chapter 3:

> "...that now to the principalities and powers in the Heavenlies (to the Heavenly Powers, themselves) might be made known by the *EKKLESIA* (this great "Body of Believers") (they will be the ones to make known) the Great and many-faceted Wisdom of God."

So, this new information, just released to the world by these Apostles of Christ, is that after this, at the end of this age,

- everything shall revolve around Jesus Christ;
- Gentiles will be fellow heirs with the people of Israel, in the Kingdom of God; and
- it will be this "Body of Christ" that will make it known to all the Universe!

That was "new information!" The Jews didn't know it, the Old Testament Prophets didn't know it! But now you and I know it! And we non-Jews have been brought into the Plan of God. We are now joint heirs of Christ.

Then, further, in Ephesians 1:11, we are told that what we have is called "an inheritance." Another great Apostle, Peter, told us more about this "inheritance" in 1 Peter 1:4. Here is how he expressed it,

> "...we have an inheritance incorruptible, and undefiled, and that fades not away, reserved in Heaven for you, who are kept by the Power of God, through faith unto salvation, ready to be revealed at the last time."

And then he added,

> "Wherein you greatly rejoice, though now for a season, if need be (and it is), you are in heaviness through many testings, SO THAT the trial of your faith, much more precious than gold that perishes, though it be tried with fire, might be found unto praise and honor and glory at the appearing of Jesus Christ; whom, having not seen, yet ye love."

So, there is this new information: we Gentiles are going to be fellow heirs in the Kingdom of God—not only with God's Chosen People, the Jews, but with Jesus, God's Special Son as well!

A last thought: so that we know what OUR "mission field" is, He has told us that this great "Task Force" that we are a part of, collectively, is going to be the instrument through which the whole Universe and everything in it, will be made to realize that God is Truly God! We have trouble imagining how He'll manage to do it, but He will!

Each of us is a working member of this "Task Force," and our place of work is right where we are.

Every morning when we hit the floor, our first thought should be, "Lord, whatever I had planned to do today, I will be happy to make that second, to what you have in mind! I'm listening for any ideas that you may have for me today!"

Lesson 4 Ephesians Chapter 1

What God Considers to Be "The Best for Us" (i.e., A Full Knowledge of God)

So far, as we have moved into Chapter 1 of this Letter, we have been told that God selected us out before the foundation of the Universe to this work that He had in mind for you and me to perform (Verse 4).

- That this included (Verse 5) our being adopted as "adult sons," "sons of God," and joint heirs with Christ!" Which is amazing, in itself!
- Then, in addition, (Verse 7) we receive the forgiveness of our sins. (Hallelujah!)
- AND (Verse 9) He has given us information about His Plan, which information had not been made known even to the Prophets, up to the time Jesus came to the earth.
- In addition (Verse 11) we have been given an Inheritance, which is a wonderful thing that Believers have to look forward to, after "Boot Camp" is over!

Then, in Verse 13 here, Paul points out the sequence of events that brought us to this amazing position that we find ourselves in. The pattern is this:

- first, we heard the Word of Truth, which is the "good news" of our Salvation;
- then, he points out, that we trusted ourselves to that which we had heard;
- then, when we did that, we "were sealed with the Holy Spirit which, he adds, is the "earnest of our inheritance, until the redemption time!"

So, God somehow presented His Truth to us; we relied on what we heard and trusted ourselves to God's Offer, and the result was that God literally "sealed" us into position by placing the Holy Spirit within us!

Paul used language here that those people would clearly understand and should be equally clear to us. The word translated "sealed" was a common business term; for example, a fragment of writing was found that said, "If the fruit is 'sealed,' then everything is in order."

Another writing said, "I gave the letter 'sealed' to the messenger."

"Sealing" marked a completed transaction, and it protected whatever was sealed from being tampered with.

So, the Holy Spirit not only acted as a "seal"; its power enabled it to safeguard from tampering, those who are sealed!

And then, in Verse 14, he used another business term, "the earnest of our Inheritance." Many samples of writing have been found by the archaeologists that speak of 'earnest money' being paid to secure a transaction until it could be completed.

God obviously wants those who would trust themselves to Him and to His Plan to know, beyond a doubt, that we are in a new position, which is "in union with Him," and what the great benefits of that new position are! Romans 8:16-17 tells us:

> "The Spirit Himself bears witness with our spirit, that wo are the children of God; and if children, then heirs; heirs of God, and joint-heirs with Christ!"

And you and I, I know, have had plenty of occasions to know God's Presence with us, which, of course, IS His Holy Spirit!

God also wants us to know—without a shadow of a doubt—that our position in Him is secure and will remain that way, until the day of our translation, when we move from this phase to the next wonderful phase of "Life." So, Paul tells us, starting here in Verse 17, what he hopes and prays will happen to us, and what we will come to experience, as we move along this thing called "Life." Of all the things there are to wish for a person that you love, here is what Paul—directed by God's Holy Spirit—prays that you will have!

And I think you may be surprised at what God considers best for us; it is not what we think of as "the easy life," nor is it good health, nor lots of money, nor any of those things that we human beings commonly think we want. Notice what it is—it's here at the end of Verse 17:

> "The Spirit of wisdom and revelation in the FULL knowledge of Him!"

Here is God's greatest desire for His People—and that is that we come to know Him fully! Not just "better" but "fully." (The Greek word here is *EPI-GNOSIS*: "full knowledge"). This is the main thing God wants for us! That's interesting, isn't it!

The Result: Divine Power in Our Life

Then he tells us what this "full knowledge of God" will provide for us and there are three things we will have forever nailed down in our mind if this "full knowledge" should become available to us, and it starts here in the middle of Verse 18:

1. "...the Hope of His calling;
2. "...what are the riches of the glory of His inheritance; and

3. "...what is the exceeding greatness of his power to us-ward who believe" (Eph. 1:18-19)

A full knowledge of our Hope; our inheritance; His Power! I seem to hear him saying to us, "If you have this, you have everything you need to make it through Life, and with perfect Inner Happiness and Peace!"

The Book of Proverbs has some wonderful information in it, as we know, and the third chapter is one of the greatest. In Verse 19 of Chapter 3, Solomon said this:

> "The LORD by Wisdom, founded the earth; by Understanding, He established the Heavens.
>
> By His knowledge the depths are broken up, and the clouds drop down the dew." (Prov. 3:19-20)

That's what the wisdom and full knowledge that God has was able to do. And God wants us to share in that wisdom and full knowledge! Solomon also said, in that same passage, starting in Verse 13:

> "Happy is the man that finds wisdom, and the man that gets understanding. For the merchandise of it is better than that of silver, and the gain thereof, than fine gold. She is more precious than rubies, and all the things you can desire are not to be compared to her" (Prov. 3:13-15)

Are you willing to take God's Word for what will do the best for you? I would think we would really want to!

And this wisdom he speaks of is not the knowledge of the world, or of all of man's thinking that has gone on through the years—the stuff that fills all our libraries—it's a "full knowledge" of God! This one Book (The Bible) contains more wisdom and knowledge than does an entire library!

And God's Word that you and I are holding is ready, willing, and anxious to tell us how to come by this "full knowledge of God!" It's here, let's find it!

In Matthew's Gospel, Jesus spoke of the Kingdom of Heaven being like a "pearl"; and we know how elusive pearls are, and that they are gathered only as a result of some considerable effort, so we are going to expend some effort!

The first clue in our search for "a full knowledge of God" is given to us right here in Verse 17, and it's in this little word "may"; that God *may* give this to you. Subjunctive mood, which is really an expression of a wish. Which means, then, that God is ready to give this to us, IF something else happens.

Then on a few words, in Verse 17 is the word "Spirit." Here's our next clue in our search for "a full knowledge of God."

I'm going to give you here a couple of passages from John's Gospel—passages that I know are very familiar to you and both are a part of what we call "The Upper Room Discourse"; words that Jesus spoke to His Disciples just before the events that came before His Crucifixion. The first is in John 14:26:

> "But the Comforter, which is the Holy Ghost, Whom the Father will send in My Name, He shall teach you all things, and bring all things to your remembrance, whatsoever I have said to you."

Then on in John 16, Jesus added to this information—this is in Verse 12-13:

> "I have yet many things to say to you, but you cannot handle them now. However, when He, the Spirit of Truth is come, He will guide you into all truth!"

So, we recognize that the Knowledge of God is imparted to a Believer through, or by means of, The Holy Spirit. The enlightenment of a

Believer in the Things of God comes only through the activity of the Holy Spirit! And yet David discovered, and made it clear to us, that:

> "If I see iniquity in my mind, I know that the Lord will not hear me!" (Psalm 66:18)

In other words, iniquity that I recognize to be in me stops the communication between God and me! The Apostle John, in First John Chapter 1, said it another way, in Verse 6:

> "If we say that we have fellowship with Him, and walk in darkness, we lie, and do not the truth!"

Dr. Harry Ironside, who was one of the great Expositors and Bible Teachers of all times, said this in his book *In the Heavenlies:*

> You would imagine that as Christians, the Lord puts a power battery into us like we do in a flashlight, then He presses a button, and then we shine for Him. Nothing of the kind: we have power only as we are living in fellowship with Him, who is the Source of all power. And as we are walking in fellowship with Him, the same power works in and through us that worked in Christ, when God raised Him from the dead.

But the Apostle John wrote out carefully for us the way to the maintenance of this "fellowship" in our most valuable little verse, 1 John 1:9 that says,

> "If we confess our sins, He is faithful and just to forgive us our sins, and to cleanse us from all unrighteousness."

We say it back to Him, what we did, and He cleanses. Then, the Holy Spirit is back in business! So, IF the Holy Spirit can do His work, then you and I can begin to learn!

But obviously, we have to get God's Word in front of our eyes! He's not going to open our head and pour the information into it! WE have to make the first move and then the Holy Spirit will begin to teach us from what we see or hear! But we have to make the first move!

Then, what do we learn first? In Verse 18, about the Hope of His Calling and about the Riches of the Glory of His Inheritance!

God has called us to this Hope. Paul stated that "Hope" in Colossians Chapter 1, Verse 5:

> "...the Hope which is laid up for you in Heaven, whereof you have already heard in the word of the truth of the Gospel."

And what does "The Gospel" say about our Hope?

> "Let not your hearts be troubled; you believe in God, believe also in Me. In my Father's House are many dwelling places, if it were not so, I would have told you. I go to prepare a place for you. And if I go and prepare a place for you, I will come again, and receive you unto Myself, that where I am, there you may be also!" (John 14:1-3)

There's the Believer's Hope! And our receiving it is the product of His Calling us. He invited us, and we accepted His Invitation!

Then there is His Inheritance. You'll notice that it says that it's His Inheritance. Why He would consider us Believers as something precious to Him is more than the human mind can grasp; but here it is stated by His Holy Word! We are His Inheritance!

And our Hope includes what God tells us is the inheritance that He has for us. It's:

> "...incorruptible, undefiled, that fades not away, reserved in Heaven for you who are kept by the power of God through faith

unto Salvation, ready to be revealed in the last time." (1 Peter 1:4-5)

The third thing that this "full knowledge of God" will indelibly place in our minds (Verse 19) is a comprehension of God's Power.

Surprisingly, He uses as the illustration of this power how it was used with the events involving the Resurrection of Jesus.

He could have talked about the tremendous force that it took to put the stars in their places, or that it took to create the Grand Canyon, or that opened the Red Sea, or many other things, but He didn't. He pointed us to the power that restored normal life to a man who was clearly and provably dead (man has not been able to do this).

That was the power that caused Him to move physically up from the earth and up and out of sight into the clouds, defying the inescapable Law of Gravity (think of all the effort and equipment that man has gone through to get people airborne—and still we can do this on only a very limited basis).

And then, there is a situation that we can only strain to imagine, and that is that this man Jesus has now been given a different physical composition, so that He could move through billions of light years of space, and is now sitting at God's Right Hand, in a place called Heaven. But we know that He is there because of the effect He has daily in our lives!

Now this power is operating, as Verse 19 tells us, to "us-ward." And I am glad that it is, because one day WE are going to die and,

- WE will be raised from the dead;
- WE will be reunited with our own bodies—bodies that, by then, may be disintegrated;
- WE will be transported through space, just like our Lord was; and
- WE know that this will happen to us, because it already happened to Him!

Now this Verse 19 has been called the "power-fullest" verse in the whole Bible. There are four different Greek words used here for "power" or for some aspect of it. The first "power" word is at the beginning of Verse 19, where it says,

"…the exceeding greatness of His 'power.'"

This word is *DUNAMIS,* which is used to describe "natural power"; the inherent power that God possesses. His Omnipotence. Then we have the word "working," "according to the working." This word is *ENERGEIA.* "Operative power," "power in action." Then we have the word "mighty." This word is *KRATOS*, the word the Greeks used for "power that shows"; something that we not only know about, but also "experience." It's what we see power "doing." And we see God's Power constantly in and around us! Then the next word, coupled with "mighty" and says, "mighty power." This "power" word is *ISCHUS,* and this is a special power, because this is the power that one person gives to another person.

So, putting it all into its literal form and into today's English—here's what Paul is hoping that we will come to know of a certainty, and that is the exceeding greatness of the inherent power that God possesses as measured by the tremendous force we see in action and that we feel in our experience which is power transmitted to us-ward—to us who keep on trusting in Him!

How could anyone express it "more tremendously" than Paul has?! And it is available to those who trust Christ!

Now, the big question: Do you feel that power existing in your life? When a problem moves in on you, do you ask, "Oh, why me, Lord?" Do you fall apart?

When my kids were growing up, we lived in a house that had big "view" windows on two sides of the living room, and every now and then a little bird would think he could fly through there. Well, obviously, he couldn't, and more than once we'd hear a thud and the girls would go look outside the window, and see the little bird lying on the ground, usually trembling, and struggling to recover.

We called it a "bird heart attack." Then usually, pretty soon the little bird would begin to recover, then would pull himself together and fly off. The process came to be a family designation for the way they would get when some sort of an interference moved into their life and then they would "fall apart" because of it.

We Believers should not be having "bird heart attacks!"

Dr. McGee handed this little poem along to us in one of his publications. You may have heard it—it goes like this:

Said the robin to the sparrow, "I should really like to know
Why these anxious human beings rush about and worry so!"
Said the sparrow to the robin: "Friend, I think that it must be
...that they have no Heavenly Father, such as cares for you and me!"

In our memory bank, there must be some of these promises:

> "My God shall supply all your need according to His riches in glory by Christ Jesus." (Philippians 4:19)

> or

> "Behold, I lay in Zion a Comer Stone; elect and precious, He who trusts in Him shall never be put to shame!" (1 Peter 2:6)

> or

> "Let your way of life be free from covetousness, being content with what you have; for He has said: 'I will never leave you nor forsake you' so that we may boldly say, 'The Lord is my helper. I will not fear! What can man do unto me?!'" (Hebrews 13:5-6)

And many more… And how do these wonderful words get into our memory? By our diligently working at getting them there! And then, with them there, we must rely on them!

All right, Paul goes on here to tell us of a great part of God's Plan to help us in getting God's Word firmly entrenched in our minds and in our lives. It's here in Verse 22:

> "God has put all things under His feet, and gave Him to be the head over all things to the *EKKLESIA*, which is His Body, the fullness of Him that fills all in all." (Eph. 1:22-23)

What's Wrong with the Word "Church"

Now, this word *EKKLESIA* that all of our Versions always translate into our English word "church" was a word that, in Paul's day, was used to identify a local "Assembly," a group of people called together for a specific purpose. That's why we can use our today's usage and call it a "task force." Then, it indicated a local group.

God's Word also, however, gives it a broader scope, as it does here in Verses 22 and 23, by describing the *EKKLESIA* as being "His Body," and in other passages speaking of all Believers as making up "The Body of Christ."

Our English word "church" complicates our thinking because it has become a synonym for the "Organized Church" or the "Church Organization," with its buildings, its management, its man-made goals.

The *EKKLESIA* is us Believers; people taken from all walks of life and blessed with a variety of proficiencies, that are, truly, gifts from God.

So, I give to you again the familiar passage from Corinthians, Chapter 12, starting in Verse 27:

> "Now you are the Body of Christ, and members of that body.
> And God has set some in the *EKKLESIA* (the "Assembly"),

> first Apostles, secondly Prophets, third, Teachers; after that miracles, then gifts of healings, helps, governments, diversities of tongues."" (1 Cor 12:27-28)

And in Ephesians 4:12, he states the purpose of these gifts:

> "...For the perfecting of the saints, for the work of the ministry, for the edifying of the Body of Christ."

Each one of us has a need for something—probably many things—that other people can meet and can supply to "building us up." For some people, it's simply "fellowship." For others it may be encouragement or admonishing or teaching, or maybe even food, or other help in our daily lives.

And no one member of the Assembly can provide it all; we each have our gift—our area of usefulness. And He, Jesus Christ, is our Head, to direct us in our work. He is the source of our strength, our direction, and our power to do what He has for us to do!

Jesus Christ is the creator of the Universe.

- He is the creator of the solar systems within the Universe.
- He is the creator of our planet within this solar system.
- He is the creator of the population that inhabits this planet.
- He is the creator of the group within the population of this planet to which He has assigned the responsibility of representing Him to the rest of the population.

Further, He did not ask of us, as He did of the Nation of Israel, that we erect a "temple building" for Him; if we were to look on to the end of Chapter 2 here, we would see that God, Himself, built a "temple" for Himself. Here's Verse 19 of Ephesians Chapter 2:

> "So then you are no longer strangers and foreigners, but fellow-citizens with the saints, and are of God's Household: and you have been built upon the foundation of the Apostles and Prophets, Christ Jesus Himself being the corner stone, in whom the whole building being fitted together, is growing into a holy temple in the Lord, in whom you also are being built together into a habitation of God in the Spirit." (Eph 2:19-22)

You and I ARE God's Temple; He lives here, inside of each Believer, as Verse 22 says there at the end. God is in us THROUGH His Holy Spirit, placed there at our moment of decision, when we decide to trust our life to Him.

So, knowing this, having this wisdom and understanding, makes this time we call "life" a bearable experience, as we understand our "Hope", as we understand our "inheritance," our "power." And as we understand the fact that our body, frail as it is, is "God's Holy Temple," created for His use!

So, there is no more occasion for you and me to have "bird heart-attacks!" He has it all under control!

Lesson 5 Ephesians Chapter 2

The "Body" is Now God's "Temple"

In this Letter to the Ephesians, we have a full explanation of where we members of the human race fit into the overall Plan of God, and it is in the same fashion that the members of the Nation of Israel were set apart to be God's Representatives here on this earth. Yet, because they failed in their mission, God set them aside, and now has put into position a new "Nation" of people, that He has identified as "The Body of Christ," the sum-total of all of those who have placed their trust in this Jesus, who IS "The Christ" — "The Anointed One of God!"

And the members of this New Nation are now to be His Representatives. As the last two verses of Chapter 2 here tell us, we constitute a:

> "...building fitly framed together into a 'holy temple' IN the Lord, and that we are to be a habitation of God, Himself, through His Holy Spirit." (Eph. 2:21-22)

A place where God's Holy Spirit, Himself, dwells. Now you and I do not have to go to a building to meet God, as did the Jews; now He dwells in His People!

Then, as Paul moves ahead, into what has been marked out for us by the translators as "Chapter 2," he explains our position as members of Christ's Body. But first he has to remind us of our previous situation, before we took the step of faith that moved us into our new position. He begins, "And you who were dead in trespasses and sins..." (Eph. 2:1). This "spiritual deadness" that we were in, didn't mean much to us then but it does now as we look back in light of what we now know, "... in which you formerly walked, according to..." (Eph. 2:2).And then he sketches out briefly the three forces that continually surround the people who live on this planet,

1. The force we call "the world." The "world system" that we have to operate in.
2. The force we call "the flesh." The built-in, physical desires that our human nature "naturally" generates.
3. The Devil, Satan, whom he describes here as "the prince of the power of the air, the spirit that works in the 'sons of disobedience.'"

People who live according to the dictates of these forces, rather than following God's direction, are in a state that God calls "spiritually dead"; Jesus expressed it, in John Chapter 3, Verse 36, when He said:

> "He that believes on the Son (here's God's Instruction) HAS Everlasting Life; and he that believes NOT the Son shall not see life, but the Wrath of God abides on him." ("continues to abide on him" Present tense! No Letup!)

So, notice Verse 3 here in Ephesians 2:

> "Among whom (among the 'children of disobedience' that he just described as the mainstream of society) also we all had our way of life in times past, following the strong desires of our flesh, fulfilling the desires of the flesh and of the mind;

> and were, then, by natural birth, the 'children of wrath,' even as others."

That is the state of the God-rejectors, and it was our original state. That describes "Phase One" of Life—the state into which we were born. A "natural" human being.

Then I like these next two words, here in Verse 4: "But God…" So often in the Examples and Illustrations that God gave to us in the Old Testament Scriptures, you will read an account, and the circumstances of it seem to dictate a sad or even disastrous result; then, we will read the words, "But God."

And I know we've felt the impact of these words often in our lives! So, Verse 4-5:

> "But God, who is rich in mercy, for His great love wherewith He loved us (aorist tense— 'a completed, past action'— 'once and for all'), even when we were dead in our sins, He has made us alive together with Christ."

Another aorist tense. Another "once and for all" statement. "He made us alive, together with Christ!" That's the first thing He has done—and that is our New Position! "Together with Christ!"

Then Paul adds a parenthesis here, to help us keep clear in our minds just how come we are here. And it's not as a result of any good that is in us, nor of any good things that we may have done, but "…by grace are you saved!" ("are delivered").

However, here, in this little statement, he changed the tense of the verb; now it's a perfect tense, which says that the action was completed in the past, but it emphasizes the fact that it has results that just go on and on and on!

But then, that isn't all—there's more to what He did for us in Verse 6:

> "...AND has raised us up together, and made us sit together in The Heavenlies, and IN Christ Jesus!"

Not just "with Christ Jesus" but "in Christ Jesus." We have been made to be an integral part of Christ, the Creator of All Things!

So here is not only a statement of our New Position, it is also a declaration of our Eternal Security: "We ARE Delivered" is a past completed action, with results that go on forever!

And as I looked at that statement, I couldn't help but wonder how in the world anyone reading the Bible could ever question the Doctrine of the Eternal Security of the Believer.

God's Word clearly says that a Believer is forever IN Christ, and seated with Him forever, in "The Heavenlies!"

Alright, we've been reminded of our past, and here we have had words about our present position, and now here's a word about our future:

> "So that in the ages 'that keep on rolling on' (literally), He might show forth the exceeding riches of His grace in kindness toward us, through Christ Jesus." (Eph. 2:7)

Why God has Created Us as "His Temple"

There are many things in the Greek language that are very revealing, and that are lost in translation. One of them is the use of the middle voice in their verbs. When they used a verb in the middle voice, they were tying the subject of the verb closely into the action of the verb; this was their way of adding the information that this action was performed for the particular benefit of the subject.

Now aren't you glad you know that! But let me point out to you what it means right here: it means that God raised us up with Christ and made us sit together up there in "The Heavenlies" with Him so that, in the ages that are still to come, God, for His benefit, can show to the

Angelic Armies, and the entire Universe, how His Grace is showered on His Creations.

As Dr. Kenneth Wuest expresses it:

> "We will be on display before the angelic world, basking in the sunshine of God's smile, enjoying the riches of His blessings—all, in order that He might be glorified by the angelic hosts."

You and I, and whatever it is that you and I may have been called on to experience in this life, all is a part of God's great Plan for the Ages. And you and I are a part of that Plan, and we certainly are the beneficiaries of that Plan! And God did all that for His Purpose!

So, in our past, we were wrapped up, dominated by this world system, totally occupied with the "details of life," as are most people. Things like family, work, money, problems, illness, people conflicts, people enjoyments, where we're going to go, what we're going to do, and on and on. The "details of life!" With nothing ahead for us but instability here on Earth. Further, we were continually under the Wrath of God. Which didn't mean much to us then, simply because we didn't fully appreciate the consequences, but it was true, nevertheless.

But now, because of our choice, we are in a new position!

- God's tremendous power is now available to us, to enable us to cope; and
- we are no longer facing "The Wrath of God!"

AND to top it all off, we are headed for a future, which the Greek text here describes as "the ages that are coming one upon another…" in which we will be enjoying this indissoluble union with the One who Created Everything!

And there's more: It all came as a gift! Notice Verse 8 here in Chapter 2:

> "For by grace are you saved through faith; and that not of yourselves; it is the gift of God, not of 'works,' lest any person should boast."

And now here's why He did this:

> "For we are His workmanship, created in Christ Jesus TO good works (works that are pleasing to Him), which God has before ordained that we should walk in them." (Eph 2:10)

"Good works" had nothing to do with our salvation, our "deliverance." But "good works" DO have a place in what we do AFTER our salvation.

So, then, we should ask: What ARE the "good works" that are expected of us AFTER our salvation? This passage tells us that they're works that were "before ordained"; probably laid out by God millions of years ago, back in the time referred to as "In Beginning." A point, as the Hebrew expressed it, a "beginning that has no beginning!"

And what KIND of works would God have planned so long ago? The Greek word translated "good" here is *AGATHOS*, which is used in the Scriptures for things that are intrinsically "Good" and "good within themselves." So, since God makes the rules and decides what's right and what's not right, we can say that they are "things that are pleasing and useful to God."

So, man doesn't have to figure out what God wants us to be doing. God had that figured out a long time ago!

What needs to be done—or how to get it done—those things are not our problem; they're God's, and He has already figured out the solution. Our responsibility is to be "always prepared" with all our equipment at hand, our motor running, our radio turned on and tuned to His wavelength, our hand on the throttle waiting for Him to give us our course, our destination, and then say, "OK, go!"

The Position of Gentiles, Before and After "Christianity"

Now, in the next verses here, Paul again brings us back to the main subject of this Letter, which is this *EKKLESIA*—this "Assembly of Believers"—that He has invited and set apart for His Purpose.

He began by contrasting our Old Position with our New Position, and now he explains those Old and New Positions in relation to the people who USED TO HAVE our position—the Nation Israel. Ephesians 2:11:

> "Wherefore remember, that in time past you were called 'Gentiles' in the flesh, and called the 'Uncircumcision' by those that are called the 'Circumcision' in the flesh made by hands."

And here are three points of difference—then and now, Old, and New.

1. In the "Old Days," the non-Jews were "without Christ," without "The Christos," "The Anointed One," "The Messiah."

   The Jews looked forward to a "Redeemer." They were confident of His Existence. This confidence made their lives bearable! But the Gentiles had nothing, only "gods" they had made up out of their imaginations or carved out of wood or stone. When you stop to think about that, those wooden 'gods' could really NOT be much help. One wonders why they even bothered to make them!

2. The second point of difference between the Old and the New: the relationship that God had with the Jews was "special" and they knew it!

But these non-Jews were Aliens; they were "foreigners!" And being a "foreigner," as you know from your travels outside the United States, is a very uncomfortable feeling! You feel very uneasy until you get back on American soil!

3. The third thing the Gentiles lacked: they were not under the amazing Covenants that God had made with these Special People, Israel. The four unconditional "one way" covenants that God had made to them:

    (a) The Covenant with Abraham, of Genesis 12:2-3:

    "I will make of you, Abraham, a great nation, and I will bless you and make your name great; and you shall be a blessing.
    AND I will bless them that bless you, and curse him that curses you; and in you shall all families of the earth be blessed!"

    These Jews were "noteworthy!" The Gentiles had no promise like this!

    (b) Then there is the Palestinian Covenant that guarantees Israel a Land, forever. The rest of the people of the world have no guarantee of ANYthing!
    (c) Then there is the Covenant God made with King David—the promise that he would have a Son who would reign forever. The world's King would be a part of their family! OUR family (us Gentiles) is "dead end!"
    (d) And then there is the "New Covenant"; Jeremiah recorded it in Jeremiah 31:33. God said, "AFTER THOSE DAYS, I will put My Law in their inward parts, and write it in their hearts, and I will be their God, and they shall be My people!"

We Gentiles are now included! And how wonderful it is to know that the Creator-God will consider you and me to be a part of His Special People!

All of these things made up what God continually refers to as "Hope," or "Wonderful Expectations." They had a "Hope," the Gentiles had none—only the frustrations of Daily Life, with nothing at the end.

There is really no better way to express the life of an Unbeliever, than in this earthy quip, that says, "Life is a bitch, and then you die."

No Hope and "without God in the world." But then we come to Verse 13, here in Chapter 2 of Ephesians:

> "BUT NOW, in Christ Jesus, you who before were far off, are brought near by the blood of Christ!"

Dr. Kenneth Wuest calls our attention to an interesting handling of words here; there at the beginning of Verse 12 we have the Gentiles' position described as being "without Christ"; but then, when Paul describes OUR new position, the name "Jesus" is added! Now it reads:

> "BUT NOW, in Christ Jesus...we are brought near...!"

It was "Jesus," in His Humanity, that came and made the difference! And now we are "with God." We are no longer "outsiders" and "foreigners." Now we have been adopted into the Kingdom of God, and we now have a great "Hope," not only for our time here on Earth, but also beyond!

We've talked about our "Hope." Hold still and let me give you a more complete rundown of all that's involved in this thing called "Hope."

First, as we know, we are going to have a new Home, in a "far-away place"; Jesus told us about it, in John 14:2:

> "In My Father's House are many dwelling places; ... I go to prepare a place for you!"

Then, further, also as we know, we are going to be "present with the Lord!" We will be, literally, "at home" with Him! Paul used a Greek word in the passage in Second Corinthians 5:6 that we would have used to say something like: "Thank Heaven, I'm home!" We know that feeling! That must have been what Paul was thinking, when he said, "I really would much rather not be 'at home' in my body, but to be 'at home' with the Lord!"

It's what Dr. Mitchell used to call "the hunkering down feeling," "right at home!" That will be how the next life will be!

The third thing involved in The Believer's Hope is that we will escape a "second" death. People don't give a lot of thought to this, but the Bible tells us that there are actually two deaths that members of the human race have to face; the first, of course, is our physical death, when our heart stops beating, and our body functions quit working. But the Bible also tells us—this is in Revelation 20:15—that:

> "...whoever was not found written in the book of life will be cast into the Lake of Fire. This is the second death!"

Believers ARE written in the Book of Life, so we will be spared this "Second Death!" In fact—and this is the fourth Benefit of our New Position: Believers will completely escape this Great White Throne Judgment! Romans 8:1 tells us:

> "There is therefore now NO CONDEMNATION to them who are IN Christ Jesus!"

Instead—and this is the fifth point of The Believer's Hope—we not only become Christ's inheritance (which in itself, is hard for us to grasp) but we're told in First Peter 1:4 that we HAVE a wonderful Inheritance! We will find that we will have been:

> "...reborn into an Inheritance, that fades not away, reserved in Heaven for us!"

The sixth thing on the list of Benefits that go to make up The Believers' Hope is the fact that pain and sorrow will all be gone! Below are the words of Revelation 21, Verses 3 and 4. The Apostle John reported this:

> "And I heard a great voice out of Heaven saying: 'Behold, the dwelling place of God is with men, and He will dwell with them, and they shall be His people, and God, Himself, shall be with them, and be their God.
>
> And God shall wipe away all tears from their eyes, and there shall be no more death, neither sorrow, nor crying, neither shall there be any more pain; for the former things are passed away." (Revelation 21:3-4)

But even that isn't all that's involved in Our Hope; the seventh thing we have to look forward to is a brand-new body—one that will be free of all weaknesses; free of the aches and pains, the problems we've had with the present one. It will be a body just like our Lord's! Here are a couple of passages about THIS:

> "For our way of life is in Heaven, from whence also we look for the Savior, the Lord Jesus Christ, who shall change our vile body, that it may be fashioned like unto His glorious body, according to the power whereby He is able even to subdue all things unto Himself!" (Philippians 3:20)

Then here's what the Apostle John had to say about it; this is First John 3:2:

> "Beloved, now are we (and we keep on being—present tense) the Sons of God, and it does not yet appear what we shall be,

but we KNOW (as a fact) that when He shall appear, we shall be exactly like Him!"

This is our Hope; the Life Ahead to be enjoyed by everyone who has trusted his or her life to Jesus Christ, God's Son.

- No condemnation;
- No having to stand before the Great White Throne judgment, to try to prove our eligibility for the Kingdom of God; because Jesus has already bought and paid for the price of Admission!
- We'll never again have to experience pain nor sorrow;
- Our new bodies will function perfectly;
- We'll have a new, permanent address, which will be in the city where God dwells; and
- All this will be complete with a wonderful Inheritance, one that will never diminish, nor disappear!

There is our Hope, and our Stabilizer. So, to end this, I'd like to remind us again of the words that the Apostle John spoke after he had recorded, in the Book of Revelation, all the amazing information he had been given.

He said, "He who testifies these things says: 'Surely I come quickly!'"

To which John responded, "Even so, come, Lord Jesus!"

Lesson 6 Ephesians Chapter 2

A Further Study of God's Grace

God had revealed something of His Plan for the human race to the Jews, the Nation of Israel, offering them special benefits if they would represent Him and His Goals to the human race.

A part of what He entrusted to them was His Code of Conduct—His Standard of Behavior—all that which we have contained in the Law as it was given to Moses. The Law that is the Ten Commandments but was also amplified and detailed out in the Books of Exodus and Numbers and Deuteronomy.

All that was a statement of His Standard, and a demonstration to them of the value of what we call "God-like qualities" such as concern for one another, longsuffering, gentleness, goodness, and self-control, as opposed to simply living an animal-like existence.

The Jews had this special position with God, with many special benefits offered to them if they accepted the challenge that God set before them; however, the rest of mankind had only the example of the Jews to look to.

And we know that some did and were benefited; for example, when the Jews left Egypt, after having lived in Egypt for about four hundred years, thousands of Egyptians elected to leave with them. "Jewish proselytes," as we call them. Attracted to Israel's God!

But the influence of the people of Israel was a weak one, and the "Gentiles"—the non-Jews—had only the Stars in the Heavens and Nature itself to direct them to their Creator.

This is what Paul has been reminding us of here in these first verses of Ephesians Chapter 2, Verse 12:

> "...at that time you were without a Messiah, being aliens from the Nation of Israel and strangers from the covenants of promise, having no "Hope", and without God in the world;
>
> BUT NOW, in Christ Jesus, you who before were far off, now you are brought near, by means of the Blood of Christ!"

Everything is changed, and the things never revealed before to the Prophets are now made clear to this New Race of People that Jesus has pronounced to be included in *THE EKKLESIA*—the people He has put together into a "task force," which He further describes as being "His Body"!

We sort of slid over one of the great passages in the New Testament, and I want to point out a couple of things in connection with it. The passage begins in Ephesians Chapter 2, Verse 4. And here it is:

> "But God, who is rich in mercy, for His great love wherewith He loved us, even when we were dead in sins, has made us alive together with Christ (by grace are you saved.)
>
> And has raised us up together, and made us sit together in The Heavenlies IN Christ Jesus,
>
> So that in the ages to come, He might show the exceeding riches of His grace in his kindness toward us, through Christ Jesus,

> For by grace are you saved through faith; and that not of yourselves; it is the gift of God, not of works, lest any many should boast." (Eph 2:4-9)

First, note that all this is "so that He (God) can show all of this to the inhabitants of the Universe." While we are the great beneficiaries of God's Act, still He has a greater purpose, and that is that the whole Universe can know and understand what? His Grace!

And He will do this through us Believers! We don't know HOW, but He will!

Which leads me to the other thing here I want you to know about, and that is some things about this word "Grace" itself. We use the word a lot in connection with Christianity, and the Bible uses it a lot; so, we should be very familiar with its meaning!

First off, the scholars that have carefully studied the language of Christ's and Paul's day tell us that this word *CHARIS* (pronounced KAAR-EES) that we translate as "Grace," meant to them "something done as a favor." But the extensive research has shown that it was a favor done always for a friend—you never did anything for an enemy.

So, what constitutes a "friend?" The word "friend"—this is the Greek word *PHILOS*—back in those Roman days had a very special meaning. It was not used loosely, like we do, when we mostly are speaking of "acquaintances"—somebody you know, even maybe quite well. But "friend," this was a title that a person earned. It spoke of loyalty and total dedication, someone for whom a person would do "favors" and even give your life for!

And a person guarded that relationship carefully. Also, if you were a "friend" of a person in high places, it could mean a great deal to you in many ways. This is why, there at the Trial of Jesus before Pontius Pilate, the thing that broke Pilate over from his leanings toward letting Jesus go free was when the mob began to say to Pilate:

> "If you let this man go, you are not Caesar's friend!" (John 19:12)

To jeopardize that position, for Pilate, would have been unthinkable! And the Apostle James used this term to illustrate the greatness of the position with God, of Father Abraham, when he said:

> "Abraham believed God, and it was imputed unto him for righteousness, and he was called the 'Friend of God.'" (James 2:23)

To them, that would be the highest title that could be granted to a person! Jesus, Himself, used that word to describe His followers. This is in John 15, in the Upper Room that last night before He left them. In Verse 13-15, He said to them:

> "Greater love has no man than this, than he lay down his life for his friends, you are my 'friends', IF you do whatever I command you."

Then Jesus added these wonderful words:

> "Henceforth I do not call you servants, for the servant does not know what his lord does; but I have called you 'friends'; for all things that I have heard of my Father, I have made known unto you!"

So now He holds us in high esteem; we are now "special" to Him! We will be the beneficiaries of His Grace—the likely beneficiary of His "favors!"

But now here is where, as someone said, "Grace moves forward an infinite leap!" Paul expresses it in his Letter to the Romans. In Chapter 5, starting in Verse 7, we have this familiar statement:

> "For scarcely for a righteous man will one die; even for a good man, some would even dare to die;

> But God demonstrated His love toward us, in that while we were sinners, Christ died for us!"

Here is the kind of action that was foreign to anybody's thinking—extending "grace" toward an obvious enemy; toward a person who continually rejected you and even worked against you! God sent Himself! And Jesus, as a human being, came and went through what He had to go through, for people who were against Him!

The Apostle John, toward the end of his life, commented with wonder on this same thing. In First John 3 he said,

> "Behold what manner of love the Father has bestowed upon us, that we should be called the Sons of God!"

So here, now, is God's attitude revealed, as it is toward those who put themselves in the position of "His Friend," as was Abraham; loyal to Him, devoted to Him, supportive of Him and what He stands for and is trying to do.

But further, here is how God has chosen to operate toward the entire human race; this thing that the world, in its ways, reserves only for those who are regarded as a genuine, true supporter—God has elected to make available to all of mankind. And Paul expresses that here in Ephesians 2:13:

> "But now in Christ Jesus, you who were formerly 'far off', now are 'made close' by means of the blood of Christ."

Our old position was "far off"; our new position is "made close"; close to the Creator of the whole Universe and all that's in it!

How did it happen? Not by anything we did, but God tells us that it came about through the instrumentality of Christ's Blood. He died, He paid our penalty, and He removed the barrier between God and man. So, Jesus literally, on our behalf, for us "made peace with God."

The Jews living in Israel today would certainly love to have a peacemaker step in on their behalf. They are war-torn, harassed, beaten down by ostracism.

And for those people you and I know, who are plagued by guilt and guilty consciences, knowing they have displeased God, here is their answer, in Verse 14 of Ephesians 2:

> "For He is our peace, who has made both one, (both Jew and Gentile) and has broken down the middle wall of partition between us, having abolished in His Flesh, the enmity."

In this reference to this "middle wall," undoubtedly Paul was referring here to the wall in the Jewish Temple that separated the Court of the Gentiles from the rest of the Temple area. A Gentile could not step beyond that wall, or the Jews would kill him!

But now Jesus, in His Death, has broken down that wall, and now in this new "Body of Christ," there should be no enmity any longer between the ethnic groups, for every Believer is on the same level—the same footing—in God's eyes!

This is a statement of what we can call the Composition of this new "Body of Christ."

But there is another thing we must note here. It's in Verse 16. In the verses we've looked at just before this, we see that Jesus, "made peace with God." He broke down the wall separating Jew and non-Jew. And, Verse 16 gives the purpose of what He did: "SO THAT He might reconcile both unto God…"

Notice it says "that He <u>might</u> reconcile…" This verb is given to us in the Subjunctive Mood, the verb form that states that there is a conditional use in mind here. Jesus made the arrangement but making it happen God always leaves up to the individual.

It's passages like this that give the lie to those people who teach that "we are all Children of God, and we'll all get to Heaven if we're good and if we really try; we're just traveling different roads…"

In spite of the fact that "The Way" that God's Word spells out may seem "unreasonable" from the world's viewpoint, it still is The ONLY Way!

Well, there's even more for us to see, here. This is in Ephesians 2:18:

> "For through Him we both have access by one Spirit unto the Father."

These words "have access" had a special connotation to the people of that day. Then an "ordinary" person didn't just walk up to, say, a governmental official and start talking; you had to have "an entrée," someone to speak for you, to introduce you, to prepare the way for your visit.

Dr. Kenneth Wuest, the Head of the Greek Department at Moody Bible Institute, expressed it this way, "God the Son provides the way into the Father's presence, through the Blood of his Cross; God the Spirit conducts the Believer in and presents him, and God the Father is the One into whose presence the Believer is brought…" That is "having access!"

Then, in these closing verses here in Chapter 2, we have more detail on the position of the members of this new "Body of Christ"—what our standing in God's community really is. Paul begins this in Verse 19, where he tells us:

> "Now, therefore, you are no longer strangers and 'foreigners'" (or "aliens", as it is in the new translations).

Paul used words here that were very familiar to the people of that day. The word "strangers" we would best translate as "tourists"—people that are just a part of a "floating population."

And the word "foreigners" or "aliens" was a technical word for people who actually resided in a place, paid taxes, maybe owned property, but they were "aliens." One of the ancient papyri they found referred to one of these "aliens." It reads:

> "Although you dwelt long among us, you were never one of us!"

But now Paul can tell us, there as Verse 19 continues:

> "You are no longer tourists and aliens, but Fellow-citizens with the saints, and of the household of God, and were built upon the foundation of the Apostles and Prophets, with Christ Jesus, Himself, being the Comer Stone." (Eph 2:19-20)

Notice what this is saying: the foundation of Christianity was the Apostles and Prophets—they were the base. The bottom layer, the "foundation." However, their purpose has passed; they are no longer a part of the scene. Now, the part that holds everything together is the corner stone, and that is Christ Jesus! And in Verse 21:

> "...it's IN Him that the whole building, being fitted together, grows!"

It is "being fitted together." Passive Voice. In other words, this is being done by a force outside itself, and it is continually growing, as a result of that "outside force." As one commentator wrote:

> "We must never get so confused as to think that you or I, through our efforts, are building up the Church of God! It is being done by a force outside of us!"

Here is what Paul said about this: "I have planted, Apollos watered, but God gives the increase!" (1 Corinthians 3:6)

So, what is this "Body of Believers" being built into? A Holy Temple, not FOR the Lord, but IN the Lord! The Universal Church, as we also call it, is actually made to be a part of the Great God of the Universe!

All right, then not only is this great group of Believers being made a part of God, Himself, Ephesians 2 Verse 22 here tells us something is happening to us as individuals:

> "In whom (in the Lord, Himself) we also are being built together for a habitation of God, through the Spirit!"

We—you and I—are being built into a place where God Himself will dwell. "Through the Spirit," it says. In other words, the Holy Spirit is alive within every Believer, here to connect us with the power and the wisdom of the great Creator of the Universe.

We are—our bodies are—His Temple! People should want to take good care of His Temple, but so many don't! We should be treating it NOT as if He really lived in it—He DOES live in it!

I have been so glad, so many times, that God doesn't just stick us people in the ground, here, and then go off and leave us. He plants us carefully in a special spot He has selected for us; then He comes regularly to look at us, see how we're doing; He waters us when we need it; He digs around us when that's needed; He fertilizes us and He even does a little pruning now and then, so that we will grow up in the right shape for what He had in mind. Then, later, when the fruit comes—through no effort of our own—He will look at us and say,

> "Well done, thou good and faithful servant; enter into the joy of thy Lord" (Matt 25:23)

Pretty amazing, isn't it! So, let's not be fighting the pruning process, or complain if He thinks it best to do a little transplanting! Right?!

The Apostle Paul experienced a great deal of the "transplanting," didn't he! We wonder if he even had a place that he could call "home!"

But here's how he looked at his life. He tells us a little about his "life" and his "calling" here in Chapter 3 of this Letter to the Ephesians,

> "For this cause, I, Paul, the prisoner of Christ Jesus for you Gentiles."

Then jump on to Verse 6, and he tells what this cause is:

> "...that the Gentiles should be fellow heirs, and of the same body, and partakers of His promise in Christ by the Gospel, whereof I was made a minister, according to the gift of the grace of God given unto me by the effectual working of His power.
>
> And to make all men see what is the *OIKONOMIA*—the "dispensation"—the 'administration' of the Mystery, which from the beginning of the world has been hid in God, who created all things by Christ Jesus,
>
> To the intent that now unto the principalities and powers in The Heavenlies, might be made known by the *EKKLESIA*—the 'Body of Christ'—the manifold wisdom of God." (Eph. 3:6-10)

Paul's Assignment was to make known to all this "mystery":

- that Jews and Believing non-Jews are to be considered by God as one;
- that to this new Organization God has committed the Administration of His Affairs on the earth; and
- that through this new Organization will be made known, to all, everywhere—in Heaven and on Earth—the great and many-sided Wisdom of God. They will then see why God has done all these things that He has done, and allowed to happen all the things that He has allowed to happen!

Now HOW He will accomplish this, He has already figured out. We, the members of the Universal Church, don't have to try to mastermind it; God already has a plan.

His Message will go out by missionaries, by radio, by television, by pastors, by teachers, and by thousands of individuals operating in the places where He has caused us to be.

What God wants of us individuals that He has scattered throughout the earth is our willingness to listen to Him for instruction and then to respond to what we hear. Paul wrote about this, in the Letter to the Romans, in Chapter 12, Verse 1:

> "I beseech you, brethren, by the mercies of God, that you present your bodies a living OFFERING, holy, acceptable unto God, which is your 'logical-rational' service."

The Greek word Paul used here to describe the word "service" is their word *LOGIKOS*. Our word "logical" comes from it. God is saying to us, "In view of all that has been provided for you, it is only 'logical' that you give back your bodies to Me." And this is certainly true! "Willing availability!"

Then Paul prays another prayer for all of us who will follow along. We've looked at this before, so I'll just remind us of his main causes for concern. It starts in Verse 14 here in Chapter 3:

"For this cause I bow my knees to the Father of our Lord Jesus Christ: that He would grant:

- (Verse 16) that we be strengthened by His Power, through His Holy Spirit;
- (Verse 17) that Christ may 'be at home' in our hearts—through the instrumentality of Faith;
- that we, being rooted and grounded in 'concern for one another,' be able to fully comprehend the breadth and length and depth

and height—and to fully KNOW—Christ's love for us—a love that passes all understanding, AND
- that we be filled with all of God's Fullness!"

These are the things that Paul sees as being the primary, basic needs of every Believer. You and I tend to think in terms of food and shelter and the "details of life" but here are the true basics for our health, and joy, and peace.

And here, once again, is Paul's great benediction:

> "Now unto Him that is able to do exceeding abundantly above all that we ask or think, according to the power that works in us;
>
> Unto Him be glory in the "Body of Christ" by Christ Jesus, throughout all ages, world without end. Amen." (Eph. 3:20-21)

Lesson 7 Ephesians Chapter 4

How We of "The Body" Bring Glory to Him...

In this great Letter of Paul's, we see him setting out the truths and doctrines of Christianity. A great broadening of the basic information that Jesus set out, and that are recorded in the last chapters of the Gospel of John, 13 through 17, that we have come to call the "Upper Room Discourse."

Here, Jesus promised that the Holy Spirit would amplify His Words that He gave to His Apostles, and here it is! All of this information was not known to the Jews; they had only a smattering of it, and things pointing to "more," and now it's made known to all.

What Jesus introduced to the human race at this point in time fulfills the Law that God gave to Moses. It replaces the Tabernacle and its liturgies and its rituals; it replaces the Order of the Priesthood, by making, now, every Believer to be his own Priest unto God.

Before, the Priests were the ones who prayed for the people; now each Believer has direct access to the Throne of God.

Before, our life after this one was hinted at; now it is spelled out for us in wonderful detail.

Before, a person's Way to God was not clearly stated; they knew it depended on many things that a person did, and tried to do; however, his ultimate deliverance—his "salvation"—would come because he was a faithful descendant of Jacob, whose name was changed to Israel.

Now, it's different! Now we know exactly what is required of us; now, we know that our ultimate deliverance has been provided for by the death of Christ and we know that our appropriation of what He did is our key for entrance into the Kingdom of God.

Before, Israel was God's chosen vessel to represent Him here on Earth, and to make Him known to mankind.

Now, this responsibility has been put in the hands of the sum-total of all Believers in Christ.

And it's the deliverance of this Message that Paul recognizes has been his responsibility. That's what he tells us in these first verses here in Ephesians Chapter 3:

> "For this cause (he says) I, Paul, the prisoner of Christ Jesus for you Gentiles, SEEING you have heard of the Dispensation of the grace of God which is given to me for you. How that by revelation, He made known to me the Mystery."

Verse 5:

> "...which in other times was not made known unto the sons of men, but is now revealed unto His Holy Apostles and Prophets by the Spirit,
>
> ...that the Gentiles should be fellow heirs and of the same body, and partakers of His promise in Christ by the gospel."

There is Paul's assignment, and he faithfully pursued it for the rest of his life, traveling, teaching, and writing. In addition, as Paul points out to us here in Verse 20 of Chapter 3, God is going to work in and through us Believers that will come along later! And what both the natural world and the supernatural world will see, as a result, will be to God's Glory.

Let me give you an expanded translation of Verses 20 and 21; the English translations we have just don't tell the whole story. Here it is:

> Now unto Him who has unlimited power, who is able to keep on doing 'above and beyond whatsoever' that we might ask as a favor for ourselves—or that we might even consider—in the measure of God's omnipotence that keeps on energizing us—unto Him be glory and worship and praise, in the Body of Believers and in Christ Jesus, unto all the generations of the age of the ages.

This sounds like a mighty long time! And to this, Paul adds "Amen!" "I thoroughly believe it!" Well, we should, by now, have some sense of the Position we have been placed in, as Believers. It's an amazing position, and it's a position that the non-believers can't in any way comprehend. When you try to tell them, they either laugh outright or they mentally tap their heads.

So, Paul deals next, here, with our "talking" about our position. And, instead of how we are to "talk," it's how we are to "walk!" Chapter 4 opens with these words:

> "I, therefore, the prisoner of the Lord, beseech you that you WALK worthy of the vocation wherewith you are called."

And how are we to do this walking?

> "With all lowliness and meekness, with longsuffering, forbearing one another in love, endeavoring to keep the unity of the Spirit in the bond of peace." (Eph. 4:2)

So, what is this "calling" that God expects us Believers to "walk worthy" of? Is it to "win souls for Christ?" Incidentally, yes; but our true calling Paul explained to us back in Chapter 3, Verse 10. All of this is:

> "To the intent that now unto the principalities and powers in The Heavenlies, might be known, by the Body of Christ, the manifold wisdom of God."

The great purpose of the Universal Church is to bring glory to God's Name before the Angelic Hosts of Heaven. It's not to glorify Man, nor is it "to bring peace to this troubled world." Our purpose is to show to the Angels that have been faithful to God, and to the Angels that defected to Satan, that God's actions through the ages have been right and just and justified.

We don't understand why that is important to God, but it clearly is!

Now we Believers are not going to bring Glory to God's Name by a haughty attitude toward those around us, nor by a "holier than thou" attitude, nor by an attitude of contempt for those who are less gifted than we are. We are to do it,

> "With all lowliness and meekness, with longsuffering, forbearing one another in love, working to keep the unity of the spirt in the bond of peace" (Eph. 4:2-3)

That's to be our mental attitude as we walk, as we use our God-given gifts. And each of us has at least one gift. Each of us is not good at everything but each of us has at least one gift, something we know how to do well. Now you may not practice that gift, but you know you have it—and if you haven't been practicing it, maybe you should work at practicing it! Use it more often. On more people!

He gives a partial list down in Verse 11:

> "Some Apostles, some prophets, some Evangelists, some 'shepherds'" (This is a part of the work of a Pastor—and the rest of that work is that of a Teacher).

Paul completed the list in 1 Corinthians 12:28. Here he added to that list:

- "Miracles" (people who seem to do amazing things);

- "Gifts of healings" (our Doctors and Nurses and Attenders, and this includes those who send cheerful and uplifting cards and letters);
- "Those who help" (this is a real gift);
- "Administrators" (people who see what needs to be done, and get it done); and
- "Translators" (people gifted with languages other than their own, so that the Written Word can reach all people on the earth).

And what is the purpose of all of these gifts? Verse 12 of Ephesians 4:

> "For the bringing to maturity of the Believers, for the work of the ministry, for the building up of the Body of Christ, until we all come in the unity of the faith, and of the knowledge of the Son of God, to a mature person, mature as measured by the stature of Christ Himself!"

You see, God wants us to be what we call "spiritually mature." "Spiritually self-sustaining." We don't need some person to cheer us up; God's Word and God's Holy Spirit will do that.

We don't need someone to pray for us; we, ourselves, are priests unto God, and providing we are in fellowship, our prayers go right to His Throne, and are heard, and are acted upon! He has promised us that!

> "The fervent prayer of a person in right standing, avails much!" (James 5:16)

A pastor's job is to be a shepherd to his flock, which means he leads them in the right paths, he sees that they get spiritual food and protection from the predators. However, he is not their priest; we are our own priests! We pray for ourselves, we whine to ourselves (if you feel like whining) and we get our strength from God's Word, not from the pastor's visits!

It is God's great desire that, as Paul has stated it here in Verse 12, that God's People get to a state of Spiritual Maturity, and God has specified certain people within the "Body of Believers" to be doing this "pushing along" of the people to maturity.

First, he has mentioned the Apostles, and the Prophets, but these categories are no longer among us. Today, this work of "bringing to maturity" is assigned to the rest on this first list: the evangelists, the pastors, and the teachers. I'm sure that's why Paul gave only an incomplete list here in Ephesians.

And then he states the intended result of this maturity here in Verse 14:

> "That we be no more children, tossed to and fro, and carried about with every wind of doctrine, by the 'double-talk' of men, by the cunning craftiness, whereby they lie in wait to deceive;
>
> Instead, speaking the truth in love, so that the Believers grow up into Him in all things—Him, the head—Christ!"

The Greek word Paul used here (*NEPIOS*), that is translated "children" in some of the versions, was their word for an "infant"; his reference here is to the "babes in Christ," as are a great many who are first saved and who know nothing of God's Word.

Without proper teaching and instruction IN God's Word, they wind up, as he describes their condition here, like a ship caught in a nasty storm. In fact, the words he used here were sailor's words: "tossed to and fro" was a word they used for a ship out of control in a storm. And "carried about" is, literally, "carried in circles."

As we know, this is the plight of too many new Believers, who fall into the hands of the cults, and the religious vultures that are around that immediately begin to talk "performance" to these new listeners. They say, "Get busy in our program"; "You must start sacrificial giving", and so on, as we know.

But instead, if and when these new Believers come into the hands, as Ephesians Verse 15 here states it, of those who:

> "...speak the truth out of a sense of 'concern' these 'infants' grow up into Christ in all things."

And the passage continues, in Verse 16:

> "Christ is the head, and from Him, the whole body is fitted and held together by that which every joint supplies, according to the proper working of each part, and 'it causes the growth of the body for the building up of itself, in the sphere of 'concern'—of love!"

It should be becoming clear to us as we move through this Ephesians Letter that, first, God DOES want this "Body of Christ" that He has set into being. He wants it to grow, but He sees it as growing, not through our knocking on doors, or talking about our Christianity in the ways that are typically pursued in so many evangelical groups, but, again as He has given it to us here in Verse 16, God's plan is for this Body to get its growth as it "builds itself up" through a showing forth of "true concern" for one another.

And this "true concern," as we know, is a product of Holy Spirit activity in the lives of Believers. We have trouble in producing this quality by ourselves, but the Holy Spirit can and does produce it when He's given the opportunity in our life!

So, Paul proceeds here to give us a contrast—a comparison of the typical "Gentile's" way of life, comparing it with what we see God pushing us toward. Here's Ephesians Verse 17 of Chapter 4:

> "This I say, therefore, and affirm together with the Lord, that you walk no longer just as the Gentiles also walk—"

And here's the first description, "...in the emptiness of their mind." If you were to walk into the Philosophy section of a library or bookstore, you'll find hundreds of books that attempt to deal with the problems of "living" but they don't have the answers—that's why people keep writing more books on the subject.

But here in this Bible, in just the twelve pages that it takes to contain these three Letters to the Ephesians, the Colossians and the Philippians, we have it all! And it works!

And how do I know it works? I've seen it work in me!

Then Paul explains WHY there is this emptiness in the minds of so many people in Verse 18:

> "...having their understanding darkened, which ignorance excludes them from the life of God because of the hardness of their mind, and they, having become callous (the New American Standard rightly translates it) have given themselves over to sensuality" (Eph. 4:18-10).

This is an interesting Greek word here that is translated as "blindness" in the King James and as "hardness" or "hardening" in the newer versions. The archaeologists have dug up a lot of valuable information for us in recent years, and this word, *POROSIS* is the word the Greeks used to describe a "callous," like one that develops on a person's hands. Layers after layer of skin build up, until there is no longer a sensitivity to reality there.

And, of course, that's the way we are about some things; every time we go against our conscience, a layer of skin is added, and the next time it's a little easier to again go against it until, after a while, a person is really "calloused" and he or she pays no attention to the warning. So, in Verse 19:

> "...being past feeling the pain, give themselves over to simply satisfying the senses, with all their desires and greed."

This is where the great mass of the people are today—living solely to satisfy their sensory urges. Nothing else matters. But in Verse 20:

> "This is not what Christ's Way teaches! And SEEING (First Class condition) you have heard Him, and have been taught by Him, as The Truth is in Jesus
>
> – that you put off the way of life of the old man, which is corrupt, since it follows the deceitful strong desires (these sensory desires that he was talking about); and
> – be renewed in your mind's spirit, putting on the new man that, after God, is created in righteousness and true holiness."

And the next verse, Verse 25, adds,

> "Wherefore, putting away (not "lying") but "The Lie"!

Note the contrasts here: In Verse 21, we have "The Truth", which is "in Jesus", contrasted with, in Verse 25, "The Lie." "The Lie" is what Satan has been feeding the Natural Man all these years, as he tells the world that "there's nothing to this Religious stuff—eat, drink, and be merry, for tomorrow we die!"

Only those are old-fashioned words. Today he's saying, "Go ahead—just do it! Live it up! Life's a bitch, and then you die!"

But what will happen to the Believer, as the Holy Spirit is able to operate inside him, is stated here in these two Passive Voice verbs: "be renewed" and "is created." The "renewing" and the "creating" is done ON the Believer by God's Holy Spirit and the mechanics of that processing is also stated right here: it takes place "in your mind's spirit."

Since we are a part of Adam's nature when we are born into this world, our Human Spirit at that point in time is totally dormant; stuck up on a back shelf and packed in a vacuum-sealed bag. But at our moment of salvation, that human spirit is brought out, given a new life, and made ready to receive Divine Instruction from God's Holy Spirit. This IS what we call "The New Birth"—the "Birth from above."

And as He is given opportunity to work, this renewal process begins to take place as in Verse 21, again,

- We HEAR Jesus speak
- We are TAUGHT by Him

And what we are taught is "The Truth"—not "The Lie!" Then, as a result of learning "The Truth," a person's life and attitudes begin to change at the rate that the Holy Spirit is able to operate. You've heard it said, I know, and it's absolutely true, "Christianity is in the business of changing lives!"

And how fast that works and to what extent it works depends on how much opportunity the Holy Spirit is given to work!

But, as the Holy Spirit does begin to work in us, we find that WE begin to monitor our actions. And this is different for each of us, of course.

With the people in Paul's day, it was a perfectly accepted way of life for a Jew to lie to a Gentile and take advantage of him whenever he could. As New Christians, they found themselves not doing this so much anymore.

God's "Code of Conduct" That He Expects Us to Live Out

Now, in our "sophisticated culture," we don't normally routinely steal and lie, but our very normal business practices include what we learned in our Economics class in high school as being "The American Way" of doing business. For example, that was that it is "the normal thing" to "charge whatever the traffic will bear"; now, however, under the leadership of the Holy Spirit's influence, we begin to think rather of charging on the basis of what is "fair and right," not on the basis of what you can get.

Then, of course, there are a lot of people around who do live on outright lies and outright stealing. Under the Holy Spirit's influence as Christians, newly appointed Ambassadors of Christ, they now begin to stop that, since they now recognize that this is not pleasing to God!

So, God expects us to monitor our actions now that we are His Ambassador; now that we are here to show the world the grace and concern that God has for His Created beings.

And where do we start? Ephesians.

> Verse 25: "Speak every man truth with his neighbor, for we are members one of another."
>
> Verse 26: "Watch how you handle your anger."
>
> Verse 27: "Do not give the Devil any place in your life."
>
> Verse 28: "The one stealing—stop it! Instead, do a good day's work, so that you can have something you earned, to give to the person that has a need!"

There are the "starters"! Before we close now, I want us to look closely at Verse 26 of Ephesians Chapter 4, where it says, "In your anger, do not sin."

Or, as the Old King James has it, "Be ye angry, and sin not..."

Here is a verse that seems to be a "contradiction." "Be angry, but don't sin!" Especially since down in Verse 31 we are commanded to "put away anger."

I'm afraid that it's too often that we run into a situation in the Bible like this. We don't quite understand it, so we just sort of slide over it and bypass the apparent "contradiction" and, in this way, miss a Truth. But this statement here is a definite command, and we shouldn't slide over His Commands!

The NIV totally distorts the Original Text. The NIV translates this as "In your anger, do not sin!" The Original Text, however, definitely commands us to "BE Angry!"

The problem here is that there are several Greek words, all of which are translated in most of our Translations with our English word "Anger."

One of these words is *THUMOS.* This is the word that is used down in Verse 31, which is the "anger" that we are to put away from us. This word *THUMOS* meant, to a Greek speaking person, a "boiling up" of our emotions. A "tantrum," in other words. It was used, for example, in Matthew Chapter 2, Verse 16, where we read that:

> "King Herod, when he saw that he had been mocked by the Wise Men, was exceeding 'angry' (our word "*THUMOS*"), and he sent forth and slew all the children that were in Bethlehem, that were under two years old."

This kind of anger we are not to have!

Then they had another word, *PARORGISMOS.* This was used to describe a "smoldering type of anger," a hatred that you sort of carry along with you over a long period of time. This word was used in Ephesians Chapter 6, Verse 4, where we have the command:

> "Fathers, provoke not your children to wrath!"

This type of anger is also prohibited to Christians!

Then we have the word we have here in Verse 26, *ORGIZO*, which is not an emotional anger, but a mental anger; a mental attitude of being angry about something. On in Ephesians 5, Verse 6, it's translated as "The Wrath of God."

Now this kind of anger we are commanded to have.

But here, again, the object of our mental anger is important. If we are "into God's Word," as we say, so that we are looking at life from the Divine Viewpoint, we will be holding a mental anger against the things that displease God!

Jesus is said to have had this kind of anger in Mark 3:5, where it's recorded that,

> "...He had looked around on them with anger, being grieved for the hardness of their hearts."

If you want a list of things to be mentally angry at, then you'll find one in Galatians Chapter 5, in Verses 19 to 21, just before the list of the Fruits of the Spirit. Here certain characteristics of Unbelievers—AND Believers out of Fellowship—are contrasted with the Fruits of the Spirit. Such things as murder and adultery but also including such things as jealousy, envy, creating discord among brethren, and so on.

So, Verse 26 here commands us to, "Be mentally in strong opposition to the things that God hates," and (the verse adds), "Do not yourself sin!"

Now, the punctuation in our English Bibles make it appear that this next phrase in Ephesians 26 is tied to the first command, but it's not. We know this because the anger that this last phrase refers to is a different "anger." It's Anger number two—the slow-burning hatred.

Here the command is:

> "Do not let the sun go down on your slow-burning hatred or bitterness toward another person!"

We ARE to be angry at what God is angry at—not at the individual, because God is concerned for him or her. God, as we say, "loves" him or her! But we are to be angry at what that individual may be practicing!

But if you feel a burning bitterness toward someone or something, put it out of your mind before the sun goes down! God wants us to have "peace within!"

If someone seems to have done you wrong, remember those wonderful words in Romans 12:19, where God commands us to:

> "...avenge not yourselves, but give place unto 'smoldering anger', for "it is written: 'Vengeance is mine; I will repay' saith the Lord!"

A quotation, by the way, from Deuteronomy 32:35. So, God is said here to expect two things from His New People:

1. to "put off" our old ways, where we rely on the things that appeal to our senses; and
2. to "put on" the New Ways, which we do, as the Holy Spirit is able to work in our life! (Eph. 4:22,24)

Lesson 8 Ephesians Chapter 4

A Continuation of "God's Code of Conduct"

In this third of the three major works that the Apostle Paul left for us, we have set out for us an explanation of this new Race of People that God set into place on this earth. People are always wanting to "get to know themselves." Here we are!

In the Letter to the Philippians, we are instructed as to how peace and inner happiness can be ours.

In the Letter to the Colossians, Paul tells us just who this Jesus Christ is, and tells us why He can be the provider to us of these great benefits.

But then there came the need for communicating all of this information to the successive generations, and to accomplish this monumental task, God's Plan called for their putting into place a great Body of Human Beings and giving that great Body a desire to extend themselves beyond themselves and communicate all these wonderful truths to those around them.

The Letter to the Ephesians contains the story of this new race of people—who they are, and how God expects them to operate, so that His Plan can be carried forward to completion.

This is something new that began with the departure of Jesus back to Heaven, from His Visit to this earth.

God, as we know from the Old Testament writings, had commissioned the offspring of Abraham and Isaac and Jacob to be His Representatives.

First, God dealt with them directly, then God appeared directly to Moses and even gave him His Thoughts in written form so that they could be passed along. Later God sent special messengers to them, men that we call Prophets, yet these people that we know of as "Jews" or "Hebrews" never did function as God instructed.

So, when God had reached the end of His Longsuffering, He detached a part of Himself and put that part of Himself into the form of a human being, and sent that Part of Himself to the earth, causing Him to be born into the human race, just as we all are ... except, in this One's case, while He had a human being for a mother, the "conceptor" was God, Himself.

Well, we know that the first order of business for Jesus was to go to the leaders of the Jewish Nation to attempt to get them to recognize Him. This should have been easy for them to do, considering the fact that their own scriptures plainly gave signs they should have recognized.

But the leaders of the Jewish people had become totally given over to following a religion that they, themselves, had created through the years—like people are still doing. For them it was a religion that consisted of following a hopeless set of rules, "dos and don'ts," with little regard for the actual teachings of their scriptures. They were so far away from God's Scriptures that when Jesus began to talk to them, they regarded His sayings as "blasphemous" and they pushed Him aside and began seriously planning to have him put to death.

So, God began to establish a new race of people to be known as "The Body of Christ," the *EKKLESIA,* followers of His Son, that the world soon began to call "Christians."

This new body started with twelve men but soon began to grow and to flesh itself out. This growth is described here in Ephesians 4:16, where it says that,

> "...from Christ, the whole body, being fitted and held together by that which every joint supplies, according to the proper

> working of each individual part, itself grows for the building up of itself, in love (in "concern" for one another)."

Then by what means is that growth going to take place? He gave us the answer to that question back in Verse 11 of Chapter 4 here:

> "He gave some to be Apostles, some to be Prophets, and some to be evangelists, and some to be pastors and teachers."

To what purpose?

> "...for the equipping of the saints (the Believers) for the work of service TO the building up of the Body of Christ—until we all attain to the unity of the Faith, and of the knowledge of the Son of God, to MATURITY!" (Eph. 4:12-13)

Now, because of the presence within each new believer of God's Holy Spirit, and the activation of our own human spirit as a result of our new birth, the Holy Spirit is going to begin to develop a set of character traits in us—traits that are really divine characteristics. "Superhuman" characteristics, really. The "fruits of the Spirit," which are:

> "...love, joy, peace, longsuffering, gentleness, goodness, faith, meekness, self-control..." (Galatians 5:22-23)

And while some non-Believers DO have some of these characteristics, the presence of them ALL is certainly limited. They are not a part of the normal, human characteristics, as we all agree. But the Holy Spirit begins to develop them, and He will accomplish this growth as fast as He is allowed to.

But in addition to what He does, we are expected to voluntarily make some changes in our own life and method of operation, as a result of The Truth that we will be learning as we study the Rule Book of this Great God of the Universe.

Here in Chapter 4, Verse 22 we are commanded to "put off" the old man that is corrupt because he was living according to his or her sensory desires, and (Verse 24),

> "...that we 'put on' the New man, which, in the likeness of God, was established in righteousness and holiness of The Truth."

And then he gives us a list of changes that we need to make in Verse 25. Start by putting away "The Lie." The article "The" is present in the Greek Text; this is contrasted with "The Truth" back in Verse 21— "The Truth" of Christ. "The Lie" is Satan's teachings of the superiority of man, the concept that "you can do whatever you set your sights on," etc., etc.

So, we get that out of our thinking; that's first. Then Verse 25 continues with,

> "...we are to speak truth to our neighbors."

> Then (Verse 26): "We are to be mentally angry at the things that God hates, yet we are to handle this anger in God's Way—with longsuffering, and letting God extract the revenge. Further, when we do find ourselves in a state of temper at someone, we are to clear out that hatred before the sun goes down."

> Verse 27: "We are not to allow Satan to influence our thinking nor our actions;"

> Verse 28: "We are to stop stealing, instead, we are to make our living by legitimate means."

It's interesting that he gives us another reason here why we "work" that's stated here at the end of Verse 28, "…so that we may have to give to him that has a need!"

That's not what people normally think of as to why we work, is it! Then the list continues in Verse 29 (and I'll give you a literal translation of this Greek phrase):

> "Let no rotten, not-fit-to-be-taken-in word proceed out of your mouth, but that which is intrinsically 'good', to the use of 'edifying'—or 'building up.'"

The word "unwholesome" that the new versions use there at the first of the verse is not strong enough. Every other place in the New Testament this word is used, it is used to describe fruit that has turned rotten or fruit that would make you sick if you ate it, as opposed to fruit that is beneficial to eat.

Instead, Paul qualifies what should come out of your mouth as always being words that will build up the listener! Words, that, as it states it here at the end of Verse 29,

> "...that will minister Grace ("beneficial help for their need") to those that hear what you have to say!"

Here is one of the greatest benefits that one human being can provide to another human being, and that is "words that provide beneficial help in time of their need."

Here in this passage, the Holy Spirit, through Paul, is asking that we give some thought to our words and our actions, now that we have become Christ's Ambassadors—that we no longer just do "as we darn well please," as we say, or that we just allow the motor of our mouth to start running, with no thought given to what comes out.

Now, the purpose of everything that we do and say is defined here for us in this Chapter 4 of Ephesians—it's stated first in Verse 11, where we have explained to us just why there are many gifts given to the various members of this "Body of Christ." It's,

> "…for the bringing to maturity of the Believers, for the work of the ministry, for the building up of the Body of Christ, until we all come in the unity of the faith, and in the knowledge of the Son of God, to a mature person."

And he states it again here in Verse 29:

> "…that our words be that which is intrinsically 'good', to the building up of Believers, and that will minister Grace—'beneficial help for their need'—to those that hear what you have to say!"

I'll admit that this admonition to control our mouth may make conversation a little more difficult, but the general idea has real merit, don't you think? Limit what comes out of your mouth to that which will build up the person you're talking to.

Now this process, if you follow it, is going to cause you to focus your attention onto the person you're talking to. And that's not all bad. This means that you are going to take your attention off yourself and focus it on the other person. This is also a pretty good idea, isn't it.

So now, what you are going to create words for is not about what YOU have been doing but on what the other person has been doing or would like to be doing.

Have you ever gone into a situation where you know you are going to have to carry on a conversation with someone and you dread it, and you get all nervous because you just know you're not going to know what to say?

Well, all you have to do is ask that person an intelligent question about himself or herself, and if it is the least bit well thought out, your question will have started the conversation and you can keep it going all afternoon with a few more questions, and that person will come away thinking you're a great conversationalist.

But, best of all—and here's the point of Paul's message here—you just may have an opportunity to say something to that person that will edify him or her. That will build him or her up. That will give a word that will help, in time of need!

Now, I'd like to take us a few pages back in our Bibles to Second Corinthians—to Chapter 1:3. Here is a wonderful passage, and yet it's one that is not fully appreciated, because of a translation matter.

When Paul wrote this letter to the members of the Assembly there in the city of Corinth that he had spent much time with he had just recovered from a serious illness; in fact, at one point, he thought he was going to die. He tells them about it briefly in Verses 8 through 10 here in Chapter 1.

But his letter begins here, in Verse 3, by blessing God, and he refers to God, our Father, as being:

> "...the Father of Mercies (of Compassion) and the God of all Comfort."

And then he tells HOW this compassionate Father operates and the purpose behind the way our Father operates. Notice Verse 4:

> "He comforts us in all our trials, so that we may be able to comfort them who are in any trouble, by this same comfort—the comfort wherewith we ourselves are comforted of God."

Now we think back to what we saw, a minute ago, as being God's Desire for our conversation that we read in Ephesians 4:29, which is that what we say,

> *"...will minister beneficial help for the need of those we are talking to..."*

And what is it that helped us—that comforted us? It was "comfort from God!" What "comforted" us wasn't little inanities, like when people say, "It's going to be all right." Or like I used to say to my girls, when they'd fall down and skin a knee, "*That's all right, dear—it'll feel better when it quits hurting!*"

That may have broken the tension, but I'm sure it didn't help a lot.

That reminds me of the story about the little boy who fell down and hurt himself and his mother picked him up and said, "Oh! Upsi-daisy!"

And the little boy stood up and looked at his mother and said, "Upsi-daisy—heck! I'm hurt!"

The inanities that we so often hand out as "words of comfort" so often don't comfort a great deal. But what WILL help are words from someone who has been through what this person is going through, and who has received help from our Heavenly Father.

> "Who comforts us in all our tribulation, so that we may be able to comfort them who are in any trouble, by the comfort wherewith we ourselves are comforted of God" (2 Cor. 1:4).

Our English word "comfort" is taken from two Latin words, *CUM FORTES,* which means "with power." So, even in our English language, the word "comfort" didn't originally mean a pat on the head or a word of sympathy, it meant bringing power into the situation.

If you are stranded in a small boat just outside the bar at Astoria, with your motor gone dead, then the roar of a Coast Guard boat pulling up alongside IS, certainly, a source of "comfort." But what really provides the "comfort" is the power that has arrived to get you out of your predicament.

If you're the victim of a gunshot wound, the help is the surgery that is necessary to remove the bullet, as painful as the surgery might be. If you're floating around in a life jacket, it's the physical act of pulling you out of the water that is the "comfort." If you're arrested for something you didn't do and you need help to establish your innocence, the "comfort" is going to be in the form of a wise attorney—an "advocate."

And for a person who has caused his life to get all screwed up, he needs good, strong advice, which can well include the calling in of help outside himself—namely our Lord Jesus Christ! He is our advocate!

Now, the Greek word translated "comfort" here, only in a different form, of course, *PARAKLETOS*, is the word that Jesus used to describe the Holy Spirit whom, He said, was "just like Him," and whom He would send in His Name to teach us and to guide us through this life. To bring Power ("comfort") to us and then deliver us safe and sound into the Next Life.

So, the action that the Holy Spirit had in mind when He had Paul write these words in Second Corinthians Chapter 1, was not often-inane words of sympathy, but real, genuine HELP, whether it be financial help, or physical labor, or words of strong advice and counsel, which could include a pointing of that person to the Real *PARAKLETOS*, the Messiah of Israel, our Lord Jesus Christ.

So, thinking back to our verse here in Ephesians 4:29, the words that God would like to see proceeding out of our mouths are words that:

> "...build up our fellow Believers, and that will minister beneficial help for their need ('Grace')—to those who hear what you have to say!"

And they will be words of God's Power and they will be given WITH God's Power because you will be looking to Him for the words you give out.

Now, Verse 30 of Ephesians Chapter 4:

> "And grieve not the Holy Spirit of God (*LUPEO*—"cause Him pain") by whom you were sealed (aorist tense 'once and for all'), unto the Day of Redemption."

We "grieve" the Holy Spirit when we allow sin to remain in our life unconfessed. This "causes Him pain." Sin in our life breaks our fellowship with the Father and stops the work of the Holy Spirit within us, which, of course, deprives us of His Guidance, His protective care, and our access to our Heavenly Father in prayer.

The application of First John 1:9, of course, restores the fellowship, and puts the Holy Spirit back in business.

Then, Verse 30 reminds us also of another one of the functions of The Holy Spirit on our behalf—He "sealed" us unto the Day of Redemption!

Seals were used in Paul's day to identify or mark out a piece of personal property. The Holy Spirit marks us out as belonging to the Heavenly Father.

A seal was also used to cover over or protect a perishable item, and that, too, is a picture of the Believer. The Holy Spirit covers us over—He preserves us through all the erosive and destructive elements that we have to pass through here on this earth, until the day that we are finally called home to Him!

Then, the conduct list is continued in Verse 31, and I call your attention to the fact that this verb here is in the passive voice; the NIV has the verse telling *you* to "do it." For YOU to put away all bitterness and wrath and anger and noisy controversy (their word for "yelling") but God knows you and I can't do this by ourselves!

The Greek, on the other hand, says, "Let this be done to you." By whom? By the Holy Spirit, of course! And the Holy Spirit CAN do this. He will get rid of these things out of your mind if you look to Him for help and give Him a chance!

Then here IS a command to us to do something that we can, consciously, do: "And be kind one to another" (Eph. 4:32).

As Dr. Robertson translates it, literally, "Keep on becoming kind one to another, tenderhearted, forgiving one another, as God, for Christ's sake, forgave you." (Aorist tense—a past, completed action!)

It's interesting that all these actions that are given to us here—these "ways of life" that He is instructing us to make a part of our pattern of life—they all are habits that He knows we can form and that we will try to make them a part of our way of life if we really trust ourselves to Him.

Now, those qualities that are called "the fruit of the Spirit" that we spoke of a while ago? They are not so easy to come by:

> "Concern (love), Joy (inner happiness), Peace (inner quietness), Longsuffering, Gentleness, Goodness, Faith, True Humility, Self-control." (Galatians 5:22-23)

So, it's interesting that God assigned The Holy Spirit to generate these qualities in us and they will be developed over a period of time. But you and I do have the ability to add these other qualities with the help of the Holy Spirit!

We can train ourselves to be kind instead of abrasive. We can school ourselves to be tender-hearted, instead of hard-hearted; to be forgiving, rather than unforgiving; to be constructive in our speech, rather than sarcastic.

And the thing that will help most in efforts to accomplish this in ourselves is to force ourselves to stop once in a while and to think of the rotten and hurtful things that we have done in our life, and then to realize that God's Son, through His Suffering, actually has wiped them all out of even God's sight!

King David, who knew about things like this, had this to say to us:

> "God has not dealt with us according to our sins, nor rewarded us according to our iniquities;

For as the heaven is high above the earth, so great is His mercy toward them that fear Him.

As far as the east is from the west, so far has He removed our transgressions from us." (Psalm 103:10-12)

Here's how, through Jesus, God's Son, and what He did when He was here on Earth—you and I can have peace and inner happiness right now—no matter what is going on around us!

Lesson 9 Ephesians Chapter 5

More About "God's Code of Conduct"

We are looking, here, at what has been called "Paul's Masterpiece"; the height of his wonderful exposition of God's Grace that He has extended to His Creations.

We remember the words that Jesus spoke there in that last meeting with His Disciples, just before His Crucifixion—they're recorded for us in John 16, where He said,

> "I have yet many things to say to you, but you cannot handle them now. However, when He, the Spirit of Truth is come, He will guide you into all Truth; for He shall not speak of Himself, but whatever He shall hear, that shall He speak, and He will show you things to come.
>
> He shall glorify Me; for He shall receive of mine, and shall show it unto you." (John 16:12-14)

And, as is God's Way, He has His Holy Spirit do His work through people and here is THAT part of the Work being accomplished through the Apostle Paul!

God has set things up for the members of this new company of people that the Bible calls "The Body of Christ," all those who have, through Time, put their lives into the Hands of God's Special Son, Jesus Christ. God has set things up for us, just like He set things up for the people of Israel. He gave them special treatment. He showed them how He could and would take care of them and their needs and He gave them great assurances of future care.

All He asked back from them was that they would acknowledge Him in their lives by following a few simple directives. Directives that were not difficult, nor were they onerous—they were sensible and practical. However, they WERE different from what people around them would be doing from time to time.

However, God even went on to demonstrate to them that those things that the people around them did (and seemed to have "fun" doing) ultimately brought about their DIS-comfort and, in many cases, their painful death. So, their course of action should have been perfectly clear.

But the Jews chose to go the way "those people around them" went, rather than God's Way, and so God, naturally, was forced to "set them aside" and put in place others to serve as His Representatives here on Earth.

And so, He created this "Body of Christ." And to us He has given great promises. And He has shown to us His power and His compassion and His ability to care for us. He has also carefully preserved for us this Book containing His Promises and the outline of His great Plan for Humanity.

And—again, as He did for Israel, He has also written out the simple list of His Instructions to us; how He knows we should operate in this "life" for our best life and to bring this "best life" to those around us.

I have placed my "paraphrase" of His List in the very front of this little book, since it's what this "little book" is all about. It's a relatively short list and its instructions are "do-able." Further, there is not an "unpleasant" thing among the items on the list. However, these things, again, are a little different from the way the majority of the people around us choose to operate.

Yet the rewards for adhering to His List are great, and the consequences of disregarding His List are not very pleasant, to say the least.

Actually, these Instructions deserve a better presentation than simply being written out on a piece of paper, as I have done it here. Look what has been done to the Ten Commandments through the years. Yet here is an equally important Statement from God! Truly, this Statement should also be embellished with beautiful letterings and written on fancy paper, carved in stone, or written on great murals! In the very least, it should be written on the wall of every child's room to be looked at daily for the rest of his or her life—but this is the best that I can do at this point.

We have covered rather carefully the first segment of these instructions given in Chapter 4. And the rest of them that are covered here in Chapters 5 and 6 we have already covered pretty well as we have gone through the Letters to the Philippians and to the Colossians.

There are some points here that I do want to call your attention to, however, so that's what I'm about to do now before we take a look at the great Presentation of the "Armor of God" at the end of Chapter 6, which is where God explains the amazing, supernatural equipment that He has made available to us.

The first is what's packed into the first two verses of Ephesians Chapter 5. The Holy Spirit has just commanded us, His People, with these words, there at the end of Chapter 4:

> "Keep on becoming kind to one another, tenderhearted, forgiving one another, as God, for Christ's sake, forgave us."

And we talked about the fact that the character traits he's asking us to cultivate here CAN be cultivated! A person doesn't HAVE to be abrasive, or unkind, or un-forgiving. God EXPECTS His People to do differently, and He will reward us wonderfully if and as we comply with His wishes!

The most direct way to start this process within us is to meditate, once in a while, on just what it was that God did arrange and what His Son went through for us!

It can be difficult to generate "real love"—that deep, sincere, honest concern for someone or someone's that are outside our immediate family. That mental attitude is not a "natural" thing; that's why it's labeled "a fruit of the Spirit." But people CAN train themselves to be kind and to be forgiving as they take time to think that someone was that way with them!

Then another thing: it's interesting that God has told us here that He arranged this forgiveness for us_for Christ's sake! Because God has this Love for His Son and He knows that it will make His Son happy if He takes care of those that His Son loves! This is too deep to try to reason out, but it's wonderful that you and I are the beneficiaries of it all!

So, Chapter 5 of Ephesians begins with "Therefore":

> "Therefore, in view of that amazing Truth, we are to be becoming Imitators of God, just as would loving children imitate their loving parents!"

This word that is translated "followers" in the King James was their word for someone who imitates you. The Greek word is *MIMETES.* We get our word "mimic" from this, and it meant to them just that—a person who mimics you, who copies your actions, who does as you do. God is asking us to work at copying Him as a child would, which we are!

Some things make a lasting impression on us. One day a bunch of our family met at a large, busy restaurant. Most of the family were already seated at this large table when my wife and I walked in.

It was Winter and I remember that I took off my coat, and since I couldn't see a place to hang it, I folded it up casually and (I thought) inconspicuously gave it a toss on to the floor, into an out-of-the-way corner. Then I turned and sat down.

Well, my grandson who was about five years old at the time got up from his chair and very seriously took his jacket that was neatly hanging on the back, folded it up just as I had done to mine and walked clear around the table in order to toss his coat over in the corner on top of mine! And then he very seriously went back to his chair and sat down.

If I hadn't fully realized it before, I certainly did then: Somebody is watching everything we do!

God is here, saying to us: I want you to work at imitating Me, just as your children imitate you!

And how do we do that? What is He saying to us? He gives us the answer right here, "Walk in love!"

That's what the English says but that doesn't really convey what the Greek text says. Their word translated as "walk" covered everything that has to do with our "moving through our daily life," our "conduct," and "how we handle ourselves."

Then the little preposition *EN* meant more to them than just "in." It meant "surrounded by" something; or an integral part of something; "all wrapped up in something." Like the kids say, today, "I'm really into that!"

And what is it we're surrounded by? It's the concern that Jesus Christ, our Creator, has for His Children, the members of His "Body."

If my thumb gets bruised, that affects me! It's an important part of me; I'm really concerned about it! So is Jesus concerned about ALL the members of HIS Body!

And as we move through our day with a consciousness of Christ's deep, personal interest in us and in what happens to us moment by moment, this attitude of "kindness," "tender-heartedness" and "forgiving" is going to grow and, as it grows, the Lord is going to be happier and happier with us!

Now, something else here in this second verse; we're commanded to "walk in love," as God and Christ do. Then, we're also told that He gave Himself for us as an "offering and a sacrifice to God." This, he says, will be a "sweet smelling savor," a "fragrant aroma" to God. Something that will please Him greatly.

Now let's think about "sacrifice" for a moment. You and I and most people who have deliberately become "Christians" really, sincerely, want to please God.

So, then, the problem that immediately confronts us is just what IS it that we're expected to do? What does He expect of us? Just what is it that pleases Him, and just what is it that DIS-pleases Him?

Well, the answers should be easy to come by. This Bible is His Book, and the answers, logically, can be expected to be in it. And they are.

The majority of Christians are not well taught. They have taken that first step of Faith—they have placed their lives in Christ's care, and they have pledged allegiance to Him, so they are, truly, IN the Kingdom of God. But then, for most of them, confusion takes over.

They are victims of what Paul was talking to his protégé Timothy about. There in Second Timothy, Chapter 2, where he points out that there are many teachers around who do not accurately present God's Truths, who spend their time talking about the things of the world and that are full of "empty chatter," with the result, as Paul states it, that ungodliness increases rather than decreases.

So, when a new, conscientious Christian comes to a passage like this in Chapter 5, Verses 1 and 2, and he sees the command to "walk in love" and he hears some teacher tell him that we are to "love everybody," then he or she thinks to himself, "No way can I do that!"

Or he sees that we are to offer ourselves, like Christ did, as a "sacrifice" to God, and he hears some teacher tell him that "sacrifice" is a part of the Christian life and it begins with "sacrificial giving to our church." When he hears and sees this, he mentally backs away.

And now, to quite an extent, this New Christian is stranded. And Satan is happy. And Christianity is of very little force in our world, as far as the great Mass of Humanity is concerned.

Didn't God anticipate all of this? Of course He did. But God's purpose for Christianity is not—and never was—to have it run the world system or to have Christians make this earth a perfect place in which to live.

This is what some elements within the Christian movement are trying to use it for—as a great "problem solver" for the ailments of human society.

Instead, one day, after the Nations of the earth have had a chance to show what they can do, and will have failed miserably, then Jesus will return to the earth, and He will set up a perfect economy.

But, in the meantime, Christianity, as an entity under the guidance of God's Holy Spirit, will have been quietly at the business of helping those people who have seen The Truth to make it through this "boot camp" that we call "life" and to prepare them for the wonderful Next Life, after this short trip is over.

We can see that there is a great similarity between God's Operation with the Jews and God's Operation with this "Body of Christ"; God gave the Jews a Law, but it was so high in principle that no Jew could live up to all its expectations.

God knew, of course, that this would be the case, and so He gave them a system of Offerings that included an acknowledgement of their known daily shortcomings. And other Offerings that would be public acknowledgments of their faith and trust in their Jehovah.

And, along with that, He asked only that they Trust Him, look to Him for guidance, and acknowledge Him with their lives.

As it was with Abraham, we're told that:

> "Abraham trusted God, and it was counted to him for Righteousness." (Gen. 15:6)

And so it was with every Jew, who trusted himself to God's care.

And now with this New Order, God has set out for us His Commandments, one of which is, as Jesus stated it in John 15:12:

> "This is my commandment, that you love one another, as I have loved you."

But, again, God knew that we, no matter how hard we might try, cannot "love everybody as Jesus loves us."

However, God provided something for us beyond that which He provided for Israel; He put within us His Holy Spirit, who will generate within us, as we give Him the opportunity, He will produce this "love" in us so that we CAN obey His Commandment!

And, along with this "love" He will generate other wonderful qualities that we call "The Fruits of the Spirit"; qualities that will bring Inner Happiness and Inner Joy to us, as we go along. Things like peace, longsuffering, gentleness, goodness, faith, humility, and self-control. And, along with all of that, the Holy Spirit is here to guide us into ALL Truth! And so, we realize that the offering and sacrifice that Jesus made to God was not something that deprived Him of anything—it was truly an "offering," patterned after the Levitical Offerings and something He gladly did!

So, our goal in this life should not be, as many people say, "to leave this earth a better place than we found it"; instead, our goal should be to please God and honor Him by our trust in Him and by our willingness to listen to His leadings and to follow His Teachings in spite of the fact that they differ markedly from what is going on around us in the world system He has asked us to live in for a while.

And here is the list of what He wants us to follow! And following will bring Him great joy and will bring us great rewards.

All right. Now, Paul continues his statement of how God says we should be conducting ourselves, and next, starting in Verse 3, he talks about sexual conduct and sexual MISconduct.

Then in Verse 5, as he talks about sexual conduct, he broadens it to include sensual conduct, which is what "covetousness" is. It's the process of letting our strong desires for "things" get our lives out of whack. "Things" that appeal to our senses and sensual pleasures.

And you'll notice that Paul always connects covetousness with "idolatry." It was a part of the way of life of the Romans, and it is a part of the way of life today. People have to have "things"; families have to have "things." That's one of the reasons why in so many families both parents feel they have to work—so they can have "things." Things that, in our younger days were never even heard of.

And the problem is that in many families those "things" come first—ahead of His Considerations. Which, from God's standpoint, is what "Idolatry" is.

The point of all of this is we are not to let our senses—our "animal instincts"—rule our lives.

In the animal world, if an animal sees something he wants, he goes after it. It may be with cunning, or it may be directly and vigorously, but at that moment, it occupies his entire attention, even to death! God expects us to NOT live like animals! As Verse 17 sums it up:

> "Wherefore, do not be UN-wise, but be understanding of what the Will of the Lord is!"

Well, the List continues, which you can read through again when you are so inclined. But let's stop at Verse 18, which reads:

> "And do not be drunk with wine, wherein is excess; but be filled with the Spirit!"

Now, you may have puzzled over why the Holy Spirit makes these contrasting commands:

> "Be not drunk with wine—instead
> Be filled with the Holy Spirit!"

I'm sure you'll agree that people—all people—have problems in living here on Earth. It was true then, it's true today.

- Problems of money
- Economic problems—making a living

- Problems of Health
- Problems with your neighbors, your children
- If you're a supervisor-type, you have problems with those under you
- If you're an employee-type, you have problems with your supervisor, or with those working alongside you
- If you are retired and have only gardening to do, you have problems with the weeds
- Or if your husband is retired, you have problems keeping him out from under your feet

Problems. Problems. Problems. Everything is filled with problems! So, what do people do? How do they cope? Well, with some it is, "I just won't think about it!" The psychologists call that "Denial," and for some, it works.

Others adjust to pressure by blowing off steam by going into a rage or kicking things.

But the most common adjustment to life's problems is through what we call "escapisms" like getting lost in Television, the Newspaper, a movie, or golf, or some more active sport, or fishing, etc.

Whatever, as we say, that "gets your mind off your problems" for a little while.

This pattern of life existed in Paul's day and it has been a forever situation. "Escapisms."

Now "sensual escapisms" are what Paul has been talking about in the first part of Chapter 5 here, and now he targets the then most prevalent "physical escapism," and what was then the most available: alcoholic beverages. And he's saying, "Don't adjust to life this way!"

We know that the things we try in our own strength don't work. Human methods of meeting our problems don't work. The problem that we try to push aside or run away from is still there.

What everyone needs is Help from outside ourselves—supernatural help. Help from someone who can actually do something about our problem! So, "Be filled ('controlled') with the Spirit!"

Adjust to life God's Way!

So, how do we arrange our life so that we are controlled by God's Holy Spirit? Simply by making it possible for God's Holy Spirit, who IS in us, to be able to operate.

He cannot operate in the presence of sin, so we clear the way by acknowledging our sin to God, in accordance with First John 1:9, and then the Holy Spirit is again able to help. A tremendous blessing you and I have available to us!

So, here we have seen another segment of God's Way for a Christian to live: trusting Him, looking to Him, obeying Him, and keeping His Holy Spirit—who is already IN us—keeping Him operating in our life!

Lesson 10 Ephesians Chapter 6

Our Defense Against Satan—God's Armor

We have been looking at God's List of Instructions for our Life here on this earth, which, if followed, will bring Inner Happiness into our life. Lists "people" have developed don't do it for the long run; God's List will!

Now I know that after reading over God's List, it is only natural that we wonder how we can ever fit the bill in the face of all the pressures that are arrayed against us—pressures from the whole world that operates contrary to our ways, such as:

- pressures from our "flesh," which we know can only stand so much pressure and then it caves in; and
- pressures from Satan himself, who we know very well is out there, quick to work against us when he sees an opportunity or a weakness.

So, how can we cope? We're told right here, starting in Chapter 6, Verse 10:

"Finally ('in summation') my Brethren, be strengthened in the Lord and in the might of His Strength."

That's how the Greek has it: "Be strengthened." "Receive strength from Him!" It's not "Be strong!" it's "Be strengthened!" It doesn't do a lot of good to tell a person who has no strength to "be strong." The old adage that "God helps them who help themselves" is not taught in the Bible!

God, on the other hand, GIVES strength to His People to do what we are asked by Him to do and to live through! Then he continues WITH a command that we can obey:

> "Put on the whole armor of God, so that we may be able to stand against the wiles of The Devil. For we wrestle not against flesh and blood, but against principalities, against powers, against the rulers of the darkness of this world, against spiritual wickedness in high places" (Eph. 6:11-12)

The Bible tells us that we have three enemies: the world, the flesh, and Satan, and Paul clearly regards Satan as our worst enemy. We have our faith to give us what it takes to overcome the man-made theories and the pressures that the world system is continually coming up with, which, by the way, will get us into trouble if we follow them, as we know.

And we can handle "the flesh." You and I have the power to RUN AWAY from the temptations of the flesh, which, by the way, includes damaging our body (God's Holy Temple) by putting the wrong things INTO our body. In other words, I firmly believe the old saying that "We are what we eat!"

But the attacks and the connivings of Satan and his followers are insidious and harder to cope with! You and I have no control over these forces! So, God has given us special help in this area; He calls it His Armor! Armor to defend ourselves against Satan!

And He commands us to put it on! Also, he used the aorist tense form here in this command, which says, "Once and for all, put it on!"

In other words, we should put God's Armor on as soon as we are aware that such a thing exists and then never take it off! It's not that we are going to be constantly under attack from Satan and his friends—but the point is that we never know WHEN his attacks will come so we need always to be ready.

Paul used lots of illustrations in his messages and, since he was chained to a Roman soldier all the time that he was writing these letters, he became very aware of the dress of the Roman soldier. And, of course, the Roman soldier, dressed in his complete equipment, was also a very familiar sight to the people of that day. The soldiers were everywhere!

Further, as Paul thought about their standard equipment, he realized how well thought out it was! So, it is a great illustration of the needs of a Christian and of God's supplying of those needs!

The First part of God's equipment for us is in Verse 14:

"...having your loins girded about with Truth..."

Around the soldier's tunic was a belt. It was wide, made of leather. Everything sort of depended on this belt. It served as a holder for his arrows if he was a bowsman, or a hanger for his sword. It held his clothing tight and out of his way. Even his breastplate was secured to it. Also, any campaign ribbons or decorations he had earned were fastened to it. It was the basic piece of a soldier's equipment.

And for the Believer, the basic piece of equipment is "Truth!"

The word "truth" is an unusual word and it actually does defy definition. "Truth" means different things to different people and the Greeks finally came to express "Truth" only in a negative way. They saw it as a situation where nothing was hidden. Everything is "out in the open," as we say.

Their word for "truth" is *A-LATHEIA,* which meant literally, "no hiding," "nothing hidden," "nothing concealed." So, we might put this thought into English and say that "Truth is the whole, honest story."

Now, you would think that a person would want to build his or her life on "the whole, honest story" but all around us are people not bothering to look and see if what they are holding to IS the "whole, honest story."

Instead, they're believing what they want to believe. They are trusting their future irresponsibly to things and to concepts that they have, in most cases, given no thought to!

So then, the question is: "Where do we find the whole, honest story?" Especially since there are so many voices claiming to be "telling you the truth." Saying, in different ways, "Just trust me."

Where can we find the standard? Well, we can find it in the statements of the One who created our whole Universe System; the One who established it and who keeps it running!

The Apostle John tells us about this during one of Jesus' early "teaching sessions." It's in John Chapter 8 and it's a familiar passage. Here, the wonders of this New Life—this Christianity—were first being explained to the world. I'll read a little of this to you. It starts in Verse 30 of John Chapter 8,

> "As He spoke these words, many believed on Him."

In other words, many realized that He was their long-awaited Messiah, so they accepted what He was saying as being "truth," and as a result, they committed themselves to Him! Then, in Verse 31:

> "Then Jesus said to those Jews who trusted themselves to Him: 'If you continue in My Word, then are you My disciples; and you shall know the Truth, and The Truth shall make you free!'"

There will no longer be things that are "hidden." Now all will be open!

So, then, we realize that "The Truth"—the "Absolute"—with nothing hidden comes from the source of Jesus Christ, and we are told here that this truth will be imparted to those trusting Him, who have committed themselves to Him, and this truth will be revealed to these trustors IF and AS they continue in His Word. That's what it says.

Then later on in His ministry, Jesus added this information from John 16, starting in Verse 12. There He said:

> "I have yet many things to say to you, but you cannot absorb them now, however, when He, the Spirit of Truth has come, He will guide you into all Truth! He shall receive of Me, and shall show it to you!"

So those whose trust is in Christ have access to the Source of Truth and it will be given to us IF and AS we live our life within the confines of His Word! And here, now, He is telling us that we HAVE that Truth, so we are to STAND on that Truth! We don't question it—we STAND on it!

It struck me that one of the most important concepts in what we can call "Christian living" is contained in Verse 13 of Ephesians 6 that begins this presentation of our Armor-plate. Notice Verse 13 again:

> "Wherefore take unto you the whole armor of God, so that you may be able to withstand in the day that evil hits and having done all **to stand**!"

Every now and then we all come to a place where, as we say, "we are at our wits end." We've done everything that we know to do, and yet the problem we're facing is still not resolved.

Here is God's Word for us at that point: "My child, having done all—now stand!"

It's what God had impressed on Moses, so that Moses could tell his people back at the beginning of their Exodus back into Palestine and when the Egyptian Army was after them. At one point, all seemed to be lost! Then we read these words from Exodus 14:13:

> "Moses said to the people: 'Fear not, stand still, and see the deliverance of the Lord, which He will show to you today!"

That was THEIR time, having done everything THEY could do to "stand, and watch the deliverance of the Lord!" And he DID deliver them. And He has delivered His People time after time. His Truth IS established. And our knowledge of this AS Truth, will enable us to Stand!

Then, there is added the "breastplate of Righteousness…"

Working from the Basis of Truth—God's Word—we will be doing the "right" things; the things that God's Word identifies as being "right."

Paul sees our "right actions" as being a "breastplate"; a protector from attack! If we DO right, neither Satan nor his emissaries can point the finger at us.

In the world all around us these days, we are constantly seeing careers being wiped out because it is discovered that some person has not always "done right." Now WE know God's Word, so we know what is "really right!"

Then, the next piece of equipment in Verse 15 states we must be properly shod! The verse translates as, *"…having shod your feet…"*

When you try to walk outside in your bare feet, you quickly realize how important a proper foot covering is! If your feet aren't properly covered, your ability to accomplish anything is greatly impaired! Our feet are very tender and our whole mobility depends on our ability to properly walk! So, we must have properly shod ourselves, if we are going to get done what God has directed us to do.

And what is it that "prepares" us? He tells us here that it's a grasp, as Paul expresses it here. It's a grasp of "The Gospel," which Paul calls "The Gospel of Peace!"

Why does he call it "The Gospel of Peace"? Well, that's what it is! It puts us in a place of "Peace with God," which, in turn, allows us to have peace within ourselves because we now know that we do have peace with God.

Further, we also know that He is busy working things for our good, so that allows us to have peace.

And with a knowledge of The Gospel, we ARE prepared to face anything. AND, as He has commanded us, "…we are prepared to give an answer to anyone who asks us, the reason for the hope that is in us!" (1 Peter 3:15).

Now, are you sure you KNOW what the Gospel message is? I know we think we do, but do we have all its points clearly in mind?

The Gospel Message is very clearly stated for us in First Corinthians 15. Here is a passage that you ought to read and re-read until you know it by heart.

Let me review the main points. They start in Verse 3 of First Corinthians 15:

> *"...how that Christ died for our sins according to the Scriptures;*
>
> *...that He was buried;*
>
> *...that He rose again the third day, according to the Scriptures;*
>
> *...that He was seen by Peter, then by the Twelve;*
>
> *...after that He was seen by about 500 Brethren all at one time, of whom the greater part are alive now but some have passed on;*
>
> *...after that, He was seen by James, then by all of the Apostles; and*
>
> *...last of all, He was seen by me also, as one born out of due time..."*

Then, he continues in Verse 20:

> "...But now is Christ risen from the dead, and become the firstfruits of them that slept. For since through man came Death, by Man came also the resurrection from the dead. For as in Adam all die, even so in Christ shall all be made alive.
>
> But every man in his own order: Christ, the firstfruits; afterward they that are Christ's at His coming.

> Then comes the end, when He shall have delivered up the Kingdom to God the Father, when He shall have put down all rule and all authority and power.
>
> For He must reign, until He has put all enemies under His feet. The last enemy that shall be destroyed is Death." (1 Cor. 15;20-26)

Then, Verse 28:

> "And when all things shall be subdued unto Him, then shall the Son also Himself be subject unto Him that put all things under Him, SO THAT God may be all in all."

There's the whole story of our faith! From beginning to end, with all its majesty! If we have this firmly in our mind, we are prepared for our own peace and to bring it to anyone that God sets up for us!

Now, the Armor continues in Ephesians 6:16:

> "In addition to all this, taking the Shield of Faith, with which you shall be able to quench all the fiery darts of the wicked."

The world system and its inhabitants are forever shooting things at us that create doubts; doubts that The Bible really IS God's Word; doubts that God does really care for us Believers, as His Word promises that He does, and that we really, underneath it all, really KNOW that He does. And God has provided for us this great Shield.

The Roman Army made use of several types of shields. There was the little round one that was fastened onto the arms of the soldiers who were apt to be involved in hand-to-hand combat.

But there was also the larger shield he speaks of here as *THUREOS*, which translates as "Door shield." It was thirty inches wide and four feet high. The Roman Army developed this super-weapon: the men in the front lines stood side-by-side against their enemy with these door shields overlapping, so it presented a solid wall of iron. If everything went according to plan, the enemy couldn't break through, and then the Javelin throwers right behind this front wall could throw their javelins and cut the enemy down! Very effective! And certainly, effective against the arrows that had been dipped in pitch, then set on fire, and shot at them!

Our "door shield" is our faith! And remember, God's Holy Spirit provides a trusting Believer with faith! It is a "fruit of the Spirit," and He causes it to grow in us as He has the opportunity to work in our life! I recall the words of the old song:

"Faith is the Victory, that overcomes the World!"

And we are to TAKE that shield of faith! When a doubt arises, fall back onto your faith! Our faith is our protector and it is right to fall back on it because our faith is well founded. It is based on "The Truth!"

By the way, if you want a wonderful presentation of just how faith works, take a careful look at Psalm 73.

Alright, now for our "head protector," we look to Verse 17:

"And take the helmet of Salvation."

Our head is where our brain is, the part of us that governs our life. Or, I should say, it's the part that SHOULD govern our life. And our thought processes should be continually shielded by our knowledge of all that our salvation—our "deliverance" provides.

And not only our Future Life but it includes "deliverance" now, today. That knowledge, as we apply it, as we keep it forever in front of our thinking, protects our brain!

Now what's left here are two things, "The Sword of the Spirit, which is the word of God," and in Verse 18, "Praying, and Watching!"

The Sword is both a defensive weapon and an offensive weapon. When you are attacked by a person with a sword, you need a sword to defend yourself; to "parry the thrusts," as they say.

And that is the context we're in here—the defense against Satanic attacks. Jesus used The Holy Scriptures this way when Satan was testing Him there in the wilderness area, back in the beginning of His Ministry in Luke 4.

Your and my defense against Satan is God's Word, since it's God's Word that tells us all about Satan and that makes it clear to us that Satan's ways lead to a person's Eternal Death. Or, if that person is a Believer, then, at least, Satan's ways lead to misery here on this earth!

I have to give you a word of caution on this passage. There are those people who take the "sword" concept out of context here and want to make it a weapon of "attack." So, they assume this means that God wants us to throw a verse of scripture at everybody we come in contact with.

The Rules of Personal Evangelism for this Age that you and I live in still govern:

1. Evangelism is the responsibility, first of all, of the Holy Spirit. That's made clear in John 16:8.
2. Believers in this Age are identified as Ambassadors for Christ—Representatives, not Warriors—and we are to be working under the orders that the Holy Spirit gives us (2 Corinthians 5), so, we listen for those orders and we don't move out without them!

The instructions regarding Personal Evangelism for us all are contained in First Peter 3:15, which, you recall, is that "…we are to be ready to give an answer to anyone who asks us about the Hope that is in us." And that calls for preparation as well as readiness!

Now, finally, as per Verse 18: "Praying," "continually praying," and "continually watching." "Praying" we understand. "Watching" was a military term for "always on guard" or "always alert."

So, we are to be:

- Watching for His Leadings
- Alert for the attacks from our enemies

And we know that:

- Our faith will handle the attacks from the things of the world;
- We run from the temptations of the Flesh; and
- The Armor that God has provided for us—including His Word—will protect us from Satan and his attacks!

The Result: We'll be delivered Home, safe and sound!

Author's Bio

Edgar "Ed" DeWitt Perry was born on November 20, 1913 in Forest Grove, Oregon in a home his father built in 1911.

He was God-fearing from his early days and devoted much of his nearly century on Earth to sharing the Word of God. One of Ed's greatest joys was studying and teaching the Bible. He was grateful for this opportunity. More about this can be found in his "Bible Teacher" recital dated June 2004.

Ed graduated from the University of Oregon. Music was always an important part of his life. In 1936, he joined Bart Woodyard's big band where he sang and played the sax and clarinet. Bart and Carolyn Woodyard introduced him to Barbara (Ketchum) Berry, the vocalist with the band. They were harmonious in every way, and Barbara soon became his wife. They had two daughters, Kay and Molly and a very full life. At one point the family moved to Hawaii and opened a candy store in the International Marketplace. Ed and Barbara believed, and instilled in their children, that the material things enjoyed on Earth were a gift from God.

Ed and Barbara were married almost fifty years. After their mother's death, their daughters found a way to re-introduce Ed to Carolyn Woodyard, who had been widowed for ten years. Ed and Carolyn married when they were both 73 and spent twenty great years together until Carolyn's passing at 93. The family believed Barbara would have been happy about this, as she and Carolyn were very dear friends for many years.

Ed worked at Boyd Coffee Co., a premier coffee purveyor founded in Portland in 1912, for twenty-five years. Among other things, he would go on to buy all of the coffee, taste all of it for restaurant distribution and serve as the company's secretary-treasurer. Subsequently, he served as financial officer for L. D. Heater Music Co. and Art Lutz & Co. During his later life he worked in accounting and setting up computer systems.

Everlasting life began for Edgar DeWitt Perry when his time on Earth ended in 2010. He was 97.

"Bible Teacher"
A recital from Edgar D. Perry
June 2004

I'm reciting all of this for you because, I believe, it makes a point, which I will spell out later.

My becoming a "Bible teacher" wasn't planned, nor even contemplated, and my exposure to formal "seminary training" was minimal, to the discomfort I know of some of other Bible teachers with whom I have rubbed shoulders. That "seminary training" consisted of one class at Multnomah School of the Bible, subject "Bible Doctrine," which consisted of a semester-long study of the Book of Romans by Dr. Ted Bradley. But my "home schooling" began in earnest in 1950 when we started attending Dr. Mitchell's Bible classes at Central Bible Church and still continues today.

Several things helped shaped my "spiritual life." The first was when my Dad took us to a week of meetings by Billy Sunday. My Dad died when I was a sophomore in high school, and this was part of the great heritage that he left me. Billy Sunday preached "hell and damnation," and literally put the fear of God into me, especially in areas of sexual immorality. His message stuck with me, and literally saved my life over the next years of adolescence from some situations that could have ruined my life.

My Dad also wrote me a wall-motto that has stuck: *If a task is once begun, never leave it till it's done. Be the labor great or small, do it well or not at all.*

And my Aunt Sarah Martine gave me a wall plaque that still is on the wall in my "office," that reads: *Lord, let me stand in the thick of the fight; let me be true as the steel of the blade. Grant me the courage to do what is right, teach me to meet every task unafraid.*

Then, after God's words in the Bible began to sink into my brain, these passages wound up first under the glass top on my desk at Boyd's, and later framed and on the wall in various offices I have enjoyed since then:

> *"And you say in your heart: 'My power and the might of my hand has got me this wealth!' but you shall remember the Lord your God; for it is He that gives you power to get wealth."—Deuteronomy 8:17-18*

> *"And it shall be, if you do at all forget the Lord your God and walk after other gods, and serve them, and worship them, I testify against you this day that you shall surely perish!"—Deuteronomy 8:18-19*

> *"Trust in the Lord with all your heart, and lean not unto our own understanding. In all your ways acknowledge Him, and He shall direct your paths."—Proverbs 3:5-6*

> *"But my God shall supply all your needs according to His riches in glory, by Christ Jesus."—Philippians 4:19*

The path that led to my Bible teaching is clear enough to me: The Lord moved a lot of people and events around me to get me ready for it and into it. First, the miracle that got me into college and that led me to Bart Woodyard and that led me to Barbara Barry, and she was led to Dr. John Mitchell's Bible classes.

Then Bart led me to the Boyd Coffee Co. and Percival Boyd. Then, he, and with Barbara's encouragement, got us listening to Dr. Charles E. Fuller and Dr. M.R. DeHaan. Next, we found ourselves in First Baptist Church (White Temple); then to the Billy Graham meetings, where I was an usher, and Barbara, along with Carolyn sang in the choir.

Then, hurrying home from our place at Tolovana Park to get to the Billy Graham meeting, we had our car accident, and I dutifully phoned the meeting office to tell them "I won't make it—get someone to take my place..." Dr. Mitchell got the message and prayed for us. Then he later "followed up" and visited me in the hospital. We moved to Central Bible Church and began many years of verse-by-verse study of God's Word. No Seminary could have offered better teaching!

Then, from our place, now, in Seaside, we spent a week with Col. Bob Thieme at the Conference at Cannon Beach, and that led to more years of listening to his taped messages with Marty and Lois and Dick and Beth. Bob Thieme's teaching was a catalyst. It took all of Dr. Mitchell's priceless teaching of the Bible and organized it in my mind, giving me an understanding of the Dispensations, the Elements of Christian Doctrine, and an appreciation for and hunger for the Greek Language.

Then my years as Choir Director at Central Bible Church had built me a relationship with Dr. Mitchell that emboldened me to ask him to let *me* teach a class in Bible Doctrine during Sunday school time. (What sheer "guts!" But some twenty or so attended, several of them members of the Church Council). Dr. Mitchell even gave me the use of his office for the purpose (there were no other rooms available). It gave me a certain amount of needed credibility! And, to my surprise, Dr. Mitchell had launched my teaching career!

In another year or so, Dr. Mitchell decided to begin to retire, and he turned his Sunday school class of three hundred members over to me. And now I am finding myself standing in front of a formidable group used to hearing the master expositor teach! It was an awesome experience, but the Lord kept me from faltering and, well-supplied with Bob Thieme's notes that were well colored with lots of history and a few carefully researched comments regarding some Greek words, I held their attention for three years, until Dr. Mitchell fully retired, after which the new pastor, Dr. Dwight Custis, retired me.

There followed a series of home Bible classes, including regular trips to a great group of Bible-loving people that Kay started in her home in Corvallis in about 1971 and has continued, with minor interruptions and changes of locations, right down to today—thirty years!

Then there was the "Sunday afternoon Bible class" that lasted for about three years and a series of Sunday morning radio broadcasts. Plus, several months of classes held at the office of Professional Careers, Inc., all sponsored by Art Lutz & Company, followed by more home Bible classes.

After Barbara left us in 1986, I moved to Hinson Baptist Church. And then later, with Carolyn now with me for support, I began teaching Sunday school class there in 1989. We're still there with the same group fifteen years later. And, in addition, there is that little audience of some twenty reached by mail every week.

I said at the beginning of this recital that there was a "point" to all of this. **What I see is the value that God places on the communication of his Word.** When you think of all the manipulating that was required of people and events to get just one Bible teacher into operation and keeping him there—then you have to realize that, just across our own United States, there are several thousand fundamental Christian churches, each with a staff of teachers just as I am. Think of what a responsibility and amount of work the "coordinator of Bible teachers for the U.S." has to enlist, train, encourage, assign and re-assign, and otherwise manage, the vast number of ordinary people. The "coordinator" needs many assistants! We can begin to see why there are plenty of "jobs" to be done in the Next Life by us people who are being trained here on this Earth in This Life!

"The Bible" is not just a collection of platitudes, wise sayings and an often disputed and questioned "history of civilization." It is a carefully crafted guidebook that the creator of the universe prepared for the human beings that He placed on **this Earth**—not some other planet. (Remember that the Bible begins with the words: "In the Beginning, God created the Heavens *and* the Earth.") This is a book that deals with "this Earth," written for the guidance and benefit of the people that He put on it. God wants every person that He put here to enjoy its bounties and benefits to the fullest and then wind up our time here with an eternal life with Him, out there in the Heavenlies. And this book explains, in detail, how that can be made a reality. You can see, in this one life that you've looked at here, how much importance God places on its communication.

And I am grateful for the opportunity of having been one of those He groomed for the job of communicating. All these other things that have been enumerated here are simply the "details of life," that He has given to us for our enjoyment and instruction; they're the things that come, and go.

And You, my beloved readers, I know will cherish His Word as I have and cling to its teachings. And remember that you, with your life, are also an equally important communicator. It clearly is important to God that His Word be communicated, and He blesses His helpers wonderfully!

The Bible's truth and reliability have been proved over and over, so it is worthy of our absolute faith and trust. Never let your faith in His book falter, nor your grip on His hand relax.

Made in United States
North Haven, CT
10 November 2024

59929245R00190